A Critical History Of The Evolution Of Trinitarianism, And Its Outcome In The New Christology

Paine, Levi L. (Levi Leonard), 1837-1902

A CRITICAL HISTORY OF THE EVOLUTION OF TRINITARIANISM

AND ITS OUTCOME IN THE NEW CHRISTOLOGY

BY

LEVI LEONARD PAINE

WALDO PROFESSOR OF ECCLESIASTICAL HISTORY IN
BANGOR THEOLOGICAL SEMINARY

"Love . . . rejoiceth with the truth."
PAUL.

" In the degree that we become true Christians,
We shall discover more brethren."
AUGUSTE SABATIER.

BOSTON AND NEW YORK
HOUGHTON, MIFFLIN AND COMPANY
The Riverside Press, Cambridge
1900

GENERAL

TO MY PUPILS

OF THIRTY CLASSES, WHOSE EAGER SPIRIT OF INQUIRY
AND CORDIAL SYMPATHY AND FRIENDSHIP HAVE BEEN
MY CHIEF INSPIRATION IN ALL MY HISTORICAL STUDIES
AND TEACHING,

AND TO MY WIFE

WHOSE CARE AND COOPERATION HAVE BEEN SO ESSEN-
TIAL TO THE COMPLETION OF MY TASK, THIS BOOK IS
AFFECTIONATELY DEDICATED.

PREFACE

THIS book is the outcome of an invitation extended to me in 1893 by the editors of "The New World" to write an article on Athanasianism. It was also suggested that I should touch on its historical relation to present New England trinitarian and christological thought. The special original study which the preparation of this article involved, and the new light thus gained, led to the preparation of a second article on the Pseudo-Athanasian Augustinianism. This was followed by a third article on New England Trinitarianism, in which it was shown that the earlier Greek Athanasian form of Trinitarianism had given place, in the Latin church, to the Pseudo-Athanasian Augustinianism, and that New England Trinitarianism in all its various developments was Augustinian rather than Athanasian. Thus the question raised by the editors of "The New World" was fully answered. I have to thank the editors for permission to publish these articles in this volume, of which they form the first three chapters. These chapters have suffered no essential change, except that the account in the first chapter of the initial stages of the evolution of the trinitarian dogma in the New Testament period has been considerably extended. The remaining chapters of the book, forming by far the larger part of it, follow out, as far as possible, the lines of trinitarian evolution already traced, and indicate what must be their logical and historical outcome and conclusion. So that the volume as a whole will be found to have a completely organic unity.

It is scarcely necessary to say that my object has been throughout to give the results of an unbiased historical and critical study of the subject. My aim has been first to ascertain the exact historical truth concerning this most important chapter of Christian theological thought, and next to state all the facts thus gained with the utmost candor, sincerity, and freedom. I know how difficult it is, even for a professed historical scholar, to divest himself of all theological prepossessions; but I can truly say that I am not aware of having been governed in my historical researches by any other motive than the simple and earnest desire to reach historical truth, and also, so far as it lies within the limits of a historian's task, such religious conceptions and grounds of theological belief as history may properly suggest and sustain. But such conclusions contain no *a priori* dogmatic element; they are wholly drawn inductively from history itself.

Of course no historian is called to divest himself of his Christian faith, or of the expression of it at times in his historical studies and writings. But, as this book itself will show, religious faith is a very different thing from theological dogma, and I can frankly declare that, while my studies in the history of Christian doctrine have led me more and more strongly away from *a priori* dogmatic positions, my religious faith has been able to rest itself more and more securely on the great fundamental verities of religion. There has been a disposition on the part of dogmatic theologians to excite a prejudice against historical studies, as if they tended to a spirit of skepticism. Such persons have a very false conception of the effect of such studies. It is true that they tend to destroy a blind faith in unhistorical traditions and in theological dogmas that are found to lack the historical basis which has been claimed for them, but such destructive results are far from being evil. On the contrary, they free the mind from skeptical tendencies by making clear the historical paths that lead towards religious truth. It has been customary to distinguish history from faith and dogma, in religious matters, as if history were not religious, and had no religious function. The Christ of history, for example, has been compared with the Christ of faith and of dogma, as if the true Christ of the Christian religion was something wholly dif-

ferent from the Christ of history, and was of a
higher supernatural order. But such a view wholly
mistakes what history is, and what its place is in
the divine order of the world. Surely the longer
one studies history, and the more deeply one enters
into an understanding of its hidden laws and forces
and movements, the more clearly does one apprehend its truly divine function as a revealer of God's
providential plans and purposes concerning this
world, and also as a continuous panorama of human events, unveiling, as the years go by, the progressive revelations of his truth and love and grace.
This book will fail of its great object if it does
not succeed in bringing out this fact that history
is God's great providential teacher of men. The
Christ of history is indeed, it must be understood,
the very Christ of God. In this view, Christ is not
reduced below his true measure, but history is raised
to its rightful place in the divine administration.
Such a conception of history tends directly toward
a truer conception of God in his relation to this
world and to man, — the noblest creature that
dwells on it. It brings all things into the closest
connection with God's fatherly providential gov-
ernance, love, and care. Especially does it raise
man himself into true fellowship with God, and
into that "full assurance of hope" which rests on
the continually increasing evidence which history
affords that God is good, and that "all things

work together for good to them that love Him."
It is under the inspiration of such a conviction,
which my historical studies have only strengthened
and illumined, that this book has been written,
and my hope and prayer is that it may lead others
into it, and, further, into the moral strength and
courage and trust that it so richly yields.

LEVI L. PAINE.

BANGOR, ME., January, 1900.

CONTENTS

CHAP.   PAGE

    I. ATHANASIANISM 1
   II. THE PSEUDO-ATHANASIAN AUGUSTINIANISM . 58
  III. NEW ENGLAND TRINITARIANISM . . . 97
  IV. THE TRINITARIAN OUTLOOK 139
   V. THE TRINITARIAN RESULT 162
  VI. THE NEW HISTORICAL EVOLUTION . . . 175
 VII. THE DEMAND OF THE HISTORICAL SPIRIT . 186
VIII. THE DEMAND OF THE RELIGIOUS SPIRIT . . 195
  IX. THE DEMAND OF THE INTELLECTUAL SPIRIT . 221
   X. THE NEW THEOLOGICAL METHOD . . . 247
  XI. THE MATERIALS OF THE NEW THEOLOGY . 263
 XII. THE CONSTRUCTION OF THE NEW THEOLOGY . 271
XIII. THE NEW CHRISTOLOGY 279
XIV. THE NEW CHRISTIAN ATONEMENT . . . 288
 XV. THE LEADING FEATURES AND BENEFITS OF THE
      NEW THEOLOGY 308
XVI. CONCLUSION 314

APPENDIX

A. THE JOHANNINE PROBLEM 319
B. A CRITICISM OF PROFESSOR A. V. G. ALLEN'S " CON-
    TINUITY OF CHRISTIAN THOUGHT " . . 368
C. PROFESSOR PFLEIDERER'S ARTICLE IN THE " NEW
    WORLD " 377

INDEX 383

"Whatever appears to me to be true, or most probable, after candid and earnest inquiry, with all reverence for the sacredness of the subject, I utter, without looking at consequences. Whoever has a good work to do must, as Luther says, let the devil's tongue run as it pleases. There are two opposite parties whom I cannot hope to please, viz., those who will forcibly make all things *new*, and fancy, in their folly, that they can shake the rock which ages could not undermine, and those who would retain and forcibly reintroduce, even at the expense of all genuine love of truth, everything that is *old*; nay, even the worn-out and the obsolete. I shall not please those hypercritics who subject the sacred writings to an arbitrary subtilty, at once superrational and sophistical; nor those, on the other hand, who believe that here all criticism — or at least all criticism on internal grounds — cometh of evil. Both these tendencies are alike at variance with a healthful sense for truth and conscientious devotion to it; both are alike inimical to genuine culture. There is need of criticism where anything is communicated to us in the form of a historical tradition in written records; and I am sure that an impartial criticism, applied to the Scriptures, is not only consistent with that childlike faith without which there can be no Christianity or Christian theology, but is necessary to a just acuteness and profoundness of thought, as well as to that true consecration of mind which is so essential to theology." — NEANDER, Preface to *Life of Jesus Christ*.

EVOLUTION OF TRINITARIANISM

CHAPTER I

ATHANASIANISM

THE New England doctrine of the Trinity is plainly passing through a critical phase in its history. That a *rapprochement* of some sort is quietly going on between so-called Trinitarians and so-called Unitarians is clear to any careful observer. Trinitarians are ready to declare themselves Unitarians in some good sense, and Unitarians are equally ready to declare themselves Trinitarians in some other good sense. Mr. Joseph Cook concludes an impassioned defense of what he calls the old trinitarian faith with a description of " God's Unitarianism," which of course is his own; while Dr. Bartol, when asked if God is in three persons, answers: " Yes, and in all persons." It is a sign of the times that the Nicene creed is enjoying a sort of revival. Trinitarians are rallying to it as the true centre of their position. Prof. A. V. G. Allen, in " The Continuity of Christian Thought," declares that " the question is not whether we

shall return or ought to return to what is called
Nicene theology; the fact is that the return has
already begun." *Homoousios* is once more the
trinitarian watchword. The latest Congregational
creed begins with it. Unitarians are equally
in favor of it. " We are all Athanasians," ex-
claims Dr. Bartol. The old Channing Arianism,
it seems, is out of date. Dr. Hedge asserts that
the Nicene Council by its homoousian doctrine
began " a new era in human thought," and claims
that it contains the essential truth. Dr. J. H.
Allen thinks the triumph of Nicene orthodoxy was
providential, and " saved Christianity as a great
social and reconstructive force." Where are we,
and what next? [1]

Meanwhile it is in order to inquire what Athanasianism really is, and whether Athanasius himself
would recognize many of his modern disciples.
This is the object of the present chapter. It pro-
poses a historico-critical survey of the Nicéne
Athanasian Trinitarianism, and its relation to earlier and later forms of trinitarian dogma. For it
must be distinctly recognized at the outset that
this doctrine is no exception to the universal law
of historical evolution. The Nicene theology was
the product of three centuries of controversy and
growth. But this evolution, in its further history,
suffered one great break. A radically new epoch

[1] Joseph Cook, Boston Monday Lectures, *Orthodoxy*, p. 68.
Prof. A. V. G. Allen, *Continuity of Christian Thought*, p. 19.
Dr. F. H. Hedge, *Ways of the Spirit*, p. 351. Dr. J. H. Allen,
Fragments of Christian History, p. 119.

in the development of the trinitarian dogma was begun by the North African Augustine. This celebrated man had a singular influence upon the whole course of Western theology. He fixed the Canon of Scripture for Latin Christendom; he introduced the doctrine of purgatory, and strengthened the materialistic ideas which ruled mediæval eschatology; he laid the foundations of that rigid view of human depravity and of divine grace and predestination which issued in Calvinism. But more far reaching still was the new turn he gave to the doctrine of the Trinity, by which the way was opened for the Sabellianizing tendencies which have infected Western theology to this day. To class Augustine with Athanasius and the Greek Fathers, as has so often been done, is to entirely misunderstand him, as well as the general relation of the Greek and Latin churches in the fifth century. In Augustine's day the Western Empire was breaking in pieces and yielding to barbarism. The Greek language and culture were dying out. Augustine himself was not a Greek scholar. There is no evidence that he ever read Athanasius or any of the later Greek Fathers. He never quotes them. His philosophical ideas were drawn from Western Neo-Platonic and Stoic sources rather than from the pure Eastern fountains of Plato and Aristotle. It is no wonder, then, that the Greek Trinitarianism assumed a new shape in his hands. He did not understand its metaphysics or its terminology. Besides, he had little respect in general for Greek theology. He refers to Athanasius in terms of admiration as a hero of the faith, but he treats Origen, the greatest and most influential thinker of the ancient Greek church, as a heretic. Thus the history of Trinitarianism divides itself into two distinct chapters, — the Greek Athanasian, and the Latin Augustinian. This chapter will deal with the former.

Athanasianism has its roots in the New Testament, and behind the New Testament is the Old. Here, then, our survey must begin. The Old Testament is strictly monotheistic. God is a single personal being. The idea that a trinity is to be found there, or even is in any way shadowed forth, is an assumption that has long had sway in theology, but is utterly without foundation. The Jews, as a people, under its teachings became stern opponents of all polytheistic tendencies, and they have remained unflinching monotheists to this day. On this point there is no break between the Old Testament and the New. The monotheistic tradition is continued. Jesus was a Jew, trained by Jewish parents in the Old Testament scriptures. His teaching was Jewish to the core; a new gospel indeed, but not a new theology. He declared that he came " not to destroy the law and the prophets, but to fulfill " them, and he accepted as his own belief the great text of Jewish monotheism : " Hear, O Israel, the Lord our God is one God." His proclamation concerning himself was in the line of Old Testament prophecy. He was the

"Messiah" of the promised kingdom, the "Son of Man" of Jewish hope. In all Christ's declarations concerning himself, as given in those Synoptic gospels, which contain the earliest traditional accounts of his teaching, there is a marked reticence as to his person. If he sometimes asked: "Who do men say that I, the Son of Man, am?" he gave no answer himself beyond the implied assertion of his Messiahship. There is no hint anywhere of a pre-incarnate life, or of a supernatural birth, or of a divine incarnation. He calls God his Father, but he also teaches that God is the Father of all, and gives his disciples the *Pater Noster*. Certainly Christ had a clear consciousness of his own intimate moral relationship with God, but there is no evidence that the idea of a peculiar metaphysical union with God ever entered his mind. At least it did not appear in his synoptic teaching.

The period of nearly a generation between Christ and Paul is one in which we are dependent on the oral traditions that circulated among the original disciples. These traditions were subsequently gathered together in various gospels, of which the three Synoptic gospels have survived. These gospels in their present shape are much later than Paul, but they contain traditions that plainly go back to the time of Christ himself, and thus antedate the period in which Paul wrote his epistles. There are also in these gospels additions that as clearly belong to a later time, and it has been the important task of historical criticism to distinguish

the original traditions from the later additions.
Of the writings of our New Testament the epistles
of Paul are the earliest in date. The First Epistle
of Peter, if genuine, as it seems to be, comes next.
The authorship of all the remaining portions is
wholly uncertain, and the dates are plainly considerably later. Latest of all are the gospel and
epistles which were attributed in subsequent times
to the Apostle John. Of the much disputed
question as to their Johannine authorship I shall
speak later.[1] Enough to say now that the whole
course and result of historical criticism has been to
show that the traditional view is without any sufficient historical foundation. The fourth Gospel is
undoubtedly a writing of about the middle of the
second century, and the author is entirely unknown.
It should also be noted that the earliest manuscript texts of the New Testament, as we have it,
are as late at least as the fourth or fifth century,
and that it is therefore impossible to know exactly
what interpolations or additions had already crept
into the original texts, though certain criteria, such
as other versions and the writings of the early
Fathers, afford some grounds of critical judgment.

With this critical explanation, we take the New
Testament writings as we find them, and ask what
evidence they give us on the question of the evolution of the dogma of the Trinity. The earliest
stratum of this evolution is contained in the Book

---

[1] See, for a full discussion of this question in its historical
aspects, Appendix A : — "The Johannine Problem."

of Acts, and in the Synoptic gospels, with the exception of the opening chapters of Matthew and of Luke, which are later additions, as we shall see further on. The doctrine of Christ in this first stratum is distinctly that of *Messiahship*. Jesus is a man of God, sent of God to declare his gospel and exhort men to prepare for the kingdom of heaven which is at hand. There is no assertion of Christ's divinity, or of his preëxistence and incarnation, or even of his miraculous birth. Jesus is everywhere described as the son of Joseph and Mary. The Book of Acts is here of primary importance. Although it evidently contains quite a large element of legend, it is equally evident that many of its accounts belong to the earliest apostolic traditions. Even when compared with the Synoptic gospels it breathes an air of historical freshness and naturalness, as if a genuine growth of the original soil. The whole picture of the Acts is that of a human Messiah, glorified by a divine mission. I have already referred to Christ's own account of himself as recorded in the Synoptic gospels. It is essentially that of the Acts. There is one feature, however, of the narrative which is common both to Gospels and Acts, that should be noticed. I refer to the miracles. It is a mistake to suppose that the miracles were a proof or intended to be a proof of Christ's divinity. The Bible contains many miracles supposed to be wrought by men. Christ's disciples also wrought miracles. The Acts contain explicit accounts of miracles performed by Peter and Paul. Such miracles were regarded as proofs of the power given by God to his servants, not as proof that any worker of them was himself divine. Belief in such miraculous power was universal in the ancient world.

The second stratum of evolution in the New Testament is found in the opening chapters of Matthew and Luke. These chapters bear on their very face the plain marks of forming a later addition. In the first place, they are historically inconsistent with the rest of the gospels. They represent Jesus as born in Bethlehem, while all the other portions, not only of Matthew and Luke, but also of the entire New Testament, make no allusion to Bethlehem as the birthplace of Jesus, and speak of him everywhere as of Nazareth, implying that he was born there. In the second place, the genealogies in these opening chapters are inconsistent with the rest of the chapters themselves. They were written to show that Jesus was the true Messiah of Jewish prophecy, who was expected to come in the Davidic line; and this line ran through Joseph, who was thus made the natural as well as putative father of Jesus. The concluding parts of these genealogies, in which Joseph is referred to, bear marks of interpolation and change, and the altered readings nullify the very object for which the genealogies were prepared. The grossly uncritical character of that age is here conspicuous. With the purpose of harmonizing a new legendary tradition that has grown up around

Christ's birth and infancy with the older genealogy, this rude alteration of the text is resorted to. The ancient Syriac manuscript of the gospels, recently discovered by Mrs. Lewis at Mt. Sinai,[1] sheds a

[1] The most recent investigations tend to prove the very early date of the Sinaitic Syriac manuscript, and its critical value and authority in establishing the original text of the gospels. Since this book was completed the first installment of an article of great critical importance has been published in *The American Journal of Theology*, January, 1900, on *The History of the New Testament Canon in the Syriac Church*, by J. A. Brewer. In the absence of external evidence the writer shows on internal grounds, by a thorough analysis and comparison of the several known Syriac versions, that the Sinaitic version is the earliest of all, which fixes its date as early as "the middle of the second century." He also concludes that this version is based on a Greek original, and that this original text is distinct from the Greek texts underlying the other Syriac versions; which gives the remarkable result that behind the Sinaitic Syriac version is to be found the earliest known Greek text of the gospels. I quote the critic's general conclusion on this point. "Unless other finds show the contrary, Ss in its original form was the first translation to which we can point with historic certainty. The extraordinary value of Ss for text-critical purposes has at once been recognized. It seems to stand on the same level of authority as ℵ and B. Merx places it even higher. Whether that, however, can be maintained, time will show. But the fact that Ss was written before T (Tatian's Diatessaron) puts it into the middle of the second century, to which the entire text bears witness; and that places it in the front rank of the witnesses for the original Greek text of the gospels."

In the course of the investigation special attention is given to Matt. i. 16, 19-25, and the writer shows by a close comparison of the different versions that the Sinaitic Syriac version, which, as we have stated above, declares the real paternity of Joseph, represents the original form of the Greek text, and that the process of textual change was from the paternity of Joseph, which was necessary to prove the genealogical descent of Christ from David, to an interpolation which avoided such paternity in the interest of a miraculous virgin birth. Thus the most advanced scholarship sustains what the natural law of historical evolution

remarkable light on this point. In that manuscript, Matthew i. 16, the verse that concludes the genealogy reads thus: " Joseph, to whom was betrothed the Virgin Mary, begat Jesus who is called Christ." Here is a plain trace of the original text, though later tradition has already begun to alter it by inserting the virginity of Mary, so that the two parts of the verse when compared in the light of the context involve a palpable contradiction. The Greek text, as we have it, seems to have suffered another alteration along the same line: " Joseph, the husband of Mary, of whom was born Jesus who is called Christ." Here the paternity of Jesus is left implicitly undecided, though what follows shows what was intended to be inferred. The genealogy given in Luke has a similar curious addition to what must have been the original text, " And Jesus himself, when he began to teach, was about

and the facts of history itself, so far as they are known, unite in declaring. The earliest Greek texts that have survived are the Vatican and Sinaitic manuscripts (B, א) which cannot be earlier than the fourth century. It is a fact worthy of note that Justin Martyr, while holding to the miraculous virgin birth, quoting Luke i. 32, and Matt. i. 21, makes no allusion to Matt. i. 16, as he surely would have done, had it been in the form which ignores Joseph's paternity. The same is true of Origen. The only ante-Nicene Father, so far as I am aware, who quotes the passage as we now read it, is Tertullian (*De Carne Christi*, c. xx.). When we realize how fluxive and unsettled the text of the gospels still was, it can be readily seen that the text of Tertullian in North Africa might be quite different from that of Justin Martyr in Syria or of Origen in Alexandria. But the point especially to be noted is that the Greek text which lies behind the Sinaitic Syriac version seems to be more than a half century earlier than Tertullian.

thirty years old, being the son (as was supposed) of Joseph." How the phrase "as was supposed" got in is easily explained. The original object of the genealogy was to carry the line of descent directly back through Joseph to David. When the theory of a miraculous birth from a virgin had gained currency, "as was supposed" was apparently inserted to cover the difficulty. In any case, the real inconsistency between the plain object of the genealogies and the later theory of the virgin birth remains conspicuous, and shows that the opening chapters of Matthew and Luke, in their present shape, are later additions to the original gospels. Scholars are to-day generally agreed in making Mark the earliest gospel. That Gospel has no account of Christ's birth or infancy, but begins with his public ministry. Such, no doubt, was the original point of departure of Matthew and Luke. But when tradition and legend had begun to grow around Christ's earlier years, the opening chapters were prefixed to these gospels.

The new theory advanced in these chapters concerning Christ is that of his true human nature on his mother's side, coupled with a superhuman miraculous birth through the agency of the Holy Ghost, thus making Christ a sort of demi-god. This theory of the miraculous conception and birth does not appear in any other portion of the New Testament, and plainly belongs chronologically to a later date. Outside of the New Testament it first certainly appears about the middle of the second century in the writings of Justin Martyr,[1] and is made to rest by him solely on the Emmanuel passage in the seventh chapter of Isaiah, of which it is supposed to be a distinct fulfillment, — a point borrowed from Matthew i. 22, 23. The passage in Isaiah has plain reference to events occurring in the prophet's own day, but was by the early Christians regarded as a direct messianic prediction. The prophet declared that a marriageable young woman would shortly bear a son who, as a sign of the fulfillment of the prophecy, would be called Emmanuel. In the Septuagint Greek version, which was universally used by the Greek-speaking Jews of Christ's day and after, the Hebrew word for " marriageable young woman " was translated " a virgin," and this mistaken translation was made the basis of the theory of the miraculous birth. It is a fact which bears directly on the question of the comparative lateness of this tradition, that Justin Martyr is the first of the post-apostolic Fathers to quote the accounts of the miraculous birth from Matthew and Luke, and he plainly follows the account in Matthew, in making that event a fulfillment of an

---

[1] It may be asked what I do with the references in the Ignatian epistles to the virginity of Mary. I answer that most of these references are in the longer recension which is allowed by Lightfoot and scholars generally to be largely interpolated and to belong to a later age. As to the one or two allusions to the subject in the shorter recension, I am convinced that the shorter epistles are not free from interpolations, and on the whole I accept the judgment of Neander that no use can be made of them on any doubtful question of early church history.

Old Testament prediction. Justin Martyr's whole argument against the Jew Trypho for Christ's miraculous birth indicates that it was a question under discussion among Christians as well as among their Jewish opponents, and he allows that " there are some who admit that he is Christ, while holding him to be man of men, with whom I do not agree." This was the position of Trypho himself, who was made by Justin to represent the Jews of his day: " We all expect that the Messiah will be a man born of men." When we consider that this is the first time that the question is raised and discussed in the historical remains of the post-apostolic Fathers, and that the opening chapters of Matthew and Luke are in this discussion first introduced in defense of the miraculous birth, the conclusion is well-nigh irresistible that these chapters were a late addition to the gospels. At all events, the whole story of the virginity of Mary and of her conception by the Holy Ghost is purely legendary, as is shown by the fact that it is closely connected with other legendary traditions, and cannot be separated from them. The account of the angels announcing by songs to shepherds the birth of Jesus, that of the Magi and the star in the east, the massacre of the little children by Herod, the flight into Egypt, are without any historical basis. They belong to a later time when legend had begun its work around the facts of Christ's early life, the results of which are seen in the so-called apocryphal gospels and acts of apostles and disci-

ples. There is a whole volume extant of these
legendary writings in which Jesus and Mary are
the principal actors. The childhood of Christ is
filled with marvels. But the legendary history of
Mary has the most remarkable growth. Her birth,
like that of her son, becomes miraculous and immaculate, and she herself is elevated into a sort
of divinity, and the way is thus prepared for the
cultus of the Virgin Mary in the Catholic Church.
The opening chapters of Matthew and Luke are
simply extracts from such apocryphal narratives.
The legendary accounts of these chapters are quite
independent of each other and wholly irreconcilable with each other, as is evident at once when
they are compared. It is true that there are still
biblical scholars who attempt to defend the historicity and harmony of these accounts. But such
attempts are worse than vain, and I need not dwell
on them. Legend has always played a prominent
part in history and biography, especially in uncritical times. Ancient literature is full of similar
legends, having their background in the mythologies of primeval ages. Gods and goddesses were
fathers and mothers of many a legendary hero,
and a halo of supernatural birth and ancestry soon
surrounded historical men of renown. Buddha
was a real historical personage, but later legend
made his birth miraculous from a virgin mother.
The same legendary element appears in the life of
Zoroaster, the ancient Persian sage. Even Plato
did not escape a partial divinization. Later Greek

tradition made his father the god Apollo. Nor did this superstition of miraculous human births, through a divine parentage, cease with the advent of Christianity. The famous "Secret History" attributed to Procopius informs us that the mother of Justinian declared that his father was a demon.

I have introduced this stage of trinitarian evolution, in which Christ's miraculous, superhuman birth is set forth, as the *second* stratum of development, because it *logically* belongs here. It is a direct evolution of the Palestinian synoptic tradition, and is based on the Messiahship of Jesus as set forth in the Acts and in the Synoptic gospels. It was natural, therefore, that the chapters which contain this new dogma should be prefixed to Matthew and Luke. They are distinguishable from the remaining portions of these gospels in this, that they illustrate the growing disposition to find proofs of Jesus' Messiahship in the Old Testament; and it was thus from certain supposed messianic predictions in the later prophets that the unhistorical tradition of Christ's miraculous birth in Bethlehem was derived. The opening chapters of Matthew make this event to be the direct fulfillment of Isaiah vii. 14 and of Micah v. 2 ; and it is important to note that Justin Martyr gives no other ground for his acceptance of the dogma of the miraculous birth than the one given in Matthew, and that Origen, the most learned of the early Christian Fathers, defends it against the

objections of Celsus on the same ground.   Origen
was scholar enough to know that the Hebrew
word translated " virgin " in the Septuagint version did not necessarily mean virgin, but he insisted that such was the meaning in the passage,
assuming the divine inspiration of the prophet to
predict the exact circumstances of the birth of the
Messiah whose advent was to be several centuries
later, and also assuming that the miraculous birth
of Jesus from a virgin in Bethlehem was a historical fact.   Thus it plainly appears that the idea
of the miraculous birth did not come from Alexandrian Greek sources, but is of Jewish Palestinian
origin, though not necessarily from Jewish Christians.   This helps to explain the entire absence of
the tradition from the fourth Gospel.   A divine
incarnation and a miraculous birth have no necessary connection, though later Christian theology
brought them together.   It is a notable fact that
they are kept wholly apart in the New Testament.
There is no incarnation in the opening chapters of
Matthew and Luke, and there is no miraculous
birth from a virgin in any other part of the New
Testament.

But while this dogma holds its place logically as
closely following the messianic doctrine of the
Synoptic gospels, it must not be inferred that it
chronologically follows these gospels in the historical evolution of Christian literature and thought.
The exact date of the opening chapters of Matthew
and Luke cannot be given, but there is little doubt

that they belong to a period subsequent to that of all the other New Testament writings. The only question would be as to the fourth Gospel. But that gospel knows nothing of the miraculous birth in Bethlehem or of the virginity of Mary. Joseph is the reputed father of Jesus, and Nazareth is supposed to be the place where he was born, as is shown in the argument of the Jews against the claim that Jesus was the Messiah. " But some said: What! doth the Christ come out of Galilee? Hath not the scripture said that the Christ cometh of the seed of David, and from Bethlehem, the village where David was?" (John vii. 41, 42.) In this argument the implied minor premise is that Jesus was in fact born in Nazareth. How then could he be the true Messiah! It is to be noted that not the slightest doubt is expressed on that point, showing again how late must have been the introduction into the Christian tradition of the legend of the miraculous birth in Bethlehem. This does not make the priority of the fourth Gospel to the opening chapters of Matthew and Luke certain, but, so far as the evidence goes, it points directly that way.

The third stratum of trinitarian evolution is marked by the intrusion of Greek philosophical thought into the Jewish Palestinian. The first two strata belong to Palestinian Aramaic soil, but the third stratum, which is introduced by the Epistles of Paul and the Epistle to the Hebrews, is of Alexandrian Greek origin and character. Paul was a Jew, and trained in Jewish schools; but he also had a Greek education, and his epistles bear plain marks of his acquaintance with Greek philosophic literature. It is an interesting question whether he had actually read the writings of the Alexandrian Jewish Philo. This cannot be conclusively proved, but there are some remarkable coincidences of thought and expression between the two writers. At all events, it must be conceded that Paul was at home in the atmosphere of Philonic thought, and we may be quite sure that he owed the real starting-point of his new theological departure indirectly if not directly to Philo himself; for his doctrine of Christ as a μεσίτης (mediator) between God and men, with all its metaphysical results, is an integral feature of the Philonic Logos doctrine. The very term μεσίτης, which first appears in Paul among Christian writers, was used by Philo again and again. The Epistle to the Hebrews gives equally clear evidence of Alexandrian and Philonic relationship. It is a most remarkable and significant fact that μεσίτης, in the special sense of a metaphysical go-between or mediator between God and mankind, is found only in Philo, Paul, and the Epistle to the Hebrews. The reason why it was not employed in later Christian writers was that λόγος took its place. The mediation theory of Paul was retained, but it assumed the form of the Logos doctrine. The μεσίτης doctrine of Paul and the λόγος doctrine of Justin Martyr, as we shall see, have one essentially com-

mon source, viz., the Greek Platonic philosophy.
How providential Paul's Greek training was to him
and to the development of Christian thought is
easily seen. The original language of the Gospel
was Aramaic, a development of the Hebrew, and
there is no good evidence that Christ or any of his
immediate disciples spoke any other tongue. Paul,
on the contrary, both preached and wrote in Greek,
and hence it was that he was so preëminently fitted
to be the apostle to the Gentiles, and to interpret
the Palestinian Jewish gospel of Christ to the
Græco-Roman world. The Gentile churches which
Paul organized, and to which he preached and
wrote, were unacquainted with the Hebrew language and literature and were trained in Greek
religious and philosophical ideas. This is the historical explanation of the entirely new stage of
christological thought. It is marked by the transi-
tion from Palestinian to Greek soil. Through Paul
the gospel passed from the world of Judaism into
the world of Greek philosophy. No other apostle
had such a wide influence or fame as he, as is shown
by the preservation of so many of his letters, and
by the frequent quotations from them in the earliest post-apostolic writings. The prominence of
Peter forms a later chapter, and was ecclesiastical
rather than theological, growing out of the fiction
of his relation to the Roman Church. The silence
of the early Fathers concerning John is remarkable, as is also the absence of all allusion to the
Gospel that is named from him. In Clement, in

Polycarp, and in the shorter epistles of Ignatius, there are quite a number of references to Paul, but not one to John. It is certainly significant that Polycarp, who was said by Irenæus to have been a hearer of John, should refer to Paul four times, and quote from all his epistles, with a single exception, repeatedly, while a complete silence is preserved concerning John and the fourth Gospel.

We are thus prepared to understand the significance of Paul in this survey of the historical evolution of the trinitarian dogma. This dogma, as it was finally developed by the theologians of the third and fourth centuries, is essentially Greek, not Jewish; Alexandrian, not Palestinian; and to Paul we must look for its real beginnings. He laid the foundations of the metaphysical bridge by which Judaism in its Christianized form passed over to Greek philosophical thought, to be metamorphosed by it into a Græco-Christian theology. Before Paul there had been no suggestion of trinity; God was "one God." Christ was "a man approved of God unto men by mighty works which God did by him." He was God's "holy servant," "a prophet," "anointed one," "exalted by God to be a prince and a Saviour." The Acts, from which these quotations are taken, are full of such expressions, and they clearly represent the christology of Paul's day. The Synoptic gospels are here in close harmony with the Acts. The Jewish Christian Messianism is the fundamental doctrine throughout. Christ is Messiah, Son of man, Master, messenger of God; but he is nowhere metaphysically distinguished from other men, as if his nature was superhuman or divine. It was Paul who with his Greek Philonic theory of a metaphysical superhuman mediator gave an entirely new shaping to the messianic doctrine, and he may be truly called the real originator of the trinitarian conception which finally issued in the Nicene creed.

What, then, was the doctrine of Paul concerning God and Christ? He nowhere gives us a full metaphysical statement. It is not clear that he had developed any precise theological doctrine of the Trinity. Certainly his view of the third person is indefinite; and it is doubtful whether he regarded the Holy Spirit as a personal being. In the two passages which contain his most discriminating utterances on the subject of the Godhead, the Holy Spirit is not mentioned: "To us there is one God, the Father, of whom are all things, and we unto him; and one Lord, Jesus Christ, through whom are all things, and we through him" (1 Cor. viii. 6). "There is one God, one mediator also between God and men, himself man, Christ Jesus" (1 Tim. ii. 5). These passages have a credal ring, and, together with the baptismal formula, seem to be the basis of the early confessions. Two points bearing upon the question of the Trinity stand out clearly. First, Paul remained a firm adherent of the Jewish monotheism. To him, as to Moses and to Christ, God was a single personal being — "the Father," "the blessed and only potentate," "whom no man hath seen, nor can see." Secondly, Paul distinguished Christ from God, as a personal being, and regarded him, moreover, as essentially inferior and subordinate to the supreme Deity. I do not press the point here that Paul, in the second passage quoted, expressly calls Christ a man, in direct antithesis with God. Other passages make it plain that the apostle conceived of Christ as superhuman and preëxistent and as having a certain metaphysical relation to God. But that Paul ever confounded Christ with God himself, or regarded him as in any way the supreme Divinity, is a position invalidated not only by direct statements, but also by the whole drift of his epistles. The central feature of Paul's christology is its doctrine of mediatorship: " One God, the Father, and one *mediator* between God and men." This is a theological advance on the messianic doctrine of the Synoptic gospels. Messiahship is the doctrine of a " Son of Man ; " mediatorship is the doctrine of a " Son of God." Paul gives no evidence of acquaintance with the Logos doctrine, but he anticipates it. He exalts Christ above all human beings. If he does not clothe him with the supreme attributes of Deity, he places him next to God in nature, honor, and power; so that, while remaining a monotheist, he takes a long step toward a monotheistic trinitarianism, giving us the one only trinitarian benediction of the New Testament (2 Cor. xiii. 14).

Passing to the post-apostolic age, we find that

these two articles of Paul's doctrine form the basis
of the faith of the church. Not only so, they continue to be the characteristic and fundamental
features of the Greek Trinitarianism through the
whole course of its development. From beginning
to end, Greek theology is distinctly monotheistic.
Clement writes: "As God lives and as the Lord
Jesus Christ lives." So Athenagoras: "We acknowledge a God, and a Son, his Logos, and a Holy
Spirit." So Dionysius of Rome: "We must believe on God the Father Omnipotent, and on Jesus
Christ his Son, and on the Holy Spirit." The
Nicene creed, in which Greek orthodoxy culmi-
nated, continues the strain in language which is
a clear echo of Paul himself: "We believe in one
God, the Father almighty," "and in one Lord
Jesus Christ the Son of God, begotten of the Fa-
ther." To be sure, the Son of God is also called
God in the added phrase, "God of God;" but
"God" is here descriptive, in the sense of divine,
since the Son of God is begotten of the Father and
hence of the same divine nature. The Father is
God in the primary or supreme sense. Christ as
Son is God only in a derived or secondary sense.
As the evolution of church doctrine went on, the
trinitarian element grew more explicit and complete, but the original Pauline monotheism was
never given up. In fact, the more pronounced the
Greek Trinitarianism became, the more tenaciously
its monotheism was declared and vindicated. God,
the Father, the eternal cause of all things, was

never confounded with either of the other persons,
or with the Trinity as a whole.

The same is true of Paul's doctrine of mediatorship. It also became a vital feature of Greek
theology, and remained its moulding principle
through all its history. A difference, however, is
to be noted. The doctrine of monotheism naturally lay in the background, as a fixed quantity,
being assumed always as a cardinal truth of Christianity which had its birth on Jewish monotheistic
ground, and carefully avoided all connection with
the pagan polytheism. Not so with the doctrine
of Christ's mediatorship. This was the new truth
of Christianity. Theologically, Christianity is a
christology. Its Trinitarianism started out of its
doctrine of Christ as the Son of God and the
mediator between God and man. Around this
point the early controversies arose, and here began
a christological evolution which became the central
factor of Greek ecclesiastical history through its
whole course. This evolution must be fully comprehended, if we would understand the Nicene
Trinitarianism. It may be naturally divided into
four sections or stages, represented by the names
of Paul, Justin Martyr, Origen, and Athanasius.

The faith of the sub-apostolic age remained
essentially Pauline. It is truly represented in the
primitive portions of the so-called Apostles' creed.
Christ was regarded as a superhuman being, above
all angels and inferior only to God himself, pre-
existent, appearing among men from the heavenly

world, the true Son of God, and hence in a sense
God, as of divine nature, though not the Supreme
One.   But no further metaphysics is yet attempted.
There is no Logos doctrine.   This doctrine which
was to so change the whole current of Christian
thought, and give such an impulse to the spirit of
metaphysical speculation, first appears in Justin
Martyr.

The question here arises and cannot be ignored:
What place should be given in this evolution to
the fourth Gospel?   The question of actual date
does not now concern us.   The point is: When
does the fourth Gospel appear in history as a document to which theological appeal is made?   Certainly the two questions are closely connected, and
I would here declare my conviction that no satisfactory conclusion can be reached on the Johannine problem, until the historical facts as to the
relation of the fourth Gospel to the origin of the
Logos doctrine are properly weighed.   Three facts
especially are to be considered.   First, setting
aside the fourth Gospel itself, no trace of a Logos
doctrine appears in the early church until Justin
Martyr; that is, more than a century after the
death of Christ.   Secondly, none of the post-
apostolic Fathers before Justin Martyr allude to
the fourth Gospel or quote from it.[1]   Thirdly,

[1] I leave out of account the Ignatian Epistles, which, if genuine, are so greatly interpolated as to be unworthy of confidence,
and also the Epistle to Diognetus, which is now properly regarded
as of later date.   The Teaching of the Twelve Apostles, the
Epistles of Clement, of Barnabas, of Polycarp, the Shepherd of

Justin Martyr plainly draws his Logos doctrine
from Greek philosophic sources, never quoting the
fourth Gospel by name in defense of it, and never
even referring to the Gospel at all, so that it is
still a disputed question whether he was directly
acquainted with it.   Whatever be the truth on
this point, it does not affect the fact with which we
are now concerned, viz., that so far as the light
of early church history goes, the Logos doctrine is
not shown to be of apostolic origin, or drawn from
the fourth Gospel.   If this gospel is Johannine, it
was, for some reason, not in general circulation
before Justin Martyr's time, and was not quoted
in connection with the Logos doctrine till quite
late in the second century.   To assume that the
fourth Gospel was written by the Apostle John,
and then conclude that the Logos doctrine of the
post-apostolic church is Johannine and apostolic,
against evidence of the clearest sort to the contrary,
is one of the most vicious and fallacious of syllo-
gisms.   I regret to say that this style of reasoning
is not yet extinct.[1]

Hermas, the Fragments of Papias, and the recently discovered
Apology of Aristides, make no allusion to a Logos doctrine or to
the fourth Gospel.

[1] See, for one illustration, Gloag, *Introduction to the Johannine
Writings*, p. 189: " The doctrine of the Logos frequently occurs
in the writings of the Fathers, especially of Justin Martyr.   They
derived their notions concerning it from the Gospel of John."
In his preface the writer allows that " the authenticity of John's
Gospel is the great question of modern criticism, and must be
regarded as still unsettled."   Yet here he assumes this " unsettled question " to be a fact, and then assumes that Justin Martyr
was acquainted with the fourth Gospel, and derived his Logos

As to the origin of the Logos doctrine in general there can be no question. It has no Jewish ancestry. The Logos doctrine is essentially a mediation doctrine. It is based on the idea of the divine transcendence and of a cosmological void needing to be filled between the absolute God and the world. Jewish theology held indeed to the divine transcendence; but by its doctrine of creation, involving a direct creative act, and of man as formed in the divine image, it brought God into the closest relations with all his creatures, and especially with man himself. God walking in the garden and conversing with Adam is a picture of the whole Old Testament conception of God's immediate connection with the human race. In fact, there lurks in Jewish thought a strong

doctrine from it. A similar piece of false reasoning occurs in regard to a quotation in the Epistle of Polycarp from the first Epistle of John (p. 101). Polycarp does not allude to John anywhere in his Epistle, nor does he give the authorship of the quotation; yet Dr. Gloag, assuming that the author of the fourth Gospel and the first Epistle of John is the same, concludes: "We have then the testimony of Polycarp in proof of the genuineness of John's Gospel, and this testimony is of great importance, as Polycarp was the disciple of John." Observe how the testimony of Irenæus, a generation later, as to Polycarp's relation to John, is here used to prop up a conclusion that is wholly without foundation. The question is not whether Polycarp was acquainted with John, but whether he gives any evidence of acquaintance with the reputed Gospel of John. There is not a hint of it in his Epistle, or even that he knew John at all. To assume that John wrote both Gospel and Epistle, and then that Polycarp, as a disciple of John, must have been acquainted with both Gospel and Epistle, and then to argue from an anonymous quotation from the Epistle that the Gospel is Johannine, is a flagrant *petitio principii*.

tincture of divine immanence in its whole theory
of theophanies, and most of all in its conception
of " the Spirit of the Lord " moving directly upon
human souls.   Thus no basis was laid in Jewish
theology for the growth of a Logos doctrine.
The " Wisdom " of the Proverbs is simply a poet-
ical personification of the divine attribute.   Christ
has much to say of his close relation to God, and
of his mission to men ; but it was a mission based
on spiritual needs, soteriological, not cosmological.
The term Logos he never uses, and the conception
was quite foreign to him.   Had the Logos mediation doctrine been a product of Jewish thought, it
would certainly have appeared in Paul ; but he
gives no hint of it.   We have indeed his doctrine
of Christ's mediatorship in a new form, and the
beginnings of a cosmological view of Christ's
nature, as being " the image of the invisible God,
the first-born of all creation ; " but this is Greek,
not Jewish, and gives evidence of his acquaintance
with Greek philosophy.   For it is in Greek philosophy that the sources of the Logos doctrine are
to be found.   It first appeared in the cosmological
Asia Minor school, in the sixth century B. C., to
explain the order of the world, as a principle of
reason and law.   As such it was employed by
Heraclitus and Anaxagoras.   When the dualistic
school of Plato arose, it became the mediating
principle between the transcendent spiritual sphere
and the world of phenomena.   It also appeared in
Stoicism, to sustain its doctrine of a divine imma-

nence in nature. Thus the Logos as a divine
principle with mediating functions had a long history in Greek philosophy before it became chris-
tologized in the early church. Justin Martyr
directly refers to Platonic and Stoic authorities
for his Logos ideas. He was himself a Platonist
before he became a Christian, and he never laid
aside his philosopher's cloak. He believed that
Greek philosophy was a partial revelation of divine
truth, and he drew from it weapons to be used in
the service of Christian dogma. Justin belonged
to the school of Paul, and in his hands the Pauline
form of doctrine was not essentially modified. The
new Logos ideas fitted quite closely to Paul's own.

But three points are noticeable in the Logos
doctrine, which became fountain heads of tendencies that were finally to change the whole current
of theological thought, and to substitute for the
Pauline christology something radically different.

First, the Logos doctrine emphasized the superhuman or divine element in Christ's nature. Paul
again and again called Christ a man. But he
also gave him a preëxistence and " form of God "
which distinguished him from merely human beings,
and thus laid a cosmological basis for his mediatorship. It is here that the Logos doctrine comes
in. The philosophical Logos was essentially cosmological and metaphysical. It was a necessary
bond of communication between the world of spiritual intelligences and this lower world of time and
sense. In itself, whether as an impersonal princi-

ple or as a personal being, it was utterly aloof from earth; but its great function was mediatorial, and thus in its relationships it touched both spheres. When Jesus Christ was identified with the Logos, his whole being was transcendentalized. His human and earthly features were transfigured, and lost in the higher glory. He was no longer the Son of man, but the Son of God, and even a *quasi* divinity. The whole point of view was changed. Paul starts with the human and proceeds to the divine. The Logos doctrine reverses the process. As a consequence, while Paul never lost sight of Christ's real humanity, the Logos theology was in danger at once of regarding Christ as essentially a transcendent being descending from the higher sphere, and entering human relations in a sort of disguise. This danger brought forth its natural fruit in the later monophysite heresies.

Secondly, the Logos doctrine in its assertion of Christ's mediatorship emphasized the subordination element which characterizes Paul's christology, and tended to magnify it. It is the essence of the Logos doctrine that the Logos mediates between what is higher than itself and what is lower. He is a middle being both in nature and function. Such is the mediating principle of Plato, the demon of Plutarch, the Logos of Philo. This cosmological view, treating the Logos principle as necessary and immanent in the universe, and not as introduced providentially into the moral order in consequence of sin, now came into Christian theology.

Paul started it, but the Logos doctrine completed it. In this view the subordination element is vital, and it became the governing note of the whole Logos school. Justin Martyr's doctrine of Christ was that of a Son of God, wholly removed in his preincarnate existence from the human sphere, and yet as completely distinguished from the Supreme Being. He regards the Logos of God as originally immanent in God, as the divine reason, and then at a point in time evolved into a personal existence of sonship and mediating activity. This development of the Logos into personality is by the divine will. Thus the Son of God is subordinate to the Father in all things, though having his origin in the Father's essence. Justin was philosophically a Platonic transcendentalist. The Supreme Being was in his view invisible and unapproachable. Hence his idea that the Jehovah of the Old Testament in his various theophanies was not the Father but the Son or Logos. He found traces of the Logos even in pagan philosophy and faith, and in the lives of such men as Socrates.

A third feature of the Logos doctrine was to be still more influential in radically remoulding Greek Christian thought. I refer to its purely metaphysical and speculative character. The Logos doctrine may be true, but if so, its truth is metaphysical, not historical. The Christ of history is not a speculation of Greek philosophy. The introduction of the Logos doctrine into Christian theology, giving a new shape as it did to the entire content

of faith, wrought an immense change in its whole
spirit and direction.   Instead of resting on historical facts, it now built itself on certain speculative
assumptions.   This is the secret of the remarkable change from the confessional character of the
Apostles' creed to the transcendental metaphysics
of Nice and Chalcedon.   It is a fact which theologians have been slow to learn, that the metaphysical words so freely used by the Greek Fathers in
theological controversy were all borrowed from the
philosophical nomenclature of Plato and Aristotle.
This becomes especially apparent in what may be
called the scholastic period of Greek theology, and
is well illustrated by John of Damascus, who pre-
faces his great work, " On the Orthodox Faith,"
with an explanatory dictionary of Aristotelean
terms.

Before proceeding to Origen, it is proper to say
·a few words as to the relation of the fourth Gospel
to the further history, and also concerning the
general character of its christology.   Although
Justin Martyr himself makes no use of this gospel
in connection with his Logos doctrine, it begins to
be quoted by his immediate successors, and soon
becomes the great repository of proof texts for the
whole Logos school.   It is pertinent, therefore, to
note that its christology is essentially Pauline,
with the addition of the Logos terminology.   Its
monotheism is decided.   God is always the Father.
Christ is the mediator sent of God, subordinate
and dependent.   Its doctrine is summed up in the

words of Christ's prayer, " This is life eternal, to
know thee, the only true God, and Jesus Christ
whom thou hast sent." In a single point, however, the Johannine christology advances beyond
the Pauline. Paul has a transcendental view of
Christ as the " form " and " image " of · God.
But the fourth Gospel develops a metaphysical
unity between the Father and the Son to which
Paul is a stranger. Just how much is involved in
the famous passage, " I and my Father are one," is
somewhat doubtful. It is clear, however, that the
unity asserted is not one of substance or being,
since Christ compares it to the unity of believers:
" that they all may be one even as we are one."

There is a general resemblance between the
Logos doctrine of the fourth Gospel and that of
Justin Martyr. Yet there are striking divergences
which indicate an independent origin. The fourth
Gospel is mystical, with a spice of Neo-Platonism,
reminding one of Philo. Justin is speculative,
with an emanation element which has a Stoic
strain. His distinction between the immanent
and the personalized Logos is wanting in the fourth
Gospel. Behind both is the shadow of Gnosticism.
But the fourth Gospel gives the clearest signs of
Gnostic influence. Its peculiar vocabulary is from
Gnostic sources. The Gnostic dualism is also
suggested in the shaping given to the doctrine of
Satan, and in the two classes of men, children of
light, who are sons of God, and children of darkness, who are of their " father the devil." The

real authorship of the fourth Gospel is obscure.
It may be that there is behind it a true Johannine
tradition ; but philosophically it plainly belongs
to the Philonic school. It is no valid objection
that Philo has no incarnation. The object of the
gospel, in part at least, was, in a Gnostic way, to
identify the Jesus of history with the mediation
Logos of Greek philosophy. This required that
the Logos should be made flesh. It seems probable that the Logos doctrine of the fourth Gospel
and that of Justin Martyr represent two separate
streams of philosophical Christian thought, which
afterwards became united in a common evolution.

We come to Origen, the boldest speculator and
the most fertile thinker of the ancient church.
The school which he founded included all the
lights of later Greek orthodoxy. Even Athanasius, who called no man master, sought the aid of
his great name, and quoted him to show that he
was a true homoousian. Origen stamped on Greek
theology the essential features that it has borne
ever since. In his hands the Logos doctrine suffered two amendments. The first is his view of
the *eternal generation* of the Son. The distinction of the Justin Martyr school between immanent
and personalized Logos Origen discarded. He
taught that the Son was *eternally* a distinct personal being. Holding to his real generation from
the Father, he insisted that it was without beginning, since the Father's activity was unchangeable
and eternal. This view placed the Logos doctrine

on a firmer metaphysical basis, since it removed
the Son of God more completely from the category
of created beings, and also opposed all theories of
a temporal evolution such as were proposed by the
Sabellians. The Origenistic doctrine of eternal
generation has recently been treated with considerable contempt, but it took a firm hold on the
Greek mind and became the fundamental note of
the Greek Trinitarianism. It has been said that
the Nicene creed does not teach it. This cannot
be sustained. It is certainly implied there. In
fact, the whole homoousian doctrine is built upon
it, and Athanasius, the great expounder of the doctrine, clearly holds it.

The second amendment of Origen was in the
line of the strict subordination of the Son to the
Father. He not only emphasized this point as
essential to the defense of the trinitarian doctrine
against the charge of tritheism, but he also gave
it an entirely new theological aspect by insisting
on *the difference of essence.* Justin Martyr made
the Son to be an emanation or product of the
Father's essence. Origen opposed all emanation
theories, substituting the doctrine of eternal generation. Hence he denied that the Son was of
the same essence with the Father, although he at
the same time denied that he was of any created
essence. The Son was truly begotten of the
Father, but his nature was different, since he
lacked the attributes of absoluteness and self-
existence, and derived his being from the Father's

will. Thus Origen reduced the Son to a sort of
middle being between the uncreated and the
created, and paved the way for Arius.

Arius has become the arch-heretic of church
history; but in the interest of historical truth I
wish to say that great injustice has been done
him. He was a sincere and thorough Trinitarian
after the type of his age, and sought to defend the
trinitarian doctrine against all taint of Sabellianism. But his polemic led him to take a step
further in the direction toward which Origen had
pointed, and which had already been anticipated
by such Origenists as Dionysius of Alexandria
and Eusebius of Cæsarea, — that the Son of God,
if truly derived from the Father and by his will,
must be *a creature*, though the highest creature
in the universe, and the creator himself, as the
Logos or mediation principle, of all other creatures.

We are thus brought to the great crisis in the
development of the Greek theology, and to its
fourth stage, — the epoch of Athanasius and the
Nicene creed. Historically and critically, Athanasianism is simply a revolt from the subordination
tendency, when carried too far, and a counter-
reaction along the Origenistic lines of eternal
generation and of an essential difference between
the Son of God and all created beings. But, as is
usual in such reactions, it went to the opposite
extreme. Arius had stretched subordination to its
farthest point. Athanasius reduced it to a mini-
mum. Origen had described the Son as " a mid-

dle being between the uncreated and the created."
The Nicene creed declared him to be of the same
essence with the Father, since he is true Son of
God, and as a Son must be of the Father's nature,
— "God of God, very God of very God." Thus
the term *homoousios* becomes the turning-point
of the Nicene epoch. Yet curiously this famous
word made much less noise in the Athanasian age
than it has since, and, besides, a new meaning has
been foisted upon it which has no ground in the
word itself or in the use made of it by the Nicene
theologians. It was put into the Nicene creed
by a sort of accident, as Athanasius explains, in
order to drive the Arians from their cover; and
although it became in this way a watchword of
orthodoxy, it was not insisted on as essential even
by Athanasius himself. What it meant to the
Nicene party is clear from Athanasius' own explanations. He declares distinctly that it was used
simply to signify that the Son was truly Son, not
putatively or adoptively, and that, as true Son, he
was of the same generic nature with the Father,
and so equal to the Father in all divine attributes.
Athanasius was ready even to accept the term
homoiousios (like in essence) as a synonym for
homoousios (completely like in essence), if it was
explained to mean a likeness of essence in kind
which would allow that the Son was a true Son
and derived from the Father his essential qualities.
This, in fact, became the basis of the union which
followed between the Athanasian and Semi-Arian

parties, resulting in the acceptance of the Nicene creed by all except the extreme Arians. It is a fact which seems not to be generally recognized, that Athanasius uses the word *homoousios* very rarely, while he employs the word *homoios* (like) very frequently, as expressing his own position concerning the relation of the Son to the Father. It is significant that in the " Statement of Faith " which was written not long after the formation of the Nicene creed, he uses simply the word *homoios*, " being *like* the Father, as the Lord says : ' He that hath seen me hath seen the Father.' " What Athanasius contended for so stoutly against the Arians was *the real divine sonship of Christ*, and *his essential equality with the Father*. When this was allowed, he cared little for words.

We are now prepared to estimate more clearly and comprehensively the trinitarianism of Athanasius. Radically it is Origenism. The Logos doctrine, in its Origenistic form of eternal generation and derived subordination, forms the backbone of the Nicene christology. Too much theological significance has been given by historical writers to the Nicene epoch, as if it created an essentially new theology. This is very far from the truth. It was a time of widespread ecclesiastical ferment, and men of action, rather than of speculative thought, came to the front. A conflict arose between two factions of the same theological school. Origenism became divided against itself. Athanasius was not a speculative, systematic thinker; he was a born leader of men, a knight of Christian chivalry, ready to point his lance at every denier of " the faith once delivered." He seized the word *homoousios* and threw it as a gauntlet into the arena, but it was a word of battle to be dropped at leisure, not a note of new theology. It was in the Latin West that a makeshift catchword of the Nicene nomenclature was taken up, its true meaning misunderstood, and a new scheme of trinitarian theology drawn from it. The difference between Athanasius and Origen is largely a matter of words. Origen disliked the term *homoousios* because it seemed to break down subordination and introduce tritheism. Athanasius adopted it because it seemed to save subordination from the annihilating *heterousianism* (unlikeness of essence) of Arius. Both were defending the same position, but from different standpoints. Yet Athanasius took one long step forward. He held to a certain subordination of the Son to the Father, as he was compelled to, in consistency with the essential character of the Logos mediating doctrine, to which he unflinchingly adhered. But he reduced it, as we have already said, to its lowest possible terms. He was ready to call Christ God, not merely in the larger sense of what is superhuman or divine, but in the strict meaning, " very God of very God," as having the same essential nature with the Father. He even declared the Son to be " equal " to the Father, applied to him the terms which characterize the highest deity, and gave him the supreme attributes of omniscience, omnipotence, and sovereignty. This is new theological language, and seems to indicate an entirely new departure. But a close study of Athanasius makes it clear that he has not departed from the Origenistic principles of generation and subordination. In fact, he could not do so without surrendering the whole Logos doctrine in its original form, and exposing himself to the charge of holding to three independent Gods. If he had felt a leaning toward the entire elimination of the subordination element, of which there is no evidence, the danger of such a charge would have deterred him. The one object of dread ever present to the Nicene and post-Nicene Fathers was the spectre of Tritheism. *To be squarely Trinitarian and yet not be Tritheistic* was the great effort of Greek theology. How was it accomplished? The answer to this question gives us the " open sesame " of the Athanasian Trinitarianism. Three distinct points are to be noted, — the view taken of the Father ; of the Son ; and of their metaphysical relation to each other.

First, the Father, with Athanasius, is the one God, the Absolute and Supreme Being. He never confounds the one God with the Trinity. The three Persons are not one Being. This, to him, is Sabellianism. His monotheism is clearly set forth in his " Statement of Faith : " " We believe in one Unbegotten God, Father Almighty, maker of all things visible and invisible, that hath his being from himself, and in one only-begotten Word, Wisdom, Son, begotten of the Father without beginning and eternally." Unbegottenness and self-existence are here made the essential attributes of the Father alone. He is the eternal cause and fountain of all being, including even the being of the Son and Holy Spirit. This point is fundamental in the Athanasian system; it is the philosophical Platonic assumption with which he starts, and on which he builds his Logos doctrine. It is the stronghold of his theism against all pantheism on the one hand, and of his monotheism against all polytheism or tritheism on the other. No Greek theologian held more firmly to the divine transcendence than Athanasius. He had no controversy with Arius here. He held equally with him that God was utterly unlike his creation, and was separated from it, in his essence, by infinite measures. Hence the prominence given by him to the Logos doctrine, which is central and dominant in his whole christology. With Athanasius the Logos in his mediation rôle is essential to the existence of the universe as well as to the redemption of mankind. In him the cosmological idea triumphs over the soteriological. Christ is much more than the Saviour of men; he is the eternal and necessary principle of mediation and communion between the transcendent God and all created things. Thus the incarnation rather than the crucifixion is made the prominent fact in the relation of Christ to men. It is not sin merely,

but nature as created, that separates man from
God.   Athanasius here departs from the Scripture,
which teaches man's essential likeness to God, and
also from Plato, who declares that "likeness to
God" (ὁμοίωσις τῷ θεῷ) is man's great prerogative
and moral duty.   Plato's doctrine of transcendence
was modified by his view of man's moral relationship. (Athanasius tended rather to *emphasize* the
divine transcendence and to separate man from
God more completely.   Hence, according to him,
the absolute necessity of the incarnation. "The
Word was made man that we might be divinized"
(θεοποιηθῶμεν).   And here appears the great reason why Athanasius insisted so earnestly upon the
homoousian doctrine.   In his view, unless the Logos
mediator was essentially divine, " very God of very
God," the chasm between God and man, between
the infinite and the finite, could not be spanned.
But let it be noted that this whole view involves
the strictest monotheism.   The Logos mediating
principle is as sharply distinguished from the
Absolute God as he is from the creation in whose
behalf he mediates.

> Secondly, Athanasius' doctrine of the Son is
the logical resultant of his doctrine of the Absolute
God as Father and of the mediating Logos.   How
does the Logos become endowed with his mediating function?   It is by virtue of his Sonship.
The Logos of God is the Son of God, and hence
able to reveal him.   Here Athanasius is a true
Origenist.   Sonship is not a superficial and tem-

poral movement of the divine activity; it is an
eternal relationship. Athanasius, moreover, holds
equally with Origen to the reality and genuineness of the sonship. He does not explain it away
as mere metaphor. The real sonship is what
he means by *homoousios*. This sonship is what
separates Christ from the category of creatures
and makes him truly divine. But real sonship
involves a real generation. This, too, Athanasius
accepts in all its literalness, though he guards
against a materialistic view of it. In one point
only does he vary from Origen, — in making the
generation an eternal fact or condition of the
divine nature, rather than a voluntary movement
of the divine will. Thus the ground is laid for
the subordination of the Son to the Father. The
Son is a generated, that is, a derived being. Consequently he is not self-existent or independent.
This is distinctly declared in one remarkable passage (fourth Oration, 3), where Athanasius argues
that if the Logos were self-existent (ἀφ' ἑαυτοῦ ὑπέ-
στη) there would result two independent causes
of existence or supreme Beings (δύο ἂν εἶεν ἀρχαί).
The subordination thus involved is not a mere
official one. The whole theory of *official* subordination is a product of Western thought; it is
unknown in Greek theology. Subordination with
Athanasius is of nature, for the Son derives his
existence " from the Father's essence." It is true
that he insists upon the equality of the Son with
the Father. Yet the term " equal " was used by

him in a relative, not absolute sense. It applied
to those attributes with which Christ was endowed
by virtue of his generation from the Father, but
not to those which make the Father the supreme
God.

Thirdly, what, then, is the metaphysical relation
of the Father and Son? At the outset let it be
noted that Athanasius has no leaning toward
Sabellianism. No stronger protests against the
Sabellian position can be found than in his writings. He sharply opposes the doctrine of one
personal Being in three modes of revelation and
activity. On this point Athanasius is as thoroughly trinitarian as Origen, and he stands
squarely in the line of all orthodox Greek theologians. He has been accused of sympathizing with
Marcellus, who was a strong defender of the
Nicene creed, but lapsed into a complete Sabellian
doctrine. There is no ground for the charge.
Marcellus was separated from Athanasius in his
whole metaphysics. He was not an Origenist; he
declared Origen to be the source of the whole
Arian heresy. He opposed the Origenistic doctrine of generation and subordination, and held
to the absoluteness of the Logos. When Athanasius came to understand the real position of Marcellus he disowned him, and his earnest plea
against the Sabellian doctrine in the fourth Oration seems to have been directed especially against
Marcellus himself, though his name is not mentioned. The truth is that Marcellus held a type

of doctrine that was gaining ground in the West, and his chief sympathizers were in that quarter. Sabellianism had its origin on Greek soil, but it was wholly rejected by the Origenistic Logos school, which finally triumphed over all monarchian tendencies and remained tenaciously trinitarian to the last; while the Sabellianism of Marcellus reappeared in a disguised form in the Western Latin church in the person of Augustine.

Athanasius, then, held to a trinity of three ∠ personal Beings. On this point there was no disagreement between him and Arius. Both stood on common Origenistic ground; both equally opposed Sabellianism. Their differences arose on the question of the nature of the second person. Arius declared him to be a creature; Athanasius declared him to be the true Son of God, of the same generic nature with the Father (ὁμοούσιος), and therefore not a creature.

That Athanasius did not mean by *homoousios* one *numerical* essence or being is not only involved in his whole metaphysics, but is expressly declared in his "Statement of Faith:" "We do not hold a Son-Father, as do the Sabellians, calling Him single in essence but not the same in essence (μονοούσιον καὶ οὐχ ὁμοούσιον), and thus destroying the existence of the Son." The charge here is that the Sabellians reduce the Father and Son to mere modes of one being, — a sort of Son-Father, and thus destroy the Son's distinct personal existence. Athanasius could not have distinguished numerical unity of essence from generic unity more pointedly than he did by the terms *monoousios* and *homoousios*. He held that the Father and the Son were both divine beings, and hence of the same divine nature (ὁμοούσιοι); but this is a very different doctrine from the Sabellian, which makes God a single essence (μονοούσιος), revealing him- self in three personal forms. Sabellianism is es- sentially monistic and pantheistic; it confounds the persons and their acts, reducing them to acci- dents of one substance. Athanasius was a theist. He held that God is a self-conscious, individual, uni-personal Being. He was equally a monotheist. He believed in " one God, the Father Almighty." Hence he was always careful to distinguish the acts of the Father and the Son as well as their .individualities.

Modern writers frequently assume that the Greek Fathers had crude ideas of what personality is, — a curious assumption to make in regard to men who were profoundly versed in the Aristotelian psychology, and whose metaphysical discrimina- tions have formed the warp and woof of theological thought to the present day. I grant, however, that modern theologians have made one psycholo- gical discovery which was unknown to Athanasius. He had not learned that "person," as a metaphy- sical term, may have two meanings, a natural and a non-natural. By it he meant an individual being, or what Mr. Joseph Cook calls derisively a person " in the ordinary Boston sense." It was reserved for Augustine and his successors down to Mr. Cook to confound all valid laws of thought by asserting that " person " may mean one thing in common speech and a very different thing in Christian theology.

· But if Athanasius held to three persons in the strict sense, how did he save himself from tritheism? I answer: In the same way as his predecessors had done before him, by the doctrine of one supreme cause. Here again Athanasius is a pure Origenist. The Origenistic doctrine of generation and subordination solved for him, as for all the Greek Fathers, the mystery of the divine unity as related to the divine trinity. The Son as begotten of the Father is a derived being, and so cannot be a separate or foreign deity. This is the point of the varied illustrations which Athanasius employs in setting forth his view, such as fountain and stream, sun and ray, king and image, parent and child. Some of these comparisons are capable of a Sabellian sense, if the object of Athanasius in using them is not understood; and in recent theology they have been thus misinterpreted. But they were intended to illustrate the community of nature of the Father and the Son, not numerical oneness. This is evident from those illustrations which cannot admit any such construction. Take the case of parent and child which Athanasius uses so frequently. Since the child is the offspring of the parent he is of the same generic nature (ὁμοούσιος); as such, he is not

foreign or exterior to the parent, but interior and
proper to him, and so *vice versa* the parent is interior to the child.   Athanasius represents a father (first Oration, 26) as replying to the question
whence his child came: " He is *not from without,*
but from myself, proper and similar to my essence,
not become mine from another, but begotten of
me; wherefore I too *am wholly in him, while I
remain myself what I am.*"   So, he adds, the Son
is interior and proper to the Father.   This doctrine of the interiorness or coinherence of the Son
in the Father has been misapprehended by Augustinian theologians.   It has been supposed to support
strongly the view of numerical unity.   But this
was not the question at issue.   Athanasius was
arguing against the Arian doctrine that the Son
is a creature, and the illustration of parent and
child was applied directly against his Arian opponents: " Let them confess in like manner concerning the Word of God that he is simply from the
Father."   The argument assumes the fundamental
postulate of the Platonic dualism and transcendence, — that the created is exterior and foreign
to the uncreated.   If the Son is a creature, he is
foreign to the Father, like all other creatures; but
if he is a true Son, of the Father's essence, he
cannot be foreign or exterior, and hence cannot be
a creature.   As a child is generically in his parent
and the parent in the child, so the Son is in the
Father and the Father in the Son; and it is to
support this argument that Athanasius appeals so

frequently to Christ's words: " That ye may know
that I am in the Father and the Father in me."
" I and my Father are one." " He that hath seen
me hath seen the Father."

In this connection further light is shed upon the
meaning of the term *homoousios*, as used by Athanasius. He applies it continually to human persons, as belonging to one human race, that is, in a
generic sense. How then can it be assumed that,
in applying it to the Son of God, he uses it in a
totally different sense, especially when the divine
relationship is being directly compared with the
human, and no hint is given that the meaning is
changed? But we are not left to conjecture.
Athanasius himself explains his meaning in one
clear passage, not to speak of others: " The sense
of ' offspring ' and ' coessential ' ($\acute{o}\mu oo\acute{v}\sigma\iota os$) is one,
and whoso considers the Son an offspring, rightly
considers him also as coessential." [1] If this passage by itself were of doubtful interpretation, the
context sets all doubt at rest, for Athanasius is
showing that the Semi-Arian doctrine of " likeness
in essence " ($\acute{o}\mu o\iota o\acute{v}\sigma\iota os$) is not in necessary disagreement with the homoousian doctrine, since it
allows that the Son is the true offspring of the
Father. But it is impossible to interpret " likeness in essence " as implying numerical unity. It
would seem unnecessary to pursue this point
further; but so ingrained in modern theology is
the view that the Nicene Athanasian doctrine of

[1] *De Synodis*, 42.

the Trinity involves a numerical unity of essence, that I propose a few additional considerations.

First, if Athanasius had meant by *homoousios* "numerically one in essence," he would not have distinguished it, as he did, from μονοούσιος and ταυτοούσιος, for this is the very point of the difference in these terms, as Athanasius himself shows, defining *homoousios* as meaning "sameness *in likeness*," in contrast with a simple unity. Further, the fact that Athanasius made such common use of the term ὅμοιος (like) as expressing his own faith, and that he was ready to accept ὁμοιούσιος as a synonym for ὁμοούσιος, if properly explained, seems wholly conclusive. But, still further, such a use of the word would have been altogether new in its history. Everywhere in Greek literature *homoousios* means generic likeness or sameness. Aristotle calls the stars ὁμοούσιοι. Plotinus uses the same term for souls, when arguing that they are divine and immortal. There is no evidence that any Greek Father ever gave the word any different meaning. Gregory of Nyssa calls not only "human souls," but also "corruptible bodies," *homoousia* (ὁμοούσια τὰ φθαρτὰ σώματα). Chrysostom describes Eve as *homoousios* with Adam.[1]

There is one more consideration that goes to the root of the whole matter. The assumption of numerical unity of essence involves another assumption, viz., that, in the case of the Trinity,

---

[1] Gregory, *Contra Eunomium*, vii. 5; Chrysostom, *Homil. in Genes.* xvi.

singleness of essence exists with a plurality of persons. But this breaks down a fundamental law of logic and psychology. Essence is the sum of the qualities of a being. Person is a being with certain qualities which constitute its essence. Essence and person then must be coincident. They cannot be separated. The distinction between them is purely logical and subjective. To assume a separation in fact, or that one may be singular and the other plural, is to confound the subjective with the objective, and create a metaphysical contradiction.[1] The Greek Fathers were never guilty of such a confusion. They were too well versed in the Aristotelian logic. The question was never even raised until the fifth century, in the compromise of Chalcedon. All through the earlier trinitarian and christological controversies the coincidence of nature and person was accepted on all sides as axiomatic. On this ground Origen and his school called the three persons three essences, meaning that each person has his own individual qualities. So Theodore of Mopsuestia, a devoted adherent of the Nicene creed, was led to his theory of two persons in Christ, or of two real Christs, by assuming that if there were two complete natures, divine

[1] While I must dissent entirely from the interpretation of Principal Robertson and Cardinal Newman in vol. iv. of the *Nicene Fathers*, I wish to express my admiration of the candor of both these critics in allowing that their view involves what is self-contradictory to the human understanding. But does not such an admission stamp the interpretation itself as false? Certainly Athanasius was not conscious of holding a self-contradictory doctrine, and he was a keen logician.

and human, two persons must result. The same
assumption led the Monophysites to their theory
of "one nature," since Christ was one person.
There is not the slightest evidence that any Greek
Father before Theodoret held any other opinion.
The Cappadocian Athanasian school stood firmly
on it. That Athanasius himself should have developed a new metaphysics on this point, so as to
change the whole character of trinitarian doctrine,
without leaving a ripple on the surface of ecclesiastical history, is inconceivable.

But the fact may be brought up that, while
Origen called three persons three essences, Athanasius and his followers refused to do so. The
explanation is simple. It was the result of a linguistic evolution, such as is common to all language.
The theological terminology of the Greek Fathers
was Aristotelian. Aristotle distinguished two
kinds of essence. By "first essence" he meant a
concrete being or thing. By "second essence"
he meant the "form" or idea, or, in Platonic
language, the universal, the genus or species,
which is the basis of all "first essences" or individual things. These distinctions underlie the
whole Greek theology. But they are brought out
explicitly and in Aristotelian form by the later
scholastic Athanasians, Gregory of Nyssa and John
of Damascus. When Origen called the Son an
"essence" he meant "first essence," that is, a
concrete being or real person. But when discussion arose in the Nicene period over the question

of the relation of nature to person, and especially concerning the use of ὑπόστασις for person, as distinguished from οὐσία, the term οὐσία became restricted in meaning to the " second " sense of Aristotle, — the universal, generic, or abstract sense ; and such was the common meaning of it in the later Greek Fathers. Gregory of Nyssa and also John of Damascus define οὐσία as κοινόν, that is, what is common or generic in contrast with the individual (ὑπόστασις). Such is the use of it by Athanasius. Hence he again and again employs the Platonic and Aristotelian names for the generic or universal (εἶδος, μορφή), as synonyms for οὐσία. No evidence could be clearer. (According to Athanasius the divine essence or form or idea is individualized and personalized in the Father, Son, and Holy Spirit, who are thus united in a metaphysical and transcendental unity, and separated from all created beings.) This is distinctly set forth by John of Damascus : " Essence does not exist by itself, but is seen in persons." It is true that Athanasius sometimes uses the term θεός as a synonym for οὐσία, but he often adds the abstract, θειότης, in explanation, and the context always shows this to be his meaning. This usage is explained by Gregory of Nyssa in the treatise Ἐκ τῶν κοινῶν ἐννοιῶν, when he says that if the name θεός signified a person, three persons would signify three gods, but since it denotes οὐσία, there is one Divinity. It cannot be too distinctly declared that the Greek theologians from Athanasius on

are philosophically Platonico-Aristotelians. With
them all, the idea or universal has concrete existence only in individual beings. The Father, Son,
and Holy Spirit are such individuals (ὑποστάσεις).
The unity of the three is not concrete or numerical but metaphysical or generic. It is easy now
to see why Athanasius declined to say "three
essences," and yet did not hesitate to say "three
hypostases" or beings. The failure to recognize
this linguistic change in the use of "essence,"
after the time of Origen, has perhaps contributed
more than anything else to the opinion that Athanasius departed radically from Origen's view. But
it was in fact a mere change of terminology, not
one of theological position.[1]

---

[1] The translator of the new volume of the *Nicene Fathers*
(*Gregory of Nyssa*) represents Athanasius as "using the older
terminology," not distinguishing ὑπόστασις from οὐσία (p. 24).
In support of his assertion he refers to a passage in *Ad Afros*, 4.
But in translating it he makes a curious blunder, leaving out of
account or misinterpreting the last clause, and thus changing the
whole meaning. A reference to the correct translation in the
fourth volume of the *Nicene Fathers* would have set him right.
In fact Athanasius did not, in this passage or in the context,
raise the question at all whether ὑπόστασις may be used in a different sense from οὐσία. It was wholly out of his thought.
That Athanasius did elsewhere use τρεῖς ὑποστάσεις in contradis-
tinction to μία οὐσία is allowed by the translator in a note.

I must make another criticism on the whole translation of
Gregory's *Contra Eunomium*. Οὐσία is translated everywhere by
the term "being" or "Being," as if it were concrete, while
ὑπόστασις is translated always by the term "person," as if person was to be distinguished from concrete being. This is unjust
both to Eunomius and to Gregory. Eunomius, as an extreme
Arian, held that the Father, Son, and Holy Spirit are three
οὐσίαι, and that each οὐσία is an individual or personal being

The Athanasian Trinitarianism is seen in its completest form in the Cappadocian theologians, Basil and the two Gregories. The idea has recently been broached that these men formed a Neo-Nicene school, falling away from the homoousianism of Athanasius to the older homoiousianism of Origen.[1] This theory rests on the assumption that Athanasius himself was not an Origenist. But, as we have seen, Athanasius had no quarrel with the genuine homoiousianism of Origen. *Homoios* was the word oftenest on his own lips.[2] His great conflict was with the Arian Heterou-

(ὑπόστασις), following the "older terminology" of Origen. Gregory, on the contrary, adopted the new nomenclature, defining οὐσία as an abstract or universal (the "second essence" of Aristotle), while ὑπόστασις was limited to individual or concrete being. The failure to recognize this difference in the use of terms creates complete confusion in the translation. Gregory explicitly holds that Father, Son, and Holy Spirit are three individuals or Beings, and that οὐσία is a generic or universal term and therefore must be singular.

The influence of Newman is clearly visible in these new translations of the Greek Fathers, and it is baneful. He failed to discern the thoroughly Aristotelian character of the Nicene metaphysics, and assumed that in the Nicene Trinity " essence " in its concrete sense and " person " are not coincident, and consequently that God is one Being at the same time that He is three Persons. See his *Theological Tracts*, pp 259, 265.

[1] Harnack's *Outlines of the History of Dogma*, p. 260. *Nicene and Post-Nicene Fathers*, second series, vol. v. p. 24. Gwatkin, *Studies of Arianism*, p. 242, with a reference to Zahn, *Marcellus*, 87.

[2] In the three *Orations against the Arians*, ὁμοούσιος is used but once, while ὅμοιος and its derivatives ὁμοίωσις and ὁμοιότης are used at least thirty-four times. The so-called *Fourth Oration* is directed rather against the Sabellianism of Marcellus. Athanasius here uses ὁμοούσιος three times, and seems to have no fear of its being charged with a Sabellian meaning.

sians.   He held out the olive branch of peace to
the Semi-Arians; and the Cappadocians were his
devoted helpers in the reunion that was finally
accomplished.   Basil was his personal‘ friend.
Gregory of Nyssa, Basil's younger brother and disciple, became the acknowledged head of the Nicene
party.   Strange would it be if these men misunderstood the theological position of their great
leader.   But there is no evidence of it in their
voluminous writings.   Their doctrinal watchwords
are the same.   They contend against Arianism and
Sabellianism alike, defending the old Trinitarianism with the old metaphysics of generation, derivation, and subordination.   It is true they were
ardent Origenists, but Athanasius himself had for
Origen only words of praise.   In one respect only
can we detect a change.   The Cappadocians were
the schoolmen of the Greek Fathers.   They introduced a more precise metaphysical treatment of
theological themes; but the substance and even
form of their doctrine is thoroughly Athanasian.

To conclude: The words of Harnack on this
closing chapter of the Greek Trinitarianism can be
truthfully applied to its whole history: "In reality under the cover of the ὁμοούσιος men indeed
continued in the Orient in a kind of homoiousianism, which is to this day orthodox in all their
churches."   Carlyle once voiced the traditional
conception of the Nicene theology when he declared that the whole controversy was about a
diphthong.   In fact, it was not a question of a

diphthong, but of an *alpha privative*. Ὅμοιος versus ἀνόμοιος was the real issue. It was Augustine and the Latin Church that changed the focus of debate, and made the diphthong a heresy, by giving *homoousios* a new meaning, and adding *filioque* to the creed. It is no wonder that a schism followed between the two churches which has continued to this day. The idea is prevalent that this schism rests on slight theological grounds. The very contrary is the truth. The addition of *filioque* to the Nicene creed was a radical overturning of the whole structure. It broke down its monotheism; it reduced generation and sonship to a metaphor; it turned three personal beings into one being revealing himself in tri-personal form; it changed the mediating Logos into absolute Deity. Such changes are revolutionary. No compromise was possible, or ever will be. The schism is complete and final.

Our survey of Athanasianism here naturally closes. But the question that was raised at the outset, Would Athanasius recognize his New England disciples? remains unanswered. This requires a further survey of the pseudo-Athanasian Augustinianism, and its outcome in the New England Trinitarianism.

CHAPTER II

THE previous chapter contained a survey of the development of the Greek Trinitarianism until its definite expression in the Nicene creed, and in the writings of Athanasius and his theological successors, Basil and the two Gregories. From this time Greek theology ceased to be creative, and has remained to this day traditional and fixed. The Nicene creed with the Constantinopolitan amendments is still the orthodox definition of the Trinity in the Greek Church. The later christological controversies issuing in the decision of Chalcedon all assumed the truth of the Nicene doctrine. Thus the term Athanasianism best expresses in a summary way the Greek orthodox Trinitarianism.

But while Athanasius himself was still living and in the very crisis of his conflict with Arianism, a man was born in Tagaste in North Africa who was to begin an entirely new evolution of trinitarian dogma. Athanasius died in 373 A. D.; Augustine was born in 354. When he died in Hippo in 430 the Vandals were besieging the city and completing the conquest of North Africa, — an event which significantly marked the political change that was rapidly passing over the Latin-Roman world. This change must be thoroughly understood in order to a full appreciation of the theological differences that now arose.

To the historical student who takes a wide chronological survey the fifth century will stand out at once conspicuously as one of the most critical epochs in the world's annals. Civilization itself hung in the balance against a resistless tide of barbarism that poured in successive waves over Europe. The names of Alaric, Genseric, Attila, Clovis, Hengist, and Horsa are simply the most famous of a long line of invading warriors with their multitudinous followers, whose inroads broke in pieces the West Roman empire. Horde after horde, Visigoths, Vandals, Burgundians, Huns, Ostrogoths, Franks, and Lombards followed each other, ravaging and pillaging, and then retreating to their forest homes, laden with spoils and captives, or settling down in the districts they had devastated. Rome herself did not escape. Sacked once and again, for years the camp alternately of contending armies, she gradually lost her old prestige and importance, ceased to be the capital of the West, and at last, as the Dark Ages came on, became the prey of warring ecclesiastical and political factions and dwindled to a city of ruins, her great Coliseum being used as a quarry, and her Forum, so full of historic memories, as a cattle pen. Thus was extinguished in Latin Christendom that splendid Græco-Roman civilization which, with all its faults and crimes, had given to the world its highest form of intellectual culture and religious faith.

The effects of these vast political and social changes were radical and momentous. Theodosius the Great, who died in 395, was the last ruler of the united empire. From this time the separation of the East from the West grew more and more sharply defined. Greek letters, art, and philosophy recrossed the Adriatic to their original home. With the surrender of the purple by the last West Roman emperor in 476, political relations between the two parts of the empire rapidly declined. The old Græco-Roman world shrank into the Byzantine, with its centre at Constantinople. Church became divided as well as state. This period marks the true birth of the Papacy, which is a Latin institution. From this time Latin creeds began to multiply. Thus the foundations were laid for the marked differences that began to appear between Greek and Latin forms of theological statement. This was especially true of the dogma of the Trinity, which received its new shaping most completely at the hands of Augustine.

In order properly to apprehend the new point of view and tendency of the Augustinian Trinitarianism, something must be said concerning the sundering of relations which had occurred between this age and the ages preceding in language, literature and philosophy. The culture of the Roman Empire was largely derived from the Greeks whom

the Romans had conquered in the second century
B. C. The Greek language became *par excellence*
the learned language of the Græco-Roman world.
The young men of the Roman nobility were sent
to Athens to complete their education. Greek
rhetoricians and philosophers like Plutarch, Plotinus and Porphyry came to Rome to lecture and
teach, not learning Latin, but using their native
tongue. Thus there came to be an essential unity
in the civilization and literature of the empire.
The early Latin Christian Fathers read the writings of their Greek brethren. Tertullian shows
his thorough acquaintance with Greek literature,
pagan and Christian. He quotes Homer, Herodo-
tus, and the Greek philosophers, and even wrote
some of his works in Greek. There was also a
constant intercourse between the Greek and the
Latin churches. Many Greeks, like Irenæus, settled in the West and became identified with Latin
Christendom. In the second and third centuries
every form of culture was cosmopolitan. Greek
teachers traveled everywhere, and Greek letters
and schools of philosophy were spread into every
corner of the Empire. This is illustrated in the
ante-Nicene theology. With minor divergences
there was a general harmony of doctrine between
the East and the West. Especially is this true of
the trinitarian dogma. Tertullian, Irenæus, Hippolytus, Novatian, Lactantius, and Hilary are in
essential agreement with Justin Martyr, Origen,
and Athanasius. It is one of the mistakes of the

traditional view of the early history of Christian
doctrine that Augustine simply developed the theology of the earlier Latin Fathers, especially Tertullian and Hilary.   Nothing can be further from
the truth.   This mistake has arisen in part from
another mistake, which I fully explained in the
previous chapter, concerning the meaning of the
term ὁμοούσιος as used by the Greek theologians.
It has been taken for granted that ὁμοούσιος meant
numerical unity of essence, and that it was so
understood by Latin as well as Greek Fathers.
Hence the "*una substantia*" of Tertullian has
been generally interpreted in the "numerical"
sense, and Augustine's doctrine of numerical unity
has been supposed to be derived from it.   This
view fails to appreciate the wide breach created by
the commotions and upheavals of the fourth and
fifth centuries.   The Latin Fathers before Augustine universally held to a trinity of three personal
beings united in a generic unity by community of
essence.   They held to the real subordination of
the Son to the Father, distinguishing the Father,
as self-existent and the first cause, from the Son as
derived and dependent.   Tertullian, whose general
view is very similar to that of Justin Martyr, even
held that the Son had a beginning and was a sort
of emanation from the Father's essence.   Hilary
of Gaul, who lived in the Nicene age and traveled
in the East, and thus became thoroughly acquainted
with the Arian and Semi-Arian controversies, expressly declared that to him *homoousion* and *ho-*

moiousion meant the same thing, and on this ground urged the homoiousian Semi-Arians to accept the Nicene creed, thus following precisely the lead of Athanasius.[1] The idea that there was

[1] In the previous chapter I showed that Athanasius was quite ready to adopt *homoiousios* as a synonym for *homoousios* if its meaning was clearly expressed as implying community of essence, and distinguishing the Son from created beings. Further, I called attention to the fact that he usually employed the term *homoios* rather than *homoousios* to set forth his own doctrine of the Son's relation to the Father, proving conclusively that he held to generic unity of essence in agreement with the Origenistic school. If he had broken with Origen and his followers in the use of the new term *homoousios*, he surely would not have continued to use the term *homoios* which was the watchword of Origenism, and which cannot be twisted to mean numerical unity. A writer in the *Biblical World* (April, 1895) takes issue with me on this point, and quotes a passage from *De Decretis* which he thinks involves the theory of numerical unity of essence of the Trinity. I wonder if the writer took care to read the original Greek, for he seems to fail to understand that the whole passage turns on the word *homoios*, and is written to explain how the Nicene bishops came to substitute for it the term *homoousios*. Athanasius says they first employed the term *homoios* to set forth their doctrine, — this Origenistic term being antithetic to the Arian term *heteros*, — but when they saw the Arians "whispering to each other" and explaining *homoios* in a sense of their own, they then insisted on the term *homoousios*, as a word that expressed more explicitly *essential likeness*. The point of contention between the Nicene Fathers and the Arians was whether the Son was uncreated or created, in other words, like or unlike to the Father in his essential being. Athanasius explicitly asserts in this passage that the bishops would have been satisfied with *homoios* if the Arians had not sought to wrest the word from its true meaning, and a clear light is thus shed on the real meaning of *homoousios*, as used by the Nicene bishops and by Athanasius himself. Let me further suggest to this critic that if he had quoted the whole of the first passage given, in its connection, instead of joining together a string of detached clauses that are wholly disconnected, he would have rendered a real service to his readers, instead of wholly

a theological difference between the East and the
West on the question of the Trinity in the third
century has no foundation in fact. The breach
was later, post-Nicene not ante-Nicene ; and it was
a breach not merely between the East and the
West, but also equally between the old Latin
world of the West Roman Empire and the new
barbarian world that settled on its ruins. Augustine sums up in himself this breach and its character. He was not a Greek scholar. In his age the
tradition of Greek culture was largely lost. There
is no evidence that he read any of the pagan or
Christian Greek writings in the original. He had
of course a general traditional knowledge of the
Greek philosophers and of the Greek Christian
Fathers. But his knowledge is vague and gained
mostly at second hand. Even Plato whom he so
reverenced was known to him chiefly through the
New Platonism of Plotinus and his school in its
Latinized form. The culture of Augustine was
essentially Latin, and even here it was mostly confined to pagan and New Platonic sources. He

confusing them. I will only add that no one can get the keys to
the understanding of Athanasianism from any English translation
of his writings extant. I have shown how defective in this respect
is the edition of the Nicene Fathers recently published. The
volumes on Athanasius and Gregory of Nyssa are translated in
accordance with the theory of numerical unity of essence, and
hence are wholly unreliable in many test passages. A scholarly
translation free from all theological bias is still a desideratum.
The critic's idea that my object in writing was " to aid in establishing a harmony between Trinitarians and Unitarians " is as
wide of the mark as the rest of his criticism. He took my irony
altogether too seriously.

shows a narrow acquaintance with the Latin Fathers before him, and quotes little from them. In short, the Trinitarianism of Augustine has little historical background. It was mostly a new creation from a new standpoint, which was drawn, not from either Greek or Latin Christian sources, but from the ideas which he had imbibed from his philosophical studies and which he applied in his own original way to the defense of what he wrongly understood to be trinitarian orthodoxy. This makes it necessary to dwell briefly on the sources and character of Augustine's philosophical views.

The various currents of Græco-Roman philosophy had gradually become concentrated, in the second and third centuries, into two great streams, the Platonico-Aristotelian with its New Platonic modifications, and the Stoic. The Greek world adhered more closely to Platonism, while Stoicism, which seems to have been especially congenial to the Romans, — witness the writings of Seneca, Epictetus, and Marcus Aurelius, — became the reigning philosophy of the Latin West. Platonism itself, as it moved westward, became mingled with the Stoic stream and lost much of its original theistic and dualistic character. Men called themselves Platonists, who were such only in name. New Platonism is essentially monistic and pantheistic, and on this side comes into close affiliation with Stoicism, though remaining spiritualistic, and in this respect, holding to its Platonic source and thus opposing the Stoic materialism. The great

question of philosophy in this period was that of
dualism *versus* monism: in other words, whether
there are two substances and separate realms of
existence in the universe, — spiritual and material,
— or whether the two are not essentially one.
Platonism held firmly to the ultimate difference
between spirit and matter, and built on this principle its dualistic and spiritualistic philosophy, making God the Supreme Spirit and the creator of
the material world. Stoicism, on the other side,
insisted on the ultimate unity of all existence, and
thus identified God essentially with the world. On
this point New Platonism fell into the monistic
current of the age, and substituted a doctrine of
evolution from the Supreme One to the lowest
forms of matter, in place of the Platonic theory of
creation, thus reducing the dualism of Plato to
unity, in harmony with Stoic ideas. The radical
difference between the two philosophies is seen in
the view taken of God's relation to the material
universe. Plato was a transcendentalist. He held
that God is essentially separate from all created
things, though explicitly accepting the doctrine of
God's providence and efficiency as active in the
upholding and governing of the world He has made.
Stoicism made God immanent in the world, reducing Him philosophically to the central principle or
force that gives life and activity to all things, thus
confounding Him with all the forms of finite existence. As a result Platonism is theistic, regarding God as a personal Being whose substance is

separated by an infinite chasm from all created or
material substance. "God," says Plato in the
"Symposium," "cannot mix with man." Stoicism,
on the other hand, is pantheistic, treating the universe as essentially of one essence evolved out of a
spermatic principle which is its only Deity. So
Platonism holds to the supernatural, a world above
nature, spiritual and eternal, while Stoicism is a
pure doctrine of nature and natural development
and knows nothing of a distinct spiritual kingdom.
Its highest form of life which it called God by a
figure is only a refined matter. The Greek Fathers were essentially Platonists. As I explained
in the previous chapter, the whole Logos doctrine
was founded on the Platonic transcendental theory.
Athanasius drew the line as clearly and sharply as
Plato himself between the uncreated and the created,— between the absolute and the conditioned.
Hence his strenuous insistence on the necessity of
a Divine mediatorship, which is the cardinal doctrine of his whole theology. A New-Platonic pantheistic strain became mingled in later Greek
thought, but no traces of it are to be found in
Athanasius. His doctrine of God and the world
is theistic and transcendental, with no tinge of
monism or pantheism.

Augustine drew his philosophical views from
the opposite quarter. The Stoicism and kindred
New Platonism that permeated Latin thought and
literature, even from the time of Cicero and Varro
and Plutarch, and became the popular philosophy

of the following centuries, entered into his very
bone and marrow.   The philosophical tendency
which was first awakened into life by the "Hor-
tensius" of Cicero was afterwards fed and ma-
tured by the writings of such New Platonists as
Plotinus, — whom he may have read in translations, — Porphyry and Iamblichus, and especially
the Latin Apuleius who was his fellow-country-
man.   Augustine in his "Confessions" gives a
clear account of the influence of these writings
upon him, and declares that they were the providential means of freeing him from the Manichean
dualism, and of preparing him for the acceptance
of Christianity.   It is to be noted that in Augustine's day there was no distinct Stoic sect as opposed to the so-called Platonists.   The eclectic
tendency which began in Cicero and Plutarch had
reached its full development in the later New
Platonism of Julian, Iamblichus, Apuleius, and
Proclus.   Platonism had become a name to cover
every form of philosophy that held to objective
truth as compared with the Epicurean skepticism.
But while Stoicism as a distinct philosophy had
merged itself in New Platonism, by means of the
pantheism which characterized them both, the inherent materialism of the Stoic philosophy still
leavened the thought of the age.   This is well
seen in Tertullian, whose whole theology is shaped
by a materialistic cast of thought, and who shows
in his writings a thorough acquaintance with the

Stoics, Zeno and Cleanthes. It is not clear how much Augustine was influenced by his North African predecessor; but the same materialistic tendency is visible in his writings, particularly in his doctrines of original sin, irresistible grace, the sacraments, and the physical punishments and sufferings of lost souls. Still more, however, was he influenced by the monism which was the eclectic and harmonizing principle that fused Stoicism and New Platonism together. Augustine's whole philosophy starts with a monistic doctrine of unity. The world is but the expression of God. Augustine seems scarcely to admit what we call second causes or laws of nature. This comes out clearly in his controversy with the Pelagians. He reduces the system of natural causation and law to a direct Divine operation. In this way he explains miracles as simply *unusual* modes of Divine efficiency in producing events. No law of nature is subverted, for there is no such law to be subverted. God's own immediate will is the sole cause of all things. This monistic theory appears also in his view of the freedom of the human will as consisting simply in voluntariness, which itself is the result of a gracious Divine efficiency. He carries his doctrine of human dependence almost to the point of the Stoic fatalism, declaring that " the will has power indeed for evil, but not for good, except as helped by the infinite Good." Thus the Stoic, New Platonic immanence, with Augustine, supplants the Platonico-Aristotelian and Athanasian transcendence.[1] This radical change of the philosophical basis of truth differentiates Augustinianism from Athanasianism along the whole line of Christian theology, and meets us at once as we pass to consider more directly Augustine's doctrine of the Trinity.

In this consideration it is needful first of all to get a clear view of the starting-point of Augustine's inquiries. His principal work on the subject is entitled "On the Trinity," and he everywhere holds himself to be a strict Trinitarian, opposing all Sabellian as well as Arian views. In the opening pages of his treatise he states the trinitarian problem as " an inquiry into the unity of the Trinity," or " how the Trinity is not three Gods but one God." That is, he seems to start from the three and to proceed to the one. This was the method of the earlier Greek and Latin Fathers. The trinitarian doctrine in its development began with the acceptance of the three scriptural beings, Father, Son, and Holy Ghost. Then arose the question whether these three divine beings were three Gods. This was the core of the controversies that began to divide the early Christians into sects. Orthodoxy, as set forth by such leaders as Justin Martyr, Origen, and Athanasius, attempted to explain how the Trinity could be accepted without a denial of monotheism. The

[1] For a criticism of the totally opposite view of Dr. A. V. G. Allen, in his *Continuity of Christian Thought*, see Appendix B.

previous chapter treats this explanation at some
length. Enough now to say that the keys to it
are the doctrines of generic unity of essence, and
eternal generation of the Son, and procession of
the Holy Spirit. Athanasius placed the Gordian
knot of the problem not in the fact of the three
persons, but in their metaphysical or ideal union.
He held that the Father is the alone eternal, self-
existent God, and that He eternally generated the
Son and sent forth the Holy Spirit, so that while
there are three divine beings in the Godhead,
there are not three eternal self-existent Gods,
since the Father is the source of being to the
others who are thus dependent and subordinate,
though receiving from the Father all divine attributes. Augustine seems to start from the same
point of view, but as he proceeds we find that the
problem really discussed is just the reverse. It
is not how the three are one, but *how the one is
three.* The explanation of this change of front,
of which Augustine himself seems not to be aware,
is to be found in the fact that he began by treating the Trinity as a problem of faith; but it soon
developed into a problem of reason. His whole
argument starts on the basis of Scripture and
revelation, but gradually passes into the remotest
regions of philosophy. In fact, the book is a most
remarkable patchwork of appeal to authority and
to reason, and contains some of the wildest specimens of theological metaphysics that can be found
anywhere in the whole range of historical the-

ology. This is one of the fundamental differences
between Athanasius and Augustine. With Athanasius Scripture is always primary and reason
secondary. The reverse is true of Augustine.
The result was that Augustine in his whole doctrine of the Trinity paid little respect to previous
theological systems or speculations. He supposed
himself, it is true, to be following in the footsteps
of his orthodox predecessors. No doubt he believed himself to be in full accord with Athanasius
and the Nicene Greek Fathers. But he had little
scholarship or critical sagacity. The whole turn
of his mind and training was toward philosophy;
and he thus at once left the beaten track of traditional Trinitarianism and moved out along the line
of his own philosophical ideas. Those ideas, as we
have seen, were wholly monistic. The New Platonic leaven in him was pervasive, though it did
not carry him to the point of absolute pantheism.
From this he was saved by the clear monotheism
of the Bible. But he took the first step toward
pantheism, as we shall see more clearly in our further consideration of his views.

Augustine starts from the assumption that there
is but one eternal substance in the universe. This
one substance is God. God then, as a being, is
essentially one. He is "*una res*," "*summa sim-
plex essentia.*" Augustine's language and whole
line of argument show that he held to the idea of
a *numerical* rather than a *generic* unity of essence.
This was his interpretation of ὁμοούσιος. With

him, essence, in the case of God, is not abstract but *concrete*. The terms genus and species he declares cannot be applied to God as they are to men. God's essence is his actual being. If God is personal, his essence is personal, that is concrete. "To God," he says, "it is not one thing *to be*, another *to be a person*, but it is absolutely the same thing." Hence he continually passes from "*unum*" as descriptive of the one essence, to "*unus*," and describes the Trinity as "*unus Deus*." For Augustine, then, the trinitarian problem is how this one God, "*unus Deus*," can be three or a "*trinitas*." He assumes it to be a fact. He continually puts *unus Deus* and *trinitas* into juxtaposition as essentially coincident. He declares repeatedly that one God and trinity are the same thing. Thus Augustine confounds monotheism with trinitarianism, and changes trinity into tri-unity. His trinity is one divine Being, not three beings. What then is the peculiarity of Augustinian Trinitarianism? He allows that Father, Son, and Holy Ghost are three. But three what? three beings? No. Three persons? Here we touch the critical point. Augustine explains how the term "person" came to be used by the Latins, but declares that it is not employed in the proper sense of a personal being. The sum of his answer is that the term "person" is used negatively rather than positively in default of any more exact term, and in order to be able to give some sort of answer to those who ask *what* three: "that we might not be altogether silent when asked, what three, while we confessed that they are three." He enters into a curious discussion of the question whether, since God is one essence, He is not also properly called one person, and on the other hand whether, if there are three persons, it is not proper to call them three essences or three Gods. He allows the logical truth of these conclusions, but refuses to accept them in the explanation of the Trinity, and frankly acknowledges that the problem is insoluble. "It is feared to say three essences," nor "can it be said that there are not three somewhats." It is plain that all through this discussion Augustine is playing with words. In fact he confesses it. "Such words are employed," he says, "that there may be something to say;" and again, "from the necessity of speaking, when copious reasoning is required against the devices or errors of the heretics."

What then did Augustine mean by "three persons" or "somewhats," if not three personal beings? Was he a Sabellian without knowing it, and even while striving to distinguish his doctrine from that of Sabellius? This cannot be affirmed without some explanation. Augustine did not start from the Sabellian premise of an evolution in God from unity to trinity; nor did he develop a Sabellian doctrine of Christ. But while he did not adopt the Sabellian premise, his own monistic New Platonic premise led him to the Sabellian conclusion, viz., that the "three somewhats" or

"persons" so-called of the Trinity are only triple
modes or relations of the one essence or being of
God.   The critical test of Sabellianism *versus* the
Nicene doctrine is whether the Trinity is essentially one Being or three Beings.   Sabellianism
says one Being; Athanasianism says three Beings.
Hence Sabellianism is monistic, while Athanasianism is trinitarian.   Here Augustine plainly sides
with Sabellius.   A remarkable passage in his
"Tractate on the Fourth Gospel" brings out his
position clearly: "The Trinity is one God; three,
but not three Gods.   Three what, then?   I reply:
The Father, and the Son, and the Holy Spirit."
But can the three be numbered, as three men can
be?   Here Augustine wavers.   "If you ask: 'three
what?' number ceases.   When you have numbered,
you cannot tell what you have numbered.   Only
in their relations to each other do they suggest
number, not in their essential existence.   I have
no name to give the three, save the Father, the
Son, and the Holy Spirit, one God, one Almighty,
and so one beginning."   Here the monism of
Augustine fully appears.   The only numbering,
he declares, that can apply to God is that of his
essence, which is one.   When the Trinity is spoken
of, "number fails."   This must mean that Augustine did not regard the "three" as real and distinct existences or individuals which, of course,
can be numbered, but only as modes or relations,
in triple form, of one existence or individual.
Hence his hesitation and play of words concern-

ing the term "person." It is to him a makeshift
for what is not a person. God, for Augustine, is
one Being and so one Person, not three Persons.
These three are *unus Deus*, that is, one Personal
Being. The three persons so-called are merely
three relative forms under which the one God is
manifested in the revelation of himself to men.
It is not to be inferred, however, that Augustine
regarded these forms or relations as superficial or
transitory. Here again he separated himself from
the Sabellians. The Trinity, according to Augustine, is the essential mode of the Divine existence.
On this point he is thoroughly Athanasian. The
one God is eternally a Trinity. Augustine does
not go so far as his later followers, in insisting
that God could not exist except in trinity, but he
regards trinity as an ultimate fact in God; so essential is it that he looks upon the whole universe
as, in some sense, trinitarian, and seeks to find
images and traces of trinity not only in man, but
in nature in all its forms, and even in the triple
character of ancient philosophy. But these very
analogies show the essentially Sabellian character
of Augustine's view. These images of trinity are
modal and relational, as, for example, the illustration of the triple nature of the human mind, or
of the body, or of the departments of philosophy.
Such illustrations fairly image forth the Sabellian
doctrine, but not the Athanasian. Athanasius frequently illustrates his doctrine by the case of a
human father and son, and of human persons gen-

erally, but Augustine expressly sets such illustrations aside as illegitimate. The reason is plain. Athanasius describes the relations which exist between three divine Beings. Augustine describes the relations or modes of existence of one Being, manifesting himself under different forms and names. The personal forms are three, but the personal centre, the personality itself, is one. This, however, is just what Athanasius flouted as Sabellianism. "For they are one (ἕν) not as of one twice named, so that the same being is in one way Father and in another way (ἄλλοτε) his Son; for Sabellius holding this view was judged a heretic; but they are two (δύο μὲν εἰσιν), since the Father is Father and is not at the same time Son, and the Son is Son and is not at the same time Father; but the nature is one (μία δὲ ἡ φύσις), and all things that belong to the Father belong also to the Son." [1]

We note here the sharp difference between Augustine and Athanasius. Augustine declares that "when the Trinity is spoken of number fails." "Three" is but a metaphor. Number only applies strictly to God as one. Athanasius reverses this. His position is that number applies properly rather to the Trinity. He insists on the numbering of the persons as essential to the truth against Sabellius. "Two," he declares, "is not a mere name for one, but is a reality." It is rather, he says elsewhere, in regard to the divine *essence*

[1] *Third Oration against the Arians,* 4.

that " number fails : " since essence is abstract and
universal, and so does not submit to number, that
is, cannot be individualized.   Only individuals can
be numbered, not universals.   This was the teaching of all the Greek Fathers.   They held to three
real subsistences or individuals in the Trinity
(τρεῖς ὑποστάσεις = *tres res*), and hence put the
numerical term τριάς into the forefront of their
doctrine   and   called   themselves   Trinitarians.
Gregory Nazianzen, for example, says the Trinity
is " divided in number " (ἀριθμῷ διαφόρη).   So John
of Damascus says that persons are distinguished
by number but not by nature.   For " a person
exists by itself, but essence does not exist by itself
but as seen in persons."   Nothing could more
clearly set forth the trinitarianism of the Greeks
as distinguished from that of Augustine ; and the
secret of that difference is that the Greek Fathers
built their doctrine on the philosophical distinctions of Plato and Aristotle, while Augustine based
his on the essential monism of New Platonism.
This appears in his whole treatment and interpretation of the Bible.   Everywhere he finds trinity
as well as unity.   The Jehovah of the Old Testament is at the same time the one God and the
Trinity.   He interprets the Divine appearances to
Adam, to Abraham, to Moses, as sometimes of the
Father, sometimes of the Son, and sometimes of
the whole Trinity, and holds, moreover, that whenever God appears as a single person (Father, Son,
or Holy Spirit), or when any act is performed in

the person of either, the whole Trinity is concerned. Thus though the Son only was incarnate, the whole Trinity wrought the incarnation, so that the Son is made to bear a part in his own incarnation. In the same way it was the Son as Christ that died, but the Father also was actively concerned in it, —a view that is perilously close to the old Patripassianism. Everything that Christ did in the flesh, the Father did also. Augustine even represents the Father as walking on the sea. Such utter confusion of the agency of the three persons was wholly foreign to Athanasius. It is true that he sometimes represents the action of the Father as involved in that of the Son in language that reminds us of Augustine. But a study of such passages in their context will show that Athanasius' point of view is entirely different. He never confounds the Father or the Son with the Trinity. To him the Trinity is always plural, never singular. He distinguishes the agency of the Son in creation from that of the Father. The Father wills, the Son executes. So in regard to the incarnation, death, and resurrection of Christ. Athanasius avoids all Patripassian tendencies. "It was not the Father that was made man. For it follows, when the Lord is called the vine, that there must be a husbandman, and, when he prayed, that there was one to hear, and, when he asked, that there was one to give. Now such things show far more readily the madness of the Sabellians, because he that prayed was one, he that heard another, one

the vine, another the husbandman." Athanasius
holds, indeed, to the unity of agency of Father and
Son, but this unity is conceived not pantheistically,
but as growing out of their metaphysical relation,
the Father being the *fons et origo* of the Son's
agency, though as agents they are two and their
acts are personally distinct. John of Damascus
represents the whole Greek theology when he says:
"The Father and the Holy Spirit have no communion with the Incarnation of the Word, except
by approbation and assent." The prayer with
which Augustine concludes his work on the Trinity
well summarizes the monistic and modalistic character of his Trinitarianism. It is addressed to the
Trinity. But the Trinity is described as "one
Lord God," and the whole prayer is in the singular number. Father, Son, and Holy Ghost are
confounded as one Person. "O Lord, the one
God, God the Trinity, whatever is said in these
books that is of thine may they acknowledge who
are thine." No wonder that Calvin, stout Augustinian as he was, should have protested against such
a form of prayer, which seems to have been common in his day. "It is a common prayer: 'Holy
Trinity, one God, have mercy upon us.' It dis-
pleases me and savors throughout of barbarism."

We are now at a point where we can understand
how Augustine was led to eliminate all subordination from his trinitarian doctrine. The traditional
view which regards Augustine as a true disciple of
Athanasianism has never been able to explain

satisfactorily this feature of Augustine's doctrine. The common explanation has been that the Athanasian homoousian doctrine makes the Son equal to the Father, and that the ground was thus prepared for the step taken by Augustine. But this cannot be allowed. Athanasius held that the Son was a derived being: he insisted strongly on the distinction between αἴτιος and αἰτιατός. The Son was not self-existent, but dependent eternally on the Father. Subordination was thus an essential element in the Athanasian doctrine. To be sure, Athanasius borrows from Paul the term "equal;" but he explains it, in harmony with his subordination doctrine, to set forth his view that the Son is of divine origin and nature and possesses by derivation all divine attributes. The step that Augustine took could never have been taken from the standpoint of Athanasius. *Subordination* has always remained the central feature of all Greek theology. It is the new philosophic starting-point of Augustine that explains the elimination of all subordination from his system. God, in his view, is essentially one; yet He is a trinity, but not a trinity of real personal beings; the personal centre is one. The three persons, so-called, are not subsistences or individuals; they are modes of the one divine existence. How Augustine explained the terms "generation" and "procession," as applied to the Son and Holy Spirit, it is difficult to say. He cannot have accepted them literally. They belong with the term "person" to Augustine's negative nomenclature. For Augustine generation did not involve any real derivation or dependence. The Son is as truly and absolutely God as the Father. God is as self-existent and eternal in the Son and Holy Spirit as in the Father. Each form or mode of the Divine Being involves the whole Divine Being. Subordination, therefore, is impossible. "Relations," as Augustine termed them, in the Trinity can have no essential significance. They are not beings or essences, but only qualities of beings. The only superiority of the Father is that he is first in order. Here is the germ of the *official* subordination that has played such a part in later trinitarian history. In Augustine's doctrine Jesus Christ is absolute Deity, the whole of God. He is the Jehovah of the Old Testament, nay, he is in fact the whole Trinity, for God is trinity; one is three and three is one, and so absolutely that the Trinity is properly addressed as a singular being, and Augustine's prayer to the Trinity was equally a prayer to Christ, to the Father, to the Holy Spirit, to all three together and to the singular whole, which is all three. Such is the amazing antinomy of the Augustinian Trinitarianism. How so logical a thinker could have thus lost himself in the mazes of monism and played jumping-jack with his own logic would be a profound mystery to any one who had not studied the history of human speculation. Curiously enough, Augustine seems to have still supposed himself to be a believer in Father, Son, and Holy Spirit as three personal agents; but there is no evidence that he ever attempted to harmonize his trinitarian faith with his unitarian theology.

Before passing to consider the outcome of Augustinianism in later history, it may be well to note several of the more radical changes in theological thought that resulted from the new Augustinian views. In the *first* place, Augustine's doctrine of the Trinity tended to break down the Christian Athanasian doctrine of *mediatorship*. This doctrine is central not only in the New Testament, but also in Greek theology. The Logos doctrine is the speculative expression of it. The redemption of man by a mediating being who partakes of divine as well as human nature is the great theme of the Athanasian argument against Arius. In Augustine's day the Atonement was not discussed. The doctrine of a Divine Redeemer was thrown into the background by the Pelagian controversy concerning man and the origin of evil. Christ's work as a Saviour was not lost sight of, but Augustine's view of him as essentially the absolute God led inevitably to a confusion of his mediatorial function with the other functions of the Godhead. The one God in Trinity was made the agent in the atonement as in all other divine activities. How far Augustine himself was affected in his views of Christ's mediatorial work by his monistic Trinitarianism his writings do not disclose. But the seed sown soon brought forth its natural fruit. Mediæval theology, which is essentially Augus-

tinian, so confounded Christ with God the Father
that instead of making him the expression and
representation of Divine mercy and intercession,
as the earlier theology had always done, it made him
rather the representative of Divine justice and
punishment.   Mediæval art is on this point a true
and telling witness.   The face of Christ, which in
early art was benignant and compassionate, becomes hard and severe, and in the frequent judgment scenes he is pictured as on the throne wrathful and vengeful, and in the act of punishing the
guilty.   No wonder that the cult of the Virgin
Mary became so popular.   Its growth, with all the
superstitions involved, was the protest of heavy-
laden souls, longing for some way of access to the
mercy of God, when the old and living way through
Christ had been closed.   Anselm's " Cur Deus
Homo " — a work which was epoch-making in its
influence upon the mediæval views of the atonement — illustrates forcibly the effect of the Augustinian type of doctrine.   The treatise is pervaded
with a thinly-disguised Patripassianism and Mono-
physitism.   The very title is suggestive.   It is not
" Why the Christ," but " Why the God-man ? "
Anselm's Redeemer is God himself, not another
mediating being, such as the Logos of Greek theology.   The question raised at the outset is, " By
what necessity and for what reason God, since He
is omnipotent, took on himself the humiliation and
weakness of human nature for the sake of its
restoration ? "   Here the mediating element is

wholly absent. A mediator implies two parties. Anselm confounds one party and the mediator together. He represents God as "descending to the Virgin's womb" and "enduring weariness, hunger, thirst, strokes, crucifixion, and death." God "the Creator," who "made Adam," "redeemed" us "by his own blood" "from sin and from his own wrath." Such language runs through the whole book. Sometimes it becomes grossly Patripassian or monistic. Speaking of the death of Christ, he says: "No one would knowingly kill God." The point of all this mode of speech is explained by Anselm himself. Christ, he says, is "the whole Trinity." "In one person the whole Godhead is meant." "Since he himself is God, the Son of God, he offered himself for his own honor *to himself*, as he did to the Father and the Holy Spirit." Thus the whole gospel idea of a daysman between God and men, a Messiah and mediator whom, "in the fullness of time," God sent, "because He so loved the world," is dissolved into the crude materialism of the early heretics. God is made to send himself, to be born, to suffer and die, and this to save men from the effects of his own wrath. Is it any wonder that modern discussions on the atonement could never reach a satisfactory result on the Anselmic basis? Anselm's God-man is both the Being to be propitiated and the Being that propitiates, a kind of Dr. Jekyll and Mr. Hyde, now the omnipotent and eternal God and anon the "man of sorrows."

This may be truth, as some still believe, but it is not the old gospel of a Messiah. Christ's voice is no longer heard saying, " If ye shall ask anything in my name that will I do, and I will pray the Father." On the Augustinian-Anselmic theory Christ prays to himself, and this is no prayer at all. The real intercessory element is gone. One of the chief results of recent Biblical investigation has been the restoration of the historical Christ, with those features of his earthly life that reveal him as our true elder brother, and thus our fit representative before God.

A *second* effect of Augustine's new Trinitarianism was to break down *the monotheistic view of God.* As I showed in the previous chapter, monotheism lies at the basis of Athanasianism. The Nicene creed gave the keynote of all Greek theology in its opening words, — " We believe in one God, the Father Almighty." Monotheism, or theism, in the philosophical sense, holds that God is a single personal being. It emphasizes personality as the true centre and test of all spiritual substance. The spiritual world is composed of persons. If God is spirit, He is a Person. Moral life involves a moral self-consciousness with its capacity of distinguishing the *Ego* from the *non-Ego*, and this is what is meant by personality. The limit of a spiritual substance is its range of self-consciousness. There are as many spiritual beings as there are centres of self-consciousness. Theism holds that God, in whose moral image we are, is such a self-conscious Being. Pantheism, on the contrary, makes self-consciousness, or personality, only a quality or accident of substance, so that there may be only one spiritual substance and yet many persons. It was the great virtue of the original Platonism, especially in its Aristotelian form, that it was firmly theistic. Zeller, in his notable " History of Greek Philosophy," declares that Plato never raised the question squarely of God's personality. This may be so; but, for all that, Plato was theistic to the core. His pronounced dualism, with its clear line between spirit and matter, rests upon a theistic basis. Call his " Timæus " a poem if you please, it speaks a true voice and tells us plainly of his faith in a personal God, the supreme maker of the universe. The theism of Plato is the monotheism of Paul and Athanasius. They never thought of calling the one God the Trinity, as if the Trinity was a single being. " To us there is one God the Father *and* one Lord Jesus Christ." But Augustine had drunk from a different philosophical stream. New Platonism is thoroughly pantheistic, and Augustine's whole theology is saturated with New Platonic influences.

It cannot be known exactly how much indebted Augustine was to the " renowned " Plotinus, as he calls him, but plainly, in some way, he had deeply imbibed the spirit of his teachings, for Plotinus was the most famous philosopher of the New Platonist school which Augustine rates so highly, —

" they approach nearest to us," he says, — as he was the most original thinker since Aristotle. Nowhere in literature can a clearer or profounder analysis of the pantheistic doctrine be found than in the " Enneads " of Plotinus, nor a more remarkable description of the New Platonic Trinity than in the first Book of the fifth " Ennead," entitled : Περὶ τῶν τριῶν ἀρχικῶν ὑποστασίων. Here are three hypostases, τὸ ὄν, νοῦς, and ψυχή, placed at the head of the New Platonic pantheon, and united by a pantheistic evolution in one eternal substance. Here, too, are found those theological terms that became the watchwords of Christian doctrine : λόγος, γέννησις, εἰκών, φῶς, ἀπαύγασμα, ὁμοούσιος. These terms are used to set forth a trinity with relations of generation, subordination, and homoousian unity that make it seem a transcript of the doctrine of Origen and Athanasius, only that it is cast in pantheistic form.   The question naturally arises whether there was any historical connection between the two doctrines, so similar in their nomenclature.   But there is no evidence of it. On the contrary, they were both plainly drawn, through independent channels, from the common sources of earlier philosophy.   Plato himself gives the basis of the Plotinian Trinity in his triad of ὁ ὤν, the Supreme God, νοῦς or λόγος, the mediating principle, and ψυχή, the world-soul.   The idea that Plotinus borrowed his doctrine from Christianity is utterly without foundation.   It is a more pertinent question whether Augustine was directly acquainted with the " Enneads " of Plotinus.   Had he read

them in a Latin translation? It cannot be asserted decisively. The several personal references
and citations in " De Civitate Dei " are not conclusive.[1] But this is certain, that his doctrine of

---

[1] Dr. Harnack seems to assert it. He says (*History of Dogma*,
vol. i. p. 358): "We know that the rhetorician Marius Victorinus translated the writings of Plotinus. This translation ex-
erted a decisive influence on the mental history of Augustine, who
borrowed from New Platonism the best it had, its psychology,
introduced it into the dogmatic of the church, and developed it
still further." There is no doubt of the profound influence of the
Plotinian school upon Augustine. But whether he ever read the
writings of Plotinus himself, either in the original Greek or in a
Latin translation is not so clear. The only authority for Harnack's assertion, that I am aware of, is what Augustine tells us
in his *Confessions* (viii. 2), viz.: that he "had read certain books
of the Platonists which Victorinus had translated into Latin."
Whether the writings of Plotinus were included among "certain
books of the Platonists " is perhaps probable, but it is not by
any means certain. There is no direct evidence of it in Augustine's own writings, beyond the passage given above. Dr. Schaff
says (*History of the Christian Church*, vol. iii. p. 1001): "It is
probable that he read Plotinus in Greek;" but he gives no good
grounds for his opinion, and when one considers how ignorant
Augustine was, by his own confession, of Greek, and also how
difficult it is to read the Greek of Plotinus, one is compelled to
reject it as wholly improbable. Dr. Schaff seems to rely on a
quotation which Augustine makes from the *Oracles* of Porphyry.
But the quotation is in Latin, and Augustine does not tell us
whose translation it is. Was it his own? I do not think so. If
Augustine could read Greek as easily as that, why did he ask
Jerome to translate the writings of Origen for him? The truth
is that Augustine made scarcely any use of the Greek writings,
even the Greek Testament, for the simple reason that he was
too ignorant of Greek to do so. His acquaintance with Greek
philosophy and theology was gained at second hand. Here can
be clearly traced the influence of Cicero. In the *City of God*
Cicero is quoted more than twenty times, and referred to frequently. It was from this source that Augustine acquired much
of his knowledge of Plato. Cicero was an admirer of Plato, calling him *quemdam Deum Philosophorum* (*De Natura Deorum*, ii.

God and of Trinity breathes the same pantheistic
strain. Plotinus declares that the Deity, though
one essence, exists by a process of evolution in
three hypostases, which have indeed a shadowy
sort of personality, and yet plainly are not regarded
by him as distinct personal beings. Personality,
with him, comes at a lower stage of evolution, as,
for example, in human souls, which being unsepa-
rated portions of the "one" or "all" in the pre-
natal state of existence, become personalized in
this present life when united with bodies. The
thorough pantheism of Plotinus made it easy for
him to adopt the theory of "three hypostases,"
as a stage of evolution between unity and multi-
plicity, without assuming that they are really personal. He had no doctrine of a personal God, in
the strict theistic sense. Personality for him is
only a temporary phase of pluralized being out
of the absolute unity. Augustine was held back
from such a position by his theistic Christian faith,
and so refused to say that the one God exists in
three real hypostases, which, in Christian trinitarian language, meant three individual persons.

12), and it was his aim, as he said, "to array Plato in Latin
dress." In a very scholarly article in Smith's *Dictionary of
Christian Biography*, written by Canon Charles Gore, the thoroughly New Platonic character of the Christian writings of Victorinus is clearly brought out, and also the probable influence of
them on Augustine. This is shown by the close affinities to be
seen in the leading doctrines held by both writers. We may well
believe, therefore, that, if Augustine did not read Plotinus himself, he at all events drank deeply of his philosophy through the
New Platonic translations and writings of Victorinus.

Thus while Plotinus had no hesitation in saying "three hypostases," as forms of the evolution of unity into plurality, since for him hypostasis, as being, did not necessarily involve individual personality, Augustine cannot refuse to allow that being and personality are coincident and involve each other, so that, if God is one as a being, he must also be one as a person, and *vice versa*, that if there are three individual persons in Deity, there must also be three essences or personal beings. Such was the dilemma in which Augustine found himself between his Christian belief and his philosophical system. The result was that he took refuge in the plea of ignorance and mystery. But his real metaphysical doctrine is plainly Plotinian. He refuses to say three hypostases or real persons, but contents himself with "three somewhats," and then, when asked "What three," answers: "Three persons, lest we should seem to be silent." But are the "three somewhats" distinct hypostases or individual beings? Augustine never says Yes, for he could not and remain Plotinian as he was. The result is that his Trinitarianism is monistic - like that of Plotinus himself. His Trinity is not tripersonal, and hence must be, in spite of himself, unipersonal, unless he drops into the open pit of extreme pantheism and makes God a mere τὸ ὄν, unconscious of himself or of the world that is evolved from Him. It is on such a foundation of pantheistic philosophy, from which, however, he shrinks back, that Augustine builds his new Trini-

tarianism and is able to say that the one only true
God and the Trinity are absolutely the same. This
is not monotheism; it is a pantheistic monism.
The great difficulty with Augustine was that he
did not know what to do with the problem of personality. He plays fast and loose with it, and
vibrates between theism and pantheism, and thus
paves the way for the amazing assumption of some
of his followers in later times, that in God essence
and person are not coincident, so that God may be
and is one Being and yet three real persons, —
an assumption that breaks down at once when
submitted to the test of reason.

A *third* effect of the new mode of conceiving
the Trinity remains to be mentioned, — *the changing of the Athanasian homoousianism from
generic to numerical unity of essence.* It is only
needful here to mark the fact that this change
resulted from Augustine's entire misconception of
the Platonico-Aristotelian nomenclature of Athanasius and the other Greek theologians. He read
the Nicene creed through New-Platonic glasses,
turning its three personal beings metaphysically
united in a Platonic universal into one being manifested under three modes of personal existence.
The result was a complete overturn of the Nicene
doctrine. Its apex became its base. Trinity
became unity. Trinitarianism became tri-unita-
rianism. The foundation was thus laid for the new
metaphysics of the Divine Being to which I have
just referred, viz., that God is one Being, while

three persons. Augustine himself was not ready
to make the jump. He simply raised the problem
and left it unsolved. But his followers were
bolder than he. God is numerically one in essence,
yet is three in personal agency; *therefore essence
and person in God are not coincident.* Already
this step was taken when the Pseudo-Athanasian
creed was framed. This creed, which is clearly a
product of the Augustinian school, declares that
" We worship one God in trinity, and trinity in
unity, neither confounding the persons, nor dividing the substance." This language assumes that
the substance or Being is one, while the persons
are three. But does the creed hold to three real
persons? Plainly not. It plays with the term
"person," as Augustine did. Its doctrine, under
all its verbal antinomies, is that of the essential Divine unity. God, it declares, is *unus Deus*, that is,
one personal Being. This creed has recently been
charged with tritheism. In fact its position is at
the opposite pole. " There are not three Gods,
but one God." True, its Sabellianism is veiled
under the assumption that God may be one Being
and yet be three persons, but its real position is
that God is one Being, whatever explanation be
given of the three persons. Thus its Trinitarianism
is only a disguise. Its hands indeed are those of
Esau, but its voice is the voice of Jacob. The
doctrine of numerical unity of essence is monistic,
not tritheistic, and the subsequent history will show
that the New Platonic leaven of the Augustinian

Trinitarianism has given a monistic and pantheistic direction to trinitarian dogma down to the present day.

To pass from Augustine to the later history of Trinitarianism is like leaving the intricate mazes of some difficult strait for the open sea. The story to be told is simple and plain. As the Dark Ages come on apace, theology becomes subject to tradition and ecclesiastical authority. Greek literature is buried; the Greek Fathers are no longer known or read, and Augustine's name is in the ascendant without a rival for a thousand years. The mediæval Catholic theology, which was slowly developed by Anselm, Thomas Aquinas, and the other great Schoolmen, is simply Augustinianism reduced to scholastic form. There were a few dissenting voices, such as Roscelin and Joachim. But they were quickly reduced to silence by papal synods. All the rest sing the same Augustinian song. Anselm may speak for them. " Although necessity compels that there be two, still it cannot in any way be expressed *what two they are*" (*quid duo sint*); and again, "one essence, yet a trinity, on account of three *I know not what*" (*tres nescio quid*). It is noticeable that in these passages Anselm refuses to use the term "person," though it is still employed by Augustinians generally, with the express understanding, however, that it is in a negative or relative sense. The great question with the Schoolmen was whether the Trinity is one being (*una res*) or three beings (*tres res*).

Roscelin held that three real persons involved three real beings (*tres res*). This was allowed by Anselm, who accepted, with Augustine, the principle that nature and person are coincident; and hence he denied that there are three real persons in the Trinity. "As God is one in substance, He cannot be several persons (*ita nec plures personæ*)." Hence his frank confession, "*tres nescio quid.*"

It is a remarkable fact that the Protestant Reformation only increased the prestige of Augustine, the great Catholic Father, as he had now become. Catholics and Protestants alike appealed to him. The question of the Trinity was not a subject of controversy, and the Augustinian form of trinitarian doctrine became a fixed tradition. The Nicene creed, as interpreted by the Pseudo-Athanasian creed, was accepted on all sides and passed into all the Protestant confessions. It is to be noted that Calvin insisted on the use of the term "person" as the only word that would unmask Sabellianism. He also held to numerical unity of essence. This would seem to indicate that Calvin believed that God was one Being in three real persons, and if so, he must have allowed that in God nature and person are not coincident. Yet he nowhere raises the question, and I am inclined to think that he was not conscious of any departure from the views of Augustine. But it was inevitable, under the increased light and freedom of Protestantism, that questioning should arise. The creeds, whether

Lutheran, Calvinistic or Anglican, described the Trinity as three persons. What did they mean? Are the three persons three Beings or only three modes of existence of one Being? It was the old question between trinitarian and monarchian in the second century, and it would not down.

We have thus reached the historical close of the undisturbed reign of the Pseudo-Athanasian Augustinianism. A further survey of the discussions that now arose, and their outcome in the New England Trinitarianism, will be given in the next chapter.

CHAPTER III

NEW ENGLAND TRINITARIANISM

THE history of the evolution of the Christian trinitarian dogma naturally falls into three divisions. The first includes the development of the Greek Athanasian doctrine, viz., that the Trinity is composed of three distinct personal beings, of whom the First Person, or the Father, is alone self-existent and absolute God, the second and third persons being derived and subordinate, the one by eternal generation, the other by eternal procession. The second division gives the history of the later Latin Trinitarianism as moulded by Augustine, which inverted the Greek doctrine, and held that each person is Absolute God, and that the whole Trinity is involved in each person, thus eliminating all subordination, making the Trinity essentially one Being, and reducing the three persons to relations or modes of existence of that Being.

But while the Augustinian form of doctrine became fixed in the faith of the Western Church through the Middle Ages, the Greek Nicene creed continued to be accepted, with the *filioque* addition, without any suspicion that the Athanasian and

Augustinian statements were in diametrical opposition to each other and based on antagonistic philosophies. The *Quicunque vult*, a Latin creed that originated in the school of Augustine, was even attributed to Athanasius, and its spuriousness was not suspected until the revival of learning was in full sweep in the fifteenth century. Even then the true meaning of the discovery was not clearly discerned. The yoke of church authority still weighed heavily on the intellects of men and forbade a full use of the light gained. The Protestant Reformers were too busily engaged in breaking the bonds of papal despotism in church and state to pay much attention to speculative questions, and the old creeds were left untouched. But as the movement proceeded, and its real significance became more fully understood, especially when the rights of individual intellectual freedom came to be asserted, a new theological movement was precipitated. Then the old creeds were subjected to criticism, and the era of Protestant symbolics began. We are thus brought to the third division of the subject, viz., the period of questioning and controversy as to *the real meaning of the creeds*, and as to *the truth of the historical and speculative assumptions involved in them*. I propose in the present chapter to consider the discussions that arose in England, and their outcome in the New England Trinitarianism.

These discussions began with the publication of Firmin's " Tracts " in the latter part of the seven-

teenth century. The position of the "Tracts" was
that "the unity of God is a unity of person as well
as of nature," and that God being unipersonal
"cannot be three persons any more than a man
can be three persons." Sherlock in reply accepted
the premises of Firmin, as to unity of person and
nature, but drew the opposite conclusion; that the
three persons are three distinct minds or beings.
But this position was wholly opposed to the Augustinian monism that had so long ruled theology;
it smacked of tritheism, a charge to which Trinitarians had always been sensitive. Had the English
theologians been thoroughly acquainted with Greek
theology, they would have had the key to the Athanasian answer, but this key was wanting to them.
Augustinian agnosticism was their only refuge.
Wallis, Jane, South, Howe, Burnet, all, in one
chorus, proclaim that the three are not real persons
in the ordinary sense of persons. Wallis says there
are three "somewhats," borrowing the word from
Augustine himself. Bishop Burnet prefers to speak
of the Trinity as "the Blessed Three," though he
would not object to the word "person" if he could
be sure it would be understood as he intended it.
This closed the discussion for the time, but it broke
out again in what is called the Arian controversy,
in the early part of the eighteenth century. The
Arians, Samuel Clarke and others, took the same
essential ground with Firmin, that God is unipersonal, and hence that the Son is a distinct personal
being, distinguishing God the Father as the abso-

lute Deity from the Son whom they regarded as
God in a relative or secondary sense, being derived
from the Father and having his beginning from
Him.

The most notable reply was that of Waterland.
His trinitarian writings have usually been regarded
by his school of theologians as the most consummate and unanswerable defense of orthodoxy that
has ever been made.   But there is nothing really
new in it, except that it loyally accepts the term
" person " in the creeds as having a real significance, and hence squarely faces and accepts under
stress the metaphysical paradox involved : that in
God nature and person are not coincident.   On
this point Waterland started a new current of trinitarian dogma.   He held, against the Arians,
that Christ is the Supreme God, a distinct person
indeed from the Father, but not a distinct Being.
To support this he allows that being is not necessarily " synonymous with person."   Yet he refuses
to take a decided stand on this point, declaring it
to be a " question about a name or a phrase, and
a scholastic question invented in later times,"
which shows to how little purpose he had read
church history.   The allied question of numerical
unity of essence which, as we have seen, lies at
the basis of this one and necessitates it, if three
real persons in one numerical essence are insisted
on, he also declines to discuss, declaring that the
subject is beyond us.   " You can never fix any
certain principle of individuation ; in short, you

know not precisely what it is that makes one being or essence." If so, what becomes of the whole metaphysics of the Nicene Orthodox Trinity, and why this excited controversy? After all, Waterland falls back on the trinitarian tradition. His "three real persons" are not individuals. It is the old modalistic monism disguised. His view of the Trinity is Augustinian. "The Lord our God is one God," does not mean, he says, "unity of person." It may mean God the Father, but "not exclusive of the other two persons." "In strictness the one God is the whole Trinity." "The word God may sometimes signify all the divine persons, sometimes any person of the three indefinitely without determining which, and sometimes one particular person, Father, Son, or Holy Ghost." This is pure Augustinianism, and shows that Waterland had not advanced a single step in the way of theological progress. His whole spirit and method are traditional.

In truth Protestantism in the seventeenth and eighteenth centuries had become reactionary and dogmatic. Its own cardinal principle of individual freedom of belief had been lost sight of, or rather it had never yet been clearly understood. Waterland gives little evidence of acquaintance with Greek philosophy or theology. His studies were confined to the Latin Fathers. He quoted Augustine to interpret or defend what he supposed to be the Nicene doctrine. The revival of Greek studies was indeed beginning to bear fruit. Such

men as Hooker, the pride of English Churchmen,
Petavius, the learned and candid Jesuit, and Cudworth, the Cambridge Platonist, were reopening
the long-closed fountains of Greek theology, in
works that are to-day rich and fruitful for all
scholars. But such cloistered voices were unheard
in this age of noisy logomachies. The ponderous
works of Waterland bore away the honors of vic-
tory, and the discussion again for the time was
closed. Henceforth the "stream of tendency"
is all one way. The Augustinian Sabellianism
sweeps on resistlessly, carrying in its wake Church-
man and Dissenter, Calvinist and Arminian alike,
and crosses the Atlantic to find a new home in
New England.

A good illustration of this period is seen in
Isaac Watts, whose hymns had such influence in
moulding English as well as American religious
thought and devotion. The Trinitarianism of
Watts was a curious amalgam of Sabellianism and
Arianism. " Person," in his view, " as applied to
the Trinity is not to be taken in the full common
and literal sense of it." " The Father, the Word
and the Spirit are so far distinct as to lay a foundation for the Scripture to speak of them in a
personal manner, as I, Thou, and He, and upon
this account they are called three persons, but
they are not so distinct as to have three distinct
consciousnesses." Watts well illustrates the general demoralization into which Calvinistic orthodoxy was now falling. He doubted whether the

Holy Spirit was anything more than the representative of the Divine principle " in a personal manner," " as the spirit of a man does not imply another being."   Watts was an Arian in his view of Christ, holding to " the preëxistence of Christ's human soul," and to its union with the immanent Eternal Logos " before the world was."   He also speculated concerning the condition of infants, suggesting that they were annihilated, in case they died before the development of moral agency. But none of Watts's peculiar views appear in his hymns, which breathe the hallowed air of traditional Calvinism.

The earliest theological divisions in New England grew out of questions connected with the prevalence of Arminianism.   The subject of the Trinity was in the background.   The Westminster catechism, with its bald trinitarian statement, was universally accepted and made the text-book of Christian doctrine.   But the theologizing tendencies that so profoundly stirred our New England forefathers could not long permit the trinitarian dogma to remain untouched.   Edwards seems to have given it little special attention ; but incidental statements show that, while he was willing to use the term " person," he was not quite clear as to its real meaning when applied to God. Hopkins deals with the subject more at length. His views are a curious mixture of Latin and Greek elements.   He held to the real eternal generation of the Son, thus far agreeing with Athanasius; but his doctrine as a whole is Augustinian. God is "the infinite three-one." Jehovah in the Old Testament is the whole Trinity. Christ is identified with Jehovah. The centre of his personality is divine, not human. Person in the Trinity "cannot be defined so as to give a clear adequate idea." Thus the Trinitarianism of Hopkins hangs on the horns of a dilemma. He held the absolute Deity of Christ, and denied all subordination, and yet insisted on his real generation from the Father. The contradiction here involved is apparent at once. Real generation supposes derivation, and consequent subordination. Hence Athanasius was a consistent subordinationist to the last. Augustinianism and Athanasianism cannot be harmonized. Hopkins does not seem to have been conscious of the difficulty. But Emmons, his greater disciple, saw and avoided it. He cut the Gordian knot in true Alexandrian fashion, declaring that "eternal generation is eternal nonsense." Emmons was a keen logician; he also had the gift of a terse and lucid theological style. No theologian since Edwards can be compared with him in these respects. Accept his assumptions and one is driven on irresistibly to the most radical conclusions. But his theology is essentially metaphysical.[1] With the rest of his

---

[1] The metaphysical system of Emmons is one of the marvels of historical theology. The links of minor premise and conclusion are forged with a consummate syllogistical skill, while the most amazing major premises, on which the whole theological edifice stands, are assumed with an ease and assurance that is

age he was wholly lacking in the historical and critical spirit. What Athanasius and the Greek Fathers taught had no interest for him. He dealt with the Trinity from the standpoint of the logical reason. "Eternal generation" is, he thought, rationally inconceivable, a mere cobweb of the speculative imagination, and he brushed it away as impatiently as did Arius himself. Thus was extinguished the last trace of genuine Athanasianism in New England theology. A new era now began, and Emmons was its prophet. He was the real founder of the New England trinitarian school.

Three points form the basis of the Trinitarianism of Emmons. (1.) He holds tenaciously to three real persons. "It is as easy," he declares, "to conceive of God existing in three persons as in one person." This language shows that Emmons employed the term "person" in the strict literal sense. (2.) He holds that the three persons are absolutely equal, and further are numerically one Being. This involves the metaphysical assumption that in the Trinity being and person are not coincident. Emmons takes this position without any evasions; and he is the first theologian that I am

simply incomprehensible in these later days when the inductive and critical process has made individual facts rather than general ideas the basis of knowledge. Professor Talcott has informed me that Emmons once said to him: "There are no chasms in my theology any more than in this floor," pointing downward   I am not disposed to question the assertion. The real chasm is not *in* the system but *behind it.* It is built on a metaphysical vacuum.

aware of in the history of the doctrine who does
so.   As I have already noted, the Pseudo-Athanasian creed assumes it implicitly, but not explicitly.
Waterland asserts that it may be so, but refuses
to make an issue of it, and falls back on the position that person has an unknown meaning.   The
language of Hopkins also implies it, but it was
reserved for so bold and speculative a thinker as
Emmons to assert that *though we cannot conceive
that three persons should be one person, we may
conceive that three persons should be one Being,*
" if we only suppose that being may signify something different from person in respect to Deity."
This wholly improbable supposition Emmons forth-
with characteristically assumes as fact.   (3.) Emmons gave prominence to the theory of " official
subordination."   " The name Father is taken from
the *peculiar office* which he sustains in the economy
of redemption.   The second person assumes the
name of Son and Word by virtue of his incarnation."   In this very statement lurks the Sabellianizing leaven which one day will leaven the whole
lump.   Father and Son are " names " " assumed "
to set forth certain activities of the one Absolute
God.   This is essential Sabellianism at the start.
But Emmons goes farther.   He had cast aside the
doctrine of the eternal generation of the Son, but
now he suggests that the names Son and Word
had no existence before the incarnation.   " They
were probably unknown in heaven until the purposes of grace were there revealed."   But if the

names Word and Son were unknown before the incarnation, how about the *real personality* of the second person of the Trinity? Did the Son exist personally before the incarnation without a name, or does the want of a name imply the non-existence of the reality? Emmons halts at this point, but his followers, Stuart and others, will take up the pregnant suggestion that he had dropped so carelessly, with what result we shall see.

Such assumptions as Emmons had employed on which to build his trinitarian system could not long pass without question. We come to the so-called Unitarian Controversy, which has left its mark on the whole further history of New England theological thought. It broke out in consequence of a sermon by Channing in 1819, in which he impugned the orthodox trinitarian doctrine as illogical and unscriptural. His position was that three persons imply " three intelligent agents possessed of different consciousnesses, different wills, and different perceptions," and that these distinct attributes constitute " three minds or beings," — the old admission of Sherlock. Moreover, he declared that the New Testament statements concerning the Father and Son involve distinct and separate personality. Channing himself was substantially an Arian, holding that Christ was a preëxistent and divine being, but dependent and subordinate to the Father who is the only Supreme Deity. Moses Stuart, in his defense of the traditional Trinitarianism, refuses to accept the term " person " as a proper one to define the distinctions in the Trinity. He wishes the word " had never come into the symbols of the churches." " I believe in a *threefold distinction* in the Godhead, and do not venture to make any attempt at explanation." It is to be noted that Stuart makes no use of the metaphysics of Emmons, who squarely insisted that God is one being in three real persons, and that in God essence and person are not coincident. Stuart rather goes back to the agnosticism of Augustine, who said " three somewhats," and of Anselm, who said " three I know not what." He had been anticipated in this by President Dwight, who declared that person is " strictly proper," but did " not know its exact meaning." The term " distinction " which Stuart substituted for person is of Sabellian origin. Calvin saw its real character and pierced it with one of the keenest shafts of his wit. It came into use in New England apparently through Watts ; but Stuart made it current coin, and from his day to the present it has largely usurped the place of person in trinitarian language. " A threefold distinction in the Godhead," which is all that Stuart dares to say, is a fit legend to be placed at the head of the latest chapter in the history of New England Trinitarianism. It is a suggestive fact that the Burial Hill declaration, and the so-called Congregational creed of 1883, both omit the word " person " from their trinitarian statements, and that out of thirty-seven church creeds that I have been able to examine only five employ it. This fact by itself illuminates our further survey. The Sabellian leaven of Emmons and Stuart did its work thoroughly, and New England Trinitarianism through all its veins became inoculated with its virus. Perhaps the most notable fact of all is that neither Emmons nor Stuart was conscious of any Sabellianizing tendency, and that their trinitarian successors to-day seem equally unconscious of it. The self-complacent assertion so frequently made that New England Trinitarianism is a lineal descendant of Athanasius and the Nicene creed vividly illustrates the power of a theological tradition even upon critical and scholarly minds.[1]

While the general course of the subsequent his-

---

[1] No historical writer has more clearly discerned the true character of the later New England Trinitarianism than Dr. George P. Fisher. I cannot forbear to quote an extract from his *Discussions in History and Theology*, p. 273. "Hopkins was the last to hold to the Nicene doctrine of the primacy of the Father and the eternal sonship of Christ. The whole philosophy of the Trinity, as that doctrine was conceived by its great defenders in the age of Athanasius, when the doctrine was formulated, had been set aside. It was even derided; and this chiefly for the reason that it was not studied. Professor Stuart had no sympathy with, or just appreciation of, the Nicene doctrine of the generation of the Son. His conscious need of a philosophy on the subject was shown in the warm though cautious and qualified welcome which he gave to the Sabellianism of Schleiermacher. What he defended against Channing, though with vigor and learning, was the notion of three distinctions to which personal pronouns can be applied, — a mode of defining the Trinity which the Nicene Fathers who framed the orthodox creed would have regarded with some astonishment. The eternal fatherhood of God, the precedence of the Father, is as much a part of the orthodox doctrine of the Trinity as is the divinity of the Son."

tory is clear, there are yet theological windings
and cross-currents which make our further survey
complicated and difficult. The trinitarian sect became divided into various tendencies which even-
tually took shape in distinct schools of thought.
My present purpose is simply to give some intelligible idea of the chief phases of the general
Sabellian movement. Four such phases may be
distinguished.

First, the modified Sabellianism of Stuart and
Bushnell. Stuart, as we have seen, followed in
the path struck out by Emmons. In his discussion with Channing he had taken simply a defen-
sive attitude, meeting Channing's metaphysics in
regard to three persons as synonymous with three
separate beings by declaring that person was used
by Trinitarians "not affirmatively but negatively,"
that is, as involving distinctions without affirming
what these distinctions are. At this point the discussion closed; but, some years after, Stuart translated with extensive notes an essay of Schleiermacher in which Schleiermacher had defended
Sabellius from the charge of Patripassianism and
interpreted the Sabellian view as essentially trinitarian, though distinguishing a trinity developed
in time from a trinity eternally immanent in the
Divine Being. Schleiermacher opposed the Nicene
doctrine of eternal generation, holding that the
Son is self-existent and independent, that is, Absolute God, and that the Trinity is a manifestation of the one God in different modes of creating

and redeeming activity.   No two names are more
historically incongruous than those of Schleiermacher and Emmons.   But their views run easily
into each other; and, in fact, Schleiermacher's
essay only fructified in Stuart's mind the seed that
Emmons had already sown.   Stuart's voluminous
notes in connection with his translation are of
great value to any one who would completely understand the further history of New England
Trinitarianism.   Bushnell confessed his obligation
to them.

The excitement caused by Bushnell's " God in
Christ " is a bygone tale.   But nothing is more
curious to-day than the history of the effort to con-
vict Bushnell of Sabellian and Unitarian heresy.
The only peculiarity of his famous book is its
Bushnellian rhetoric and genius.   Its christology
is borrowed from Schleiermacher and Stuart.   Yet
Stuart sat secure in his chair at Andover, in all
the odor of orthodoxy, while the theological air
was hot with accusations against his eloquent disciple.   In fact the doctrine of both was thoroughly
Sabellian, though a modification was introduced
which, it was claimed, changed its whole character.
Sabellianism holds to the eternal immanent uni-
personality of God, but introduces a trinity of developments of God in time for purposes of Divine
manifestation in creation and redemption.   These
developments are in personal modes, but not such
as constitute three personal beings.   This is the
doctrine also of Stuart and Bushnell.   But Stuart

laid hold of the idea of Watts and Emmons that there is "laid a foundation in the Divine nature" for these distinctions. Bushnell was at first agnostic on this point, though later he tentatively accepts it. But this qualification did not affect the essential Sabellianism of the whole doctrine. Stuart and Bushnell both, following Schleiermacher, declare that God is not eternally tripersonal, but unipersonal. The Trinity is not fully developed until the incarnation. Here Stuart takes up the suggestion of Emmons that the names Word and Son were not known in heaven before the birth of Christ, which implies that the Trinity came into real existence with this event. Stuart seems at times to hold a developed trinity of real persons, and seeks to hide his Sabellianism under this cover. But, in fact, his persons are not real any more than the Sabellian persons are; they are modes of personal existence of the One Divine Being. He talks about the Son's personality, but he frankly confesses that he uses person "to designate a distinction which cannot be comprehended or defined, and would not employ it if it had never been used." Personality as related to God is for Stuart the great enigma, as it was for Augustine. Accepting "a numerical unity of substance" in the Godhead, he declares that "this excludes such personality as exists among men." He even suggests that personality cannot be essential to divinity, — a pantheistic idea which shows whither New England Trinitarianism was pointing. Stuart's doctrine was modalistic and he frankly allows it, quoting and appropriating Turretin's phrase "modal distinctions."

One great merit, however, must be accorded to Stuart. He was a Greek scholar, and comprehended the true character of the Nicene Trinitarianism, allowing that *homoousios* in the Nicene creed did not mean numerical unity, and that its doctrine was essential subordinationism, and on this ground rejecting it. Thus Stuart, in his interpretation of the Greek theology, placed himself in line with Petavius and Cudworth and anticipated the results of later scholarship. I have styled the doctrine of the Stuart-Bushnell school a modified Sabellianism. It ought to be said, however, that in one respect they differed widely from the Sabellians of the early church. These regarded Christ as a semi-divine and semi-human being whose personal existence would end at the close of the Christian dispensation, when God would be all in all. Stuart on the other hand made Christ the incarnation of the Absolute God. "The Son," he said, "is αὐτόθεος." Hence his denial of eternal generation and of subordination. It was the great objection of Stuart to the Nicene creed that it made the Son a derived and dependent being, and so broke down, as he declared, his true Deity. But Stuart was equally afraid of tritheism. There cannot be three αὐτόθεοι. One refuge only remained for him,—a Sabellian denial of three real persons.

The *second* phase of trinitarian thought to be described is the transcendental modalism of H. B. Smith, Shedd, and Dorner. I mention Dorner because he represents a German element of influence which profoundly affected this whole school, and also because his writings have been widely read in New England. The renaissance of German literature first made itself felt philosophically and theologically on this side the ocean through Unitarian scholars like Hedge and Norton, and it leavened the transcendental movement, which found its great prophet in Emerson. But the influence of Goethe, Kant, Schelling, and Hegel could not be limited to a sect. It entered the ranks of the so-called Evangelicals. H. B. Smith, who may be selected as the best exponent of this second phase of New England Trinitarianism, spent several years in a German university and drank deeply at the springs of German transcendental thought. The subjective transcendental character of the school must be clearly understood in order to appreciate the peculiar turn given by them to the trinitarian dogma. It explains the remarkable fact that though they laid claim to historical and exegetical learning, they paid scant respect to the historical and Biblical aspects of Christian doctrine. They belonged to the slowly ebbing tide of an intensely metaphysical age, and represent a curious mixture of New England Edwardsianism and German Hegelianism. Hence the subjective deductive method rules and shapes their thinking,

and history and exegesis are twisted, if necessity
arises, into harmony with their metaphysical assumptions. I need only refer for illustration to
Dorner's interpretation of the Nicene theology in
his " History of Christian Doctrine," and to Shedd's
interpretation of the Augustinian anthropology in
his " History of Christian Doctrine," unreliable as
they are for historical or critical purposes, and
only valuable as representing their own theological
opinions.

This school was thus peculiarly fitted to give a
new impulse to the waning Augustinian metaphysical method of treating the dogma of the
Trinity. They started, as Augustine himself did,
with a purely metaphysical assumption, viz., the
absoluteness of the divine unity. " God," says
H. B. Smith, " is the one supreme personality."
Dorner calls Him " the Absolute Personality."
God then is personal, which seems to avoid pantheism. But is He unipersonal? No, his personality is tripersonal. Is He then one Being? Yes;
but " not an individual like a man." God cannot
in his essence be individualized. But can He
be individualized in his personal form of being?
Is He three individual Persons? No; for this
would be tritheism. Can God then be defined?
Not clearly. Smith 'says, " God is not one of a
class." Yet this school ventures into the hidden
depths of the divine nature with a bold and firm
step. Smith says, " God is triune." Shedd says,
He is " a plural unit." But what do these terms

mean ?   Smith answers, — and Dorner agrees
with him, — " The one Supreme Personality exists in three personal modes of being, but is not
three distinct persons." This is the old modalism
which constitutes the real warp and woof of the
whole theory.   Note the remarkable metaphysical assumption involved, viz., that personality and
person in God are different. *God is one personality, but not one person.*   But how can this be ?
Is personality here used in an abstract sense?
Then God is not one concrete Being, and pantheism again confronts us.   Or is He one concrete
Being and also personal, then He must be unipersonal.   Such is the metaphysical puzzle involved
in the view of Smith and Dorner.   Shedd explains
his " plural unit " somewhat differently, but comes
to a similar paradoxical result.   God, he says, is
both unipersonal and tripersonal, that is, of course,
both one Person and three Persons, or, mathemat-
ically stated, $1 = 3$.   But what is the real doctrine
that lurks under this strange guise ?   It is a modalistic pantheistic Sabellianism.   Let Dorner state
it in his own German way.   " The absolute Personality is present in each of the divine distinctions in such a way that though they are *not of
themselves and singly personal,* they have a share
in the One Divine Personality, in their own manner."   " The eternal result of the trinitarian process is the eternal presence of the divine Personality in different modes of being."   Here is
modalism and Sabellianism and pantheism in one
conglomerate.

Lest I may seem to be unjust in my statement, which is largely in the very language of these writers, I quote a passage from H. B. Smith. He derides the doctrine of God "as an individual being" as "Unitarian," "Deistic" and "anthropomorphic," and adds: "God is the supreme intelligence, the one supreme Personality and Causality, but not one as an individual in the sense in which one man is an individual." But the doctrine of God "as an individual being" is not Deism, it is Theism, the doctrine of Plato and Athanasius; while the doctrine of the Smith-Dorner school is the first step to a complete pantheism. The question between the theist and the pantheist is concerning the nature of personality as related to substance. The theist holds that a person is a single self-conscious being with its own substance. The pantheist holds that there is but one substance in the universe, and that personality is an accident or quality or mode of existence of substance, so that there may be and in fact are many persons included in the one universal substance of things. The first step toward such a pantheistic result is to regard the three persons of the Trinity as personal self-conscious modes of existence of the one absolute self-consciousness. This is the doctrine of Smith and Dorner. The second step is to resolve *every* individual and personal self-consciousness, that is, every personal being, into a mode of the absolute self-consciousness. The final step is to resolve all personality, whether individual or absolute, into a specialized and accidental mode of existence of the one eternal absolute, the τὸ ὄν of the New Platonists, which is above all limitations, even self-consciousness itself, — the doctrine commonly attributed to Spinoza. Pantheism can go no further; and the road to it is straight. When Augustine declared that he did not know what he meant by "three persons" in the Trinity, he left firm theistic ground, and his followers have ever since been moving forward toward a pantheistic end. In this evolution the Smith-Dorner school took one decisive step. It brought out clearly the metaphysical pantheistic premise involved in the Augustinian position, though it struggled hard to preserve the appearance of a theistic Trinitarianism.

But the air of this transcendental school was too rare and ethereal for common minds. The genius of its leaders gave it celebrity, but its followers formed only a coterie. Its refined metaphysical distinctions and paradoxical antitheses could not take the place of the popular theology. Trinitarian faith wavered between a crude tritheism and a veiled unitarianism. Meanwhile the new age of historical inquiry had fairly dawned. The Bible became a subject of critical study. Traditional orthodoxy was in a state of flux, and its ancient theological foundations were in danger of upheaval and ruin. The man for the hour was needed, and he appeared, as was supposed, in the person of Mr. Joseph Cook.

This brings us to the *third* phase of the later

New England Trinitarianism, marked by a revival
of a type of doctrine which comes nearer to that
of Sabellius himself than any other of recent times,
and of which Mr. Joseph Cook, Dr. Lyman Abbott,
and Dr. A. H. Bradford may be selected as representatives. These names can hardly be said to
form a school. They are widely apart from each
other in many respects. I link them together because of their essential agreement in their theories
of the Trinity. When Mr. Cook delivered his three
lectures on the Trinity in 1887 there had been a
long lull in public discussion, and the supporters
of orthodoxy were quietly waiting for the next
" moving of the waters." For Mr. Cook himself
the time was opportune. He was at the zenith of
his peculiar reputation. Boston had installed him
" in Moses' seat." The orthodox *élite* of Massachusetts sat at his feet and hung upon his lips.
When he announced his theme there was a universal hush of expectation and sympathy. Truly the
opportunity was great. But unfortunately Mr.
Cook was not properly equipped for the work
he took in hand. His genius is rhetorical, not
metaphysical. Especially was he lacking in the
scholarship which such a discussion required. He
was seemingly innocent of all knowledge of the
Greek Fathers. The Latin Pseudo-Athanasian
creed was for him the most perfect statement of
orthodoxy. The character of his acquaintance
with ecclesiastical Greek is shown in his remarkable use of the term ὑπόστασις, which he prefers to

person, because, as he supposes, it means less than
person; whereas Dr. Shedd rejected it for the
very good reason that it cannot mean less and may
mean more. Mr. Cook might have learned something from Jerome, who was afraid to use the
term ὑπόστασις for *persona*, as the Greeks desired,
because it seemed to involve tritheism, — the very
thing that Mr. Cook so feared. But no man can
be omniscient, and I should not here refer to Mr.
Cook's shortcomings in church history if he had
not boldly entered historical ground and made
statements which his cultured audience accepted
apparently as true on his authority.

Mr. Cook's aim in his addresses was to defend
trinitarian orthodoxy as he understood it. He
especially proposed to exorcise the " paganism," as
he called it, of " three Gods." To this end he
appealed to the " scientific method." But it must
be frankly said that there is little science in Mr.
Cook's discussion, and little that is original, saving
always his remarkable rhetoric. After giving a
definition of the Trinity, which Sabellius would
have found no fault with, he introduces an old
illustration which had been used by both Trinitarians and Unitarians in the early church, but with
opposite application, — that of the sun and its
rays. There is nothing new in the illustration,
but the use made of it by Mr. Cook is certainly
original, and I challenge any one to find anything
to compare with it in the history of trinitarian
dogma. To be appreciated, it must be read in

full; but I will endeavor to give a clear outline of it. "Sunlight, rainbow, heat, one solar radiance; Father, Son, Holy Ghost, one God. As the rainbow shows what light is when unfolded, so Christ reveals the nature of God." "As at the same instant the sunlight is itself and also the rainbow and heat, so at the same moment Christ is both himself and the Father, and both the Father and Holy Ghost." "As the solar rainbow fades from sight, and its light continues to exist, so Christ ceases to be manifest and yet is present." "As the rainbow is unraveled light, so Christ is unraveled God." "When the rainbow faded from the East, I did not think it had ceased to be. It had not been annihilated; it had been revealed for a while, and, disappearing, it was received back into the bosom of the general radiance, and yet continued to fall upon the earth. In every beam of white light there is potentially all the color which we find unraveled in the rainbow; and so in all the pulsations in the will of God the Father in his works exist the pulsations of the heart of Him who wept over Jerusalem," "for there is but one God." So the Holy Ghost, figured by heat, is "Christ's continued life." Such is Mr. Cook's doctrine of the Trinity as set forth by himself, and he immediately proceeds to declare it both scientific and scriptural.

Perhaps the most remarkable thing about this illustration is the unstinted applause with which it was received by his audience, made up largely of

Massachusetts ministers. Surely there could be
no clearer evidence of the chaos that had befallen
theological thought in New England than that such
a bald Sabellianism was enthusiastically indorsed
by such an assembly, and that from that day to
this no note of criticism or dissent has been heard,
that I am aware of, in trinitarian circles. It may
be said that Mr. Cook should not be judged by a
metaphor. But the metaphor was employed on
purpose to set forth his doctrine, — a doctrine that
is essential modalism, going beyond Sabellius himself, and coming close to the Patripassianism out
of which Sabellianism sprang. It is true Mr.
Cook struggles to save himself from the charge of
holding a modalistic view, but he struggles in vain.
His defense is that "the peculiarities of Father,
Son, and Holy Ghost are incommunicable," and
he illustrates this from the properties of light,
color, and heat, which he assumes to be likewise
incommunicable. But are the peculiar properties
of light, color, and heat incommunicable? Is not
light always colored and always warm? Are not
the seven colors of the rainbow always forms of
light? And when the prism by a single movement
of the hand changes a beam of white light to blue
and yellow and violet, has there been no intercom-
munication of light and color? And are we to be
soberly assured that the rainbow which appears
and disappears with all the changefulness of April ·
skies is a true illustration of the second person of
the Trinity, and that his peculiar properties are

yet "incommunicable"? Truly science has at
last assumed a strange garb. Wisdom, as in the
"Encomium Moriæ" of Erasmus, puts on cap and
bells and plays the part of Folly. But suppose
for the moment that the properties of light and
color and heat are incommunicable, and fitly represent the relations of Father, Son, and Holy
Ghost, even then Mr. Cook is not saved from
modalism, for the properties of light, color, and heat
are *not personal :* neither, in his view, are Father,
Son, and Holy Ghost persons. What is this but
modalism stark and clear!

But lest, peradventure, we have misunderstood
Mr. Cook's rhetoric, we pass to his second lecture.
Here we have, not metaphor, but philosophy. The
premise is that "a personal ·God is immanent in
all matter and mind." Hence all nature and
spirit, the world, the soul, Christ himself, are but
manifestations of God as a person. There are
three special revelations of God, — in nature, in
moral law, and in Christ. "*But there are not
three persons ; He is one person in the strict sense,
for natural law is a unit in the universe, and
reveals but one will.* These revelations of God
are all one person, although in each revelation He
is a person." (The italics are Mr. Cook's.)
This surely is English unadorned, and what is its
doctrine if not modalistic unitarianism! God,
the lecturer elsewhere declares, is "one will, one
heart, one conscience," "the Infinite Personality."
He talks about "the Trinity of the Divine Nature,"

"the three spheres of God's self-manifestation," "in each of which the Ineffable Immanent Person says something new." This trinity of divine manifestations Mr. Cook holds to be "scientifically demonstrable," and he winds up a whole page of italics with this conclusion : "A Personal Trinity, of which Creator, Redeemer, and Sanctifier are *but other names*, is scientifically known to exist," and then he adds directly : "This is the Trinity which Christianity calls Father, Son, and Holy Ghost." Had Mr. Cook given this remarkable exposition of a modal trinity simply as his own theological opinion, I should take no exception to it, so far; but when he declares that it represents historical Christianity, I must, in the interest of historical truth, emphatically demur. Mr. Cook's three lectures are a travesty of history. His so-called trinitarianism is neither Athanasian, nor even Augustinian, no, nor even that of the Pseudo-Athanasian creed. It is not early New England unitarianism. Channing would have denounced it as a hybrid unitarianism, and such it is. No wonder Mr. Cook closes his third lecture with a grand cosmic description of the dome of the sky, and uses it to illustrate what he calls "God's unitarianism." History must call it Mr. Cook's.

I have spoken of Mr. Cook as a leader in a new phase of trinitarian evolution. It is noticeable that he no longer wavers on the question of God's single personality. Traditional orthodoxy had said, "one God in three Persons." H. B. Smith

and Dorner said, " one absolute Personality in
three personal modes of being," denying, however,
that the Divine Personality is unipersonal. Dr.
Shedd said that God is both unipersonal and tripersonal. But Mr. Cook is innocent of such transcendental ambidexterities. He declares boldly,
" There are not three persons. God is one person
in the strict sense." This is what Smith called
" Deism," but it is theism, as we have already
shown, and Mr. Cook is to be heartily commended
for helping to rescue theological thought from that
German " Serbonian bog;" though it may be a
question whether he has mended matters by accepting the other horn of the dilemma. The Smith-
Dorner school seemed to emphasize the trinitarian
side of the Divine personality, but Mr. Cook
throws the emphasis completely on the side of
unity. He has thus saved Monotheism, but utterly
broken down Trinitarianism.

It is at this point that Dr. Lyman Abbott and
Dr. A. H. Bradford join hands with Mr. Cook.
According to both of them God as a Trinity is
unipersonal. They declare themselves Trinitarians,
but their trinitarianism is merely nominal. Dr.
Abbott, in a published sermon, criticises the formula "three persons in one God," which, he says,
" is a good phrase not to use." He assumes that
three persons are three Gods, as Mr. Cook also
did, and asserts with emphasis: " There is one God,
only one God." But is Christ this " one God "?
Dr. Abbott seems to give a clear affirmative answer.

He declares that " Jesus Christ is God living a
human life," " the incarnate God." In his "Evolution of Christianity" he makes Christ " the
cause rather than a product of evolution," and
describes him as " the Infinite entering into human
life and taking on the finite." More explicitly
still he says: " In Jesus Christ *in propria persona*
God has entered human life in order that He might
show us who He is." " Incarnation," he says, " is
the indwelling of God in a unique man." This is
plainly a doctrine of Christ's essential Deity. But
is the Son a distinct person from the Father?
And is the Spirit a distinct person from the Son?
Let Dr. Abbott's exegesis of John xiv. concerning
the Comforter give the answer. " Another Comforter," he says, is simply an assumed name for
Christ himself. Father, Son, and Holy Ghost are
simply different names for one person. " Now it
is ' another Comforter,' now it is himself (' I·will
come unto you '), now it is the Father, now it is
all three; there is no difference." It is " One
God revealing himself" in these varied forms.
Dr. Abbott is somewhat wary, and makes other
statements which look toward a more humanitarian
view of Christ, but it is difficult to distinguish his
trinitarianism from Mr. Cook's modalistic patripassian unitarianism. Dr. Bradford is more outspoken. " The problem of the Trinity is simply
this: Are Father, Son, and Holy Ghost three names
for one being, or do they denote three distinct persons?" And the answer is squarely given. " The

Trinity does not mean three distinct persons, but three distinctions in one person." Father, Son, and Holy Ghost are names of three impersonal distinctions. "Whenever the Father is represented as coming into relations with men, the name is Son or Logos." It is then the Father under the name of Son or Logos that became incarnate and died on the cross; but this is unadulterated Patripassianism. Thus curiously has the evolution of so-called trinitarianism from the time of Augustine swung around the circle and reached its final logical result in the oldest known form of unitarianism in the early church, — the doctrine that the one God, the Father Almighty, became man and suffered and died.

Our survey has brought us to a position where it can be clearly seen that we have come to a critical turning-point in the history of trinitarian thought. The old cycle has run itself out, and a new cycle must inevitably begin. This fact will be illustrated in the *fourth* and last phase to which I shall call attention, — *the doctrine of the essential divineness of humanity and preëminently of Christ, the unique representative of mankind, who was, in this sense, a true incarnation of Deity.* This type of dogma is so new and unformed that it is somewhat difficult to fix it; but Dr. Phillips Brooks, Dr. J. M. Whiton, and Dr. George A. Gordon may be mentioned as representatives of its essential elements and tendencies. The underlying idea of this school, viz., that man was created

in the divine image and is thus a real "partaker of
the divine nature," is of course not new. It is not
only Biblical, it vitalized the noblest philosophies
and religions of the ancient world. The filial
relation of man to God, and the capacity and duty
of man to become like God, was a fundamental
note in the faith of Socrates and Plato centuries
before Christ uttered his parable of the Prodigal
Son. But the new dogma of "the essential divineness of humanity" is something more than this.
There lurks in it a metaphysical monistic strain
that reminds us of Plotinus and the Stoics. Plotinus ("Enneads," iv. 7, 10) expressly argues for
the divineness and immortality of the soul, on the
ground that it is *homoousios* with Deity. So this
school proclaims the consubstantiality of man with
God, borrowing the Nicene watchword, and applying it to all mankind, as being equally constituted
Sons of God. We have seen why Athanasius
restricted the term *homoousios* to the second person of the Trinity. He drew the line sharply
between the uncreated and the created. The uncreated divine Three are *homoousioi*, but all created beings are *heterousioi*. This was the point
of his controversy with Arius. If Christ is a created being, as Arius held, then he is not *homoousios* with the Father, and so ceases to be truly
divine. Such was the reasoning of Athanasius,
grounded on his dualistic Platonic ideas. We
have also seen how Augustine's doctrine of Divine
immanence drawn from New Platonic sources gave

a new monistic direction to western thought, and we have traced its onward movement, growing more and more pantheistic in its spirit down to the present day. Recent developments in physical science have done much to strengthen this monistic current. Monism is no doubt the last word in all the sciences. There is one ultimate force, one law, one evolution, one universe. But science properly stops with matter; it raises no question concerning the transcendental background of material existence. The dualistic theism of Plato and Athanasius has no controversy with the monism of science. It is a monistic *philosophy*, not a monistic *science* keeping within its own bounds, that crosses the border line between the transcendental and the material sphere, and proclaims a homoousianism that covers both. But can this step be taken? Is it necessitated by the discoveries of science? And if so, what then? What is the relation of spirit and matter, of the eternal to the temporal? Are all things essentially spirit? Or are they essentially matter? And, whether spiritual or material, are they *homoousioi?* Is there something of divinity, as Plotinus thought, in the lowest forms of existence?

Such are the questions that lie in the background of present theological thought. It is to be said at once that the new school does not leave the monistic track of its predecessors. The leaven of German metaphysical idealism which we saw working in the school of Smith and Shedd reappears in a

still more pronounced form in this latest phase of
Trinitarianism. Especially is the influence of R. W.
Emerson and F. H. Hedge discernible. Phillips
Brooks's sermon on " Identity and Variety," and
Dr. Gordon's use of " the principle of identity and
difference " in setting forth his view of the Trinity
and of Christ's deity, seem to have their common
source in Emerson's definition of philosophy, as
based on " two cardinal facts, the one and the two ;
unity or identity and variety, oneness and other-
ness." So the new language concerning the Incarnation reminds one strangely of Emerson's
description of Christ: " One man was true to what
is in you and me. He saw that God incarnates
himself in man, and evermore goes forth anew to
take possession of his world," and in that sublime
consciousness " he declared ' I am divine.' " But
perhaps the influence of Hedge has been quite as
potent. He more than any other man has set the
current toward the new doctrine of the consubstantiality of man with God. He accepts the Athanasian homoousianism as true. " God in man and
man in God," he declares, " is its underlying idea."
Only " Athanasius did not perceive that what was
true of Christ is true of other men." " The fault
of the trinitarian doctrine is what it omits to teach."
This is the very line of the new trinitarian departure. Its fundamental premise is " the essential
kinship of the divine and the human." The sermons of Phillips Brooks are pervaded with this
idea. The underlying assumption everywhere is

the dignity and worth of man in virtue of his essential and eternal relation to God. In one remarkable sermon especially, entitled "The Eternal Humanity," Brooks has given a clear metaphysics of his theology. The text is, "I am Alpha and Omega, the Beginning and the End, the First and the Last." "Here Christ asserts his *own eternity*." "Before man was made, the man-type existed in God." "This man-type is part and parcel of the everlasting Godhead." The God-man was eternal, and the incarnation was only the "exhibition" of his "eternal manhood in the Godhead." "Human nature" therefore "did not begin with Adam," who was only the copy of an eternal original; hence man is in the divine image or *homoousios*. This is certainly a new theological metaphysics. Dr. Brooks does not break with the orthodox creeds; but what precisely is his doctrine of the Trinity? Is it Sabellian? It looks that way. And what of the Incarnation? If the Word was eternally human, how could he "become flesh," in the sense of becoming man? There was then no true incarnation in the historic sense. The eternal God-man, when Jesus was born, only *appeared* to assume human nature. But this is the old Gnostic Docetism.

Dr. G. A. Gordon's book, "The Christ of To-Day," may be regarded as a metaphysical interpretation of Phillips Brooks's sermons. Its aim is avowedly speculative. Dr. Gordon insists that Christ's gospel cannot be adequately preached

without an " intellectual appreciation " of his person and nature. " Ethics are the outcome of metaphysics." Moreover, Dr. Gordon thinks that the
time has come for " a new conception of Christ,"
that is, a new christology. But he frankly acknowledges the " difficulty " and "embarrassment "
of the " problem," which is, — " whether Jesus is
the supreme and unique representative of the humanity of God, the proper incarnation of the Filial
in the being of the Infinite." This assumes " that
in God there is the Eternal Prototype of humanity." Hence " man is constituted in the Eternal
Humanity." This " consubstantiality of man with
God " is revealed through the incarnation " which
is the assertion of the divine meaning of history."
But the speculative question is not yet answered,
*how Christ is so uniquely related to God and
man.* What is Christ's metaphysical being? and
what is the metaphysical character of the incarnation? Dr. Gordon faces these questions, and a
large part of his book is occupied with their consideration. But I must confess that I do not find
a clear answer. " This Eternal Prototype of humanity in the Godhead," who is he, or what is it?
Is he the " Son of God " of the Nicene creed, or an
impersonal form of existence of the one God? I
find but one intelligible answer, — the old familiar
Sabellianism. Dr. Gordon holds to " one absolute
Person " in the Godhead, and his trinitarianism,
which he unfolds with such elaborate ingenuity
by means of " identity and difference," is wholly

modalistic and monistic, not to say pantheistic.
His Eternal Humanity is "ideal," as he himself
confesses, and so is his "Eternal Christ." Who
then is the "historic Christ"? Is he the same
with the "Eternal Christ"? By no means. Dr.
Gordon is continually putting them into sharp contrast. Jesus is "the supreme person in time" over
against "the supreme person beyond time." As a
person, then, he belongs to the temporal and not
to the eternal. But did Christ's earthly personality
begin with his human birth, or was he personally
preëxistent? Athanasianism says he was eternally
the Son of God. Patripassianism says he was the
Father himself. What is the answer of the new
school? Dr. Gordon seems to beg the question;
but I do not understand him to be Athanasian or
Patripassian. His "Absolute Personality" is not
three Persons certainly, in any ordinary sense of
person. If "God is a self-conscious being," as Dr.
Gordon affirms, he must be a personal being, and
if the Infinite consciousness is one, as Dr. Gordon
also affirms, then God must be unipersonal. But
since God's consciousness is infinite, it must, according to Dr. Gordon, include all things. "All
creatures, all persons are, in a true sense, modes of
the one Infinite consciousness." Then "why not
three Eternal Distinctions behind these multitudinous temporal distinctions?" Surely, why not!
And this is the argument from "Identity and
Difference" for the Christian Trinity. Is it any
wonder that Dr. Gordon declares that "historical

pantheism is in error only through its exclusiveness"? But if Christ is not an eternal Divine Person in the old trinitarian sense, what metaphysical basis is left for his moral supremacy? May not Ritschlianism, Dr. Gordon's *bête noir*, which rests Christ's claims on moral grounds, rather than metaphysical, be a safer position after all?

The essential metaphysical weakness of this school which starts from the idea of the essential divineness of human nature is *its inability to construct any clear doctrine of the incarnation.* If God is eternally human and humanity is eternally divine, why is an incarnation necessary? In this view the very ground of an incarnation, that is, the incoming of divinity into humanity, is taken away. Athanasius made an incarnation the central doctrine of his theology, because " God must be made man so that man may be made divine." But monism finds no such necessity. Further, suppose incarnation a reality, why is not *every* human birth also a divine incarnation? And if so, what was there " unique" in Christ's incarnation? The logical result of this view is to deny any metaphysical or " physiological " incarnation at all, and to reduce it to an ethical movement of the Divine spirit realized in others besides Christ; and such is the actual position taken by Dr. Whiton, who boldly carries this position to its final conclusions. In an article on " A Way out of the Trinitarian Controversy," [1] Dr. Whiton declares the old doctrine of

[1] The *New World*, September, 1893.

Divine incarnation "a paganish notion." "The physiological notion of incarnation must give place to the ethical one." Dr. Whiton squarely classes himself with Christian monists. Dualism is "now discredited." "There is but one spiritual nature, and that may be indifferently spoken of as divine or human." "This one nature belongs equally to God, to Christ, and to mankind." The universal God is "individualized in each personal conscience." "The centre of the trinitarian conception is that God is ever immanent and ever incarnating himself."[1] "The incarnation of God is not a mere event, but an age-long process." Christ is not the only Son of God. There are many sons, and many incarnations. Surely; why not? as I above suggested. And who is Christ? A man, with a "full and natural humanity." His "uniqueness" consists in his moral perfection, which "entitles him to be called divine, in distinction from those who by nature are partakers of one life with him and sons of God, as he is." Yet, strangely, Dr. Whiton calls himself a Trinitarian, and takes special pains to deny all affinity with Sabellianism or pantheism. The thing to be noted is that, under all this Sabellianizing, pantheistic trinitarianism, Dr. Whiton holds Christ to be *a man essentially like other men;* and this view is plainly gaining ground among professed Trinitarians. Such is the view of Dr. A. J. F. Behrends, as given in a sermon recently published, and also of W. Beyschlag. Both

[1] *Gloria Patri*, pp. 152, 129.

hold to a modalistic Trinity, and yet to Christ's essential humanity. How two such contrasted conceptions can be speculatively harmonized is an unsettled question. But plainly behind all this style of thinking is Hegelianism.[1]

Two impressions are made on me by this review of recent theological thinking. First, *its thoroughly dogmatic character*. The historical spirit which has so deeply penetrated our age has plainly made little impression as yet on orthodox theologians. They still deal in the ideal and the abstract, and seek to build theology on metaphysical foundations. Dr. Fairbairn's volume, "The Place of Christ in Modern Theology," well illustrates this. In that book the historical spirit wrestles with the dog-

---

[1] Fichte, who anticipated Hegel, in his later thinking made much of the proem of the fourth Gospel, because it seemed to him to sustain the idea of a timeless revelation of God in the world. The incarnation he explained in a transcendental way as occurring in the case of all spiritual men, in the same manner as in Jesus Christ. Such an incarnation of the Logos in man, in his view, merges him in God and he becomes "all in all," — a pantheism that outreaches Plotinus himself (see Schwegler's *Handbook of the History of Philosophy*, p. 276, translated by Stirling).

Dr. A. H. Strong, in a recent series of articles on Ethical Monism, says: "It is not too much to say that the monistic philosophy, in its various forms, holds at present almost undisputed sway in our American universities." He gives it welcome and sums up his own doctrine: "There is but one substance, God. The Eternal Word, whom we call Christ, is the only complete expression of God." "Matter, humanity, and the incarnation" are "self-limitations of Christ." Wherein Dr. Strong's view differs from Spinoza is not easy to say. Spinoza's "extension and thought," which are "empirically derived determinations" of "one absolute substance" which Spinoza calls God, correspond quite closely to Dr. Strong's "matter and humanity." Yet Dr. Strong is a stanch Calvinistic Trinitarian.

matic, but unsuccessfully.   The watchword, " Back
to Christ," with which the book begins, dies into
an echo, and we have " the lame and impotent
conclusion " that the consciousness of Jesus gives
us an Augustinian fifth-century christology.   Dr.
Gordon well says that " philosophy must always be
tried at the bar of history."   It is the truest word
in his brilliant but inconclusive book.   To that
Cæsar must final appeal be made.   But the historical method that sits in judgment to-day on all
human knowledge demands facts, not fancies.
Metaphysics has its function, but it is useless for
practical ethics and religion, unless based on a
solid scientific induction.

Again, it is impressed upon me that *theological
thought is still largely cast in the old theological
moulds*.   Trinity, generation, consubstantial, incarnation, God-man, — terms invented and made
current coin by Greek philosophers and theologians, are still the familiar watchwords of orthodoxy.   The bottles are old, but the wine is new
and the old flavor has gone.   The law of evolution
that runs through all history has done its work
here as elsewhere.   The notable thing is that men
are so unconscious of the change.   A Catholic
writer has charitably declared that good Protestants are " unconscious Catholics."   It would not
be surprising if it should be found that there are
some Trinitarians who are " unconscious " Unitarians.

As I close this survey of the evolution of the
trinitarian dogma, I recur to the question with

which I began: Is Trinitarianism in New England to-day Athanasian? Certainly I have failed to accomplish what has been the chief aim of these chapters, if the answer to this question is not now clear. With Hopkins the last trace of genuine Athanasianism disappears; and from Emmons down to the present day Augustinianism has been completely in the ascendant. The idea so widely prevalent that we are having an Origenistic or Athanasian renaissance is one of the "curiosities of literature." Origen's "eternal generation," in its Origenistic meaning, is as dead as Pan. His Platonism, with its idealistic dualism and Logos doctrine, shows no sign of revival. Plato is still enthroned in the hearts of men, by reason of his splendid genius, but the real interpreter of Plato to this age is the disciple whose writings are still mostly buried in their original Greek, but whose subtle thought has been reincarnated in a long succession of illustrious thinkers, — Augustine's "*renowned Plotinus.*"

CHAPTER IV

THE TRINITARIAN OUTLOOK

IN the previous chapters the history of the evolution of the Christian dogma of the Trinity has been sketched down to the present day. Here our task as a historian would seem to end. History, strictly speaking, deals only with what is past. But the historical spirit easily and naturally passes into the prophetic spirit. The truly critical and philosophic historian is also a prophet. The great prophets of Israel were simply religious interpreters of history to their own age. Their prophecies so called were the true reading of passing events in the light of the spiritual laws that govern all historical movements. For history is no exception to that principle or law of orderly sequence in all living things which we call evolution. Even free will, which might be regarded as an uncertain factor in human affairs, because free and contingent, and so under no law of necessity, yet acts under motive and a law of rationality which removes its volitions from the sphere of chance to the sphere of moral causation. Cause and effect have their place just as surely in human events as in the events of nature. In all organic life,

whether lower or higher, there is "first the blade,
then the ear, then the full corn in the ear." In
everything human "the child is father of the
man." There was a large element of historical
truth in Lessing's comparison of the world to "a
colossal man," for it too has its childhood and
youth and manhood; and its laws of growth,
maturity, and decline may be clearly discovered.
It required only a clear historical insight to predict the sure downfall of the Roman Empire in
the days of Tiberius and Nero and Domitian, as
Israel's prophets had already done in the times of
its national backslidings and degeneracy. So there
is a law of *intellectual* evolution that works out
its results in the history of human beliefs and
speculations. From the standpoint already reached
in the survey of trinitarian history we may extend
our outlook into the coming years and read with
measured confidence the broad outlines of its now
hidden issues. Such is the purpose of this chapter concerning the future prospects of New England Trinitarianism. But it must not be forgottèn
that all true prophecy rests on true history, and
cannot for a moment be dissociated from it.

First of all, then, let us sum up and get clearly
in view the result of our previous studies. New
England Trinitarianism to-day is in a disorganized,
inchoate condition. It is passing through a radical turning-point in its evolution, sloughing off its
old shell and developing a new one. At such a
time it is always difficult to give an exact diagnosis

of theological opinions. But, bearing in mind the most recent trinitarian tendencies, as we have sketched them in a previous chapter, and watching the direction of the theological winds from the straws of local and individual as well as more ecumenical dogmatic declarations, it may be said, speaking broadly, that present New England Trinitarianism is characterized by three principal features: First, its Sabellian Patripassianism. I unite these two terms which really represent two quite distinct forms of trinitarian doctrine, because the whole tendency of New England trinitarian belief along the line of the Sabellian type of theological thought has been more and more strongly toward the Patripassian type. The preceding chapter fully illustrates this fact. Sabellianism allows a trinity of distinctions in God, or of divine modes of existence, using the word " person " in a secondary sense to describe those distinctions or modes, but not accepting a real tri-personality. In this view the Son or second person is distinguished from the Father or first person in some real manner, though it may be difficult to gather precisely in what manner. But Patripassianism loses sight of all real distinctions of any kind and wholly confounds the Son with the Father, making the Son so called to be actually the Father, but in a sort of disguise. We have seen that the earlier New England trinitarian leaders such as Emmons, Stuart, Bushnell, H. B. Smith, Shedd, remained on Sabellian ground. But Mr. Joseph Cook moved

on to the Patripassian position, and Drs. Lyman
Abbott and A. H. Bradford and others followed
in the same general path. According to these
thinkers, Father, Son, and Holy Ghost are but
different names and manifestations of one and the
same personal Being. This Being has his completest manifestation in Jesus Christ. Thus the
Deity of Christ is made the central and most vital
doctrine in their theology. He is manifested God
or "God manifest in the flesh." This phrase
"God manifest in the flesh" is now being constantly employed by defenders of the dogma of
Christ's true Deity and has become a sort of
watchword and shibboleth of orthodoxy. But it
contains a gross interpolation, as all scholars are
aware. The original language of Paul was "He
who was manifest in the flesh;" and he was de-
scribing Christ in his incarnate life, with no hint
of any allusion in the whole passage to God, whom
Paul never confounded with Jesus of Nazareth.
Several interpolations of a like sort are to be found
in the New Testament, made in a similar theological interest in times that were wholly wanting in
historical criticism, and when such interpolations
and changes in the text were difficult of discovery,
since new transcriptions of manuscripts were continually being made. The history of this interpolation and of its discovery, showing how ὅς was
changed into θεός, is one of the most curious and
remarkable chapters in textual criticism. The new
version of the New Testament has restored the

true text, and removed "God" from the passage. Why scholarly men should continue to use a phrase that has been so clearly proved to be spurious is somewhat difficult of comprehension. The persistency with which they employ it shows how easily it suits their Sabellianizing and Patripassianizing type of thinking. Certainly the phrase is a good one to juggle with. It has a breadth and elasticity that makes a wide interpretation possible. There is a monistic pantheistic flavor about it that commends it to our age. But even assuming that Paul wrote the clause as interpolated, it cannot be interpreted to mean that Christ is Absolute Deity. Paul held firmly to the Jewish monotheism. "There is one God and one Mediator between God and man, the man Christ Jesus." Paul never confounds Christ with God. God for him is always the one only eternal and invisible. Jesus Christ was a manifestation of God in the flesh. But what kind of a manifestation? There are many manifestations of God. Nature is a manifestation of God. Paul declares that God's power and divinity are known by the things that are made. So is man a manifestation of God, having been created in his true image. But nature and man are not identical with God. The thing formed is not the same with him who formed it. Such identity is pantheism. There is no such doctrine in Genesis or in Paul. If Christ was a manifestation of God in that natural scriptural sense, what ground is there in this passage for claiming

Christ's supreme Deity? Yet this is just the interpretation given by the trinitarian theologians who are so frequently quoting it. In illustration I wish to call attention to the addresses made at the recent semi-centennial anniversary of the Plymouth Church in Brooklyn.

I do this the more readily because this series of meetings was made the occasion of setting forth "the new Puritanism," in other words, the new New England theology, on two special points, the Calvinistic anthropology and the Nicene Trinitarianism. With its new statement of Calvinism I am not now concerned, but the "new Trinitarianism" was here proclaimed in what seemed no uncertain language. In all the addresses the real personal Deity of Christ was made the central theme. Mr. Beecher's doctrine was given in the following extract: "Could Theodore Parker worship my God? Jesus Christ is his name. All that there is of God to me is bound up in that name. A dim and shadowy effluence rises from Christ, and that I am taught to call the Father. A yet more tenuous and invisible film of thought arises, and that is the Holy Spirit. But neither is to me aught tangible, restful, accessible." Dr. Abbott also quoted from Mr. Beecher's address to the London ministers: "Do I believe in the divinity of Christ? I do not believe in anything else." "There is nothing else to me when I am thinking of God." Mr. Beecher was a man of extraordinary emotional genius, and his language in the

heat of extemporaneous speech should not be too
critically interpreted. But Dr. Abbott himself
declared that "the heart of Mr. Beecher's teaching was this : that Jesus Christ was God 'manifest in the flesh,' " and significantly added, "And
what Mr. Beecher held and this church holds on
this subject, I hold no less earnestly." Now certainly nothing can be plainer than Mr. Beecher's
meaning, whatever latitude we may allow to his
language. He held that Christ was very God,
and that the whole Godhead was incarnate in him.
"My God ? Jesus Christ is his name." And this
was plainly Dr. Berry's interpretation of Mr.
Beecher's views. In his address on the same occasion he said that Mr. Beecher drew his "doctrine of the Deity of Jesus Christ from his own
Christian experience," on which basis he rested
his faith in the incarnation, since it was "obliga-
tory for God to come to man and work for him
and die for him." The bald Patripassianism of
Dr. Berry's words is noticeable ; but it is a just
conclusion from Mr. Beecher's own language, and
reveals clearly the thorough Patripassian character of the "new Trinitarianism." Christ is no
longer the incarnation of the Son of God, the
second person of the Trinity, — that was the old
Trinitarianism, — but the very incarnation of God,
the Father Almighty, the Absolute One. The distinctions of Father, Son, and Holy Ghost have
faded out. God in his own single person, whatever name or names be given him, Father, Son, or

Holy Ghost, God, the one and only God, " came to man, worked for him, and died for him." Thus Christ is all the Father there is, as well as Son and Holy Ghost. All divinity is centred and summed up in him. It is hardly needful to say to any historical scholar that all this " new Trinitarianism " is no trinitarianism at all. It is simply another example of the now common practice of retaining the old bottles and filling them with new wine.

The theological declarations of this notable church anniversary are the more significant, because they have been published in book form and widely read, and have called forth little dissent from the upholders of Trinitarianism, and it is my impression that this type of belief is now increasingly prevalent in the New England Congregational churches. The doctrine of the Trinity in its ancient Nicene form and meaning is never preached. The very phrase " three persons " is passing out of our creeds and church confessions. In place of the old Trinitarianism, with Father, Son, and Holy Ghost as three distinct personal beings united by community of nature, yet distinguished by an essential subordination, the Son and Holy Ghost being derived from the Father and possessing all their divine attributes from the Father as the one eternal self-existent fountain of all being, the supreme Deity of Christ is now pushed to the front and made the great test of evangelical faith. In short, Trinitarianism is being *unitarianized*. One person, Christ, has become for all such believers the one only God. He is God incarnate. The Father was incarnate in him. The Holy Ghost, as Joseph Cook says, is only "Christ's continued life."

It is one of the most singular facts in the present theological situation, that the theologians who are the stanchest supporters of the trinitarian " faith once delivered," as they believe, are themselves drifting directly to a unitarian form of heresy which the early church condemned and cast out. It is also remarkable that these persons are so unconscious of what this new Trinitarianism involves. They suppose themselves to be building new buttresses of the old trinitarian dogma. They stoutly oppose what they call Unitarianism, whatever that may mean. They are ready to use the strongest trinitarian language. They recite the Nicene creed, and baptize in the name of Father, Son, and Holy Ghost, and continually repeat the trinitarian benediction. But what does all this signify, if they read into all these forms and symbols of the ancient faith a meaning that did not originally belong to them. Their dogma of Christ's essential and absolute Deity is wholly foreign to ancient orthodoxy. It is the old heresy revived of Patripassian Unitarianism. Of course in this view God is one personal being, and if Christ is God incarnate, and as such is the one personal Deity, what becomes of the Father, — the one absolute and unseen God of the Old Testament, — of Christ himself, and

of Paul? He is reduced to a metaphor, a shadow,
of which Christ the Son is the true substance. In
such a doctrine, not only Trinitarianism but even
Monotheism itself, the apostolic basis of the
Athanasian trinity, suffers collapse. Of course
the reply is at hand, — and we are familiar with
it, — that there may be three real personal distinctions, though not three personal beings in the one
being of God. But this Sabellian evasion is a
pure psychological assumption which carries a
fallacy on its very face, and which we owe to the
bold *ipse dixit* of the great Hopkinsian Emmons.
He it was who first dared to declare that while
" it is evident that no man can conceive three
divine persons to be one person, it does not hence
follow that no man can conceive that three divine
persons should be one divine Being. *For if we
only suppose that being may signify something
different from person in respect to Deity* (italics
are my own), then we can easily conceive that God
should be but one Being and yet exist in three
persons." Sure enough, how easy! " *If we only
suppose!* " But can we " suppose "? Is not a
moral being, whether he be man or God, necessarily a person? Is not a person necessarily a
being? But Emmons, as we have already seen,
jumps the whole logical difficulty and assumes his
monstrous supposition to be an actual fact. Perhaps the most amazing thing of all is that men
who claim to be consistent thinkers can so naively
assume such a patent logical fallacy to be axio-

matic truth in respect to God. The simple truth is that a personal triunity is a Gordian knot that can never be logically untied, and can be cut only by the sharp sword of a logical paradox. It is interesting to recall the fact that Cardinal Newman, whose finely spun discriminations have furnished much of the material of modern trinitarian speculation, frankly allowed the truth of this view of the case, and boldly accepted its consequence, viz., that there are three persons in one personal being, or, to put it as H. B. Smith and Dorner did, that there are three persons in one personality; and this barefaced logical paradox was for him an article of evangelical faith. His New England followers are only saved from a similar logical dilemma by their pantheistic tendencies, from which Newman was apparently free. I have dwelt more at length on this point because it represents the primary and cardinal note in the present stage of trinitarian or more truly unitarian evolution.

The *second* notable feature of the Trinitarianism of to-day is the doctrine of the consubstantiality or community of essence of God and man. This feature has a close affinity with the Sabellian-Patripassian one, and the two are usually found together. Such men as Phillips Brooks and George A. Gordon, who have been prominent in setting forth the view of the essential divineness of humanity, and who base on it their doctrine of Christ's divinity, are clearly Sabellian, if not

Patripassian, in their doctrine of the relation of
Christ to God; while it is equally true that such
men as Lyman Abbott, who more directly represent the Sabellian-Patripassian position, also
accept the closely affiliated idea of man's essential
divineness and God's essential humanness. Dr.
Abbott squarely asserted this view in an address
lately delivered at Bangor. He told us that a
theological student on being asked : " Do you
think the divinity of Christ differs in *kind* or in
degree from the divinity in man ? " replied : " In
degree." Dr. Abbott defended this reply. " There
are not two kinds of divinity," he said. " We are
in God's image. That means that we are in *kind*
like God. We are children of God." This is,
no doubt, a good gospel, on the face of it, and
there is nothing new in it. The newness appears
in the tacit assumption that lies behind it, viz., that
if man is in *kind* like God, he is therefore truly
and essentially divine, in other words, *of divine
nature.* There lurks here a confusion between
moral likeness and *essential* likeness which dis-
closes the pantheistic mode of thought into which
our modern Trinitarianism is passing, as we shall
note more directly soon. The Nicene Trinitarianism held to Christ's *essential* likeness to God, and
so declared him divine, but it distinguished Christ
from mankind by holding that man's likeness to
God was *moral* rather than *essential.* This distinction was based on the Platonic dualism which
separated the uncreated from the created by the

broad chasm of an *essential difference*. This
dualistic view made Christ, the Son of God, essentially different, that is, different in *kind*, from men.
But monism allows no such chasm between the
uncreated and the created, between the divine and
the human, between God and man. Such is the
philosophical background of the new Trinitarianism. The created is evolved from the uncreated,
and is of the same essential nature. Man is as
truly divine as God is. " There are not two kinds
of divinity." Of course not. The real question is
whether the *one kind* of divinity includes man.
Dr. Abbott says Yes just as plainly as Phillips
Brooks or Dr. Gordon. It is not surprising that
these two apparently distinct schools of trinitarian
thought should coalesce. They are in close philosophical affinity, and their partisans are united
moreover in a common aim, viz., to save, in form
at least, the old orthodox Trinitarianism. This
aim gives the true clue to this new doctrine of
man's consubstantiality with God. Traditional
trinitarian orthodoxy had placed the centre of
Christ's personality in his divine nature, thus reducing his human nature to a sort of superficial
appendix of the divine, and destroying its real
individuality. Christ's humanity thus became a
docetic and unmeaning show. How could it be
said that Christ was a true man, with real human
needs, susceptibilities, desires, and free will, involving temptability to evil and sin, so that it could be
said of him that " he was tempted in all points

like as we are," if the central and governing principle of his personality was divine and so raised
above all changeableness and temptableness? Such
a construction of Christ's person was no longer
possible in these days of historical research and
criticism, by means of which the real historical
human Jesus, so long lost to view, has been once
more unveiled. When the historical facts of
Christ's earthly life are disentangled from the
legendary traditions that have grown up around it,
there is clearly revealed in his human nature a
human will central and regnant over his whole
being, — a will moved by human motives, affections, interests, appeals, desires, hopes, aspirations,
faith, yes by human fears also, sensitiveness to
suffering and weaknesses of the flesh. What
more touching proof of all this than that scene in
Gethsemane! Now how can this historical picture
of Christ be accepted, and the old orthodoxy, with
its doctrine of two natures and two wills, divine
and human, — the divine ruling the human, —
remain secure? This is the very problem that the
theory of man's essential divineness seeks to solve.
Man, it is said, is consubstantial with God. He
is essentially divine, for he is in the divine image.
His humanity is a divine humanity. Every man
is not only a true son of man, but also a true son
of God. But supremely was this true of Jesus,
the unique representative of both man and God.
He is wholly man and yet wholly God. But how
is this amazing assumption, this apparent psycho-

logical contradiction, to be explained and defended? The answer is: There is in God's own nature an eternal humanity which in Christ became personalized by the incarnation and so was made manifest to men. And here again the interpolated phrase, "God manifest in the flesh," is made to do duty, and lo! the knot has been successfully untied. Christ on his earthly side is a mere man, unique indeed, but none the less a true son of humanity, while in his heavenly aspect he is the absolute and eternal God. The Sabellian and pantheistic character of this solution has been already pointed out. But as a metaphysical explanation of Christ's relation to the Trinity it is an utter failure, for it leaves clearly exposed to view a vast unbridged chasm between the human Jesus and the eternal humanity of the absolute God which even the befogging speculations of old or new Hegelianism are unable to conceal.

It is somewhat difficult to decide how far this idea of man's divinity has penetrated into the popular mind and faith. But it belongs to a class of ideas that is more and more permeating the very air of the age. Our literature is steeped with it. Emerson and his transcendental school, the most potent literary factor in recent thought, have done much to give it currency. Still further, it has close affinity with the reigning scientific monism which is rapidly passing from science to philosophy, and which as a philosophic principle constitutes *the third marked feature of the new Trinitarianism of to-day.*

Philosophical monism must be carefully distinguished from scientific monism. The latter is limited to the material and phenomenal world, the former covers the whole universe, spiritual as well as phenomenal. Certainly scientific monism, or the doctrine " that the whole cognizable world is constituted and has been developed in accordance with one common fundamental law," to adopt a definition of Haeckel, is the greatest discovery of modern natural science, and any religious or philosophical dogma that is to hold its ground must not only reckon with it, but also accept its conclusions. But while this is true, it is quite another thing to extend this monistic law of natural evolution over the spiritual and moral as well as natural world. It is easy to see at once that the consequences of such a step are radical and momentous. If the whole material and spiritual universe may be reduced to one ultimate principle, which is it: matter or mind? Hence two classes of monists are to be distinguished, which are in direct antagonism, viz., materialistic monists and idealistic or spiritual monists. Materialistic monism, as a philosophical and not merely a scientific doctrine, holds that matter is the first principle of all things out of which are evolved even the highest forms of organic life, including man's intellectual and religious nature. Thus the " soul " is only a form of matter, " a function of the brain," which is its material base and organ. The difference between the human soul and that of lower animals is one of degree and not of kind. This view of course involves the denial of the soul's separate individual existence after the death of the body, together with all the other spiritual dogmas which rest upon it. Haeckel's "Confession of Faith of a Man of Science" is a conspicuous example of materialistic philosophical monism. Of course most students of natural science adhere closely to their own field of labor and do not allow themselves to cross the line which separates science from philosophy and religion. But it is difficult if not impossible to prevent the mind from philosophizing on the facts that are brought before it. Haeckel declares his firm conviction that his monistic "Confession of Faith" "is shared by at least nine tenths of the men of science now living," "although few have the courage (or the need) to declare it openly." Whatever the truth may be as to exact numbers, the trend of thought and belief among "men of science" is plainly towards philosophical as well as scientific monism, — such men as Tyndall and Huxley and Haeckel being the more outspoken representatives. It ought to be noted here that materialistic monism, though modern in its present shape and lineage, is not new in the history of philosophic thought. Greek philosophy began on a materialistic monistic basis and remained such until the Socratic-Platonic dualism arose, and afterwards had its representatives in the widespread and popular Stoic and Epicurean schools. In fact, materialism in one or other of these forms was the

prevailing religious belief during the golden age
of the Roman empire, — the period from Augustus
to Marcus Aurelius.

The idealistic monism starts from the opposite
pole. It reduces all things, even the lowest forms
of matter, to a spiritual substratum. Matter itself
is but an evolution of spirit. Idea, to adopt Hegelian language, is the essence of the universe.
There is a wonderful charm in the idealistic philosophy, and it is no wonder that it has drawn to
itself the loftiest and noblest spirits. Man loves
to disengage himself from the dull round of earthly
temporal things and put on wings with Plato and
soar upward to the transcendental and eternal.
Poetry which speaks man's highest moods and
aspirations is idealistic in its very nature. Wordsworth, who struck the keynote of the most splendid
poetry of the century, theist though he was in
faith, is ever rising into that heaven of idealistic
vision where God is both one and all, as in the
" Excursion," in a passage full of mystical pantheism, from which I quote but a single clause : —

> "Thou, Thou alone
> Art everlasting, and the blessed Spirits,
> Which Thou includest, as the sea her waves."

But idealism has its weak side. There are, it may
be said, two kinds of mind. There are minds
that naturally seek facts, the facts of nature, of
history, and of experience. There are also minds
that as naturally live in the region of thought, of
the abstract, and who seek to project out of the

world of their own abstract thinking a world of concrete realities. Here lies the great danger to which idealistic monism is exposed. The bridge from the abstract to the concrete, from the genus to the individual, is wholly a subjective creation, and can never be made the objective basis of a natural evolution from idea or spirit to matter and the organic material world. This is the rock on which idealism in its extreme form has ever split, from Plato and Plotinus to Spinoza and Hegel. But still another danger lurks in a monistic idealism. The "idea" of Plato was not individual or personal, it was a universal, and his highest idea of the good was the *summum genus*. So the absolute "one" of Plotinus was simply the highest point of abstraction which thought could reach. Plato himself was a religious thinker, but his idealistic philosophy had no personal God, while Plotinus was a consistent and avowed pantheist. A religious idealist may attempt to hold to a personal God, but the whole tendency of this philosophy will be quite away from such a God toward a Platonic Plotinian abstraction. Emerson's criticism on Christianity well sets forth the natural attitude of monistic idealism toward personality as an element of being, and especially of the highest form of being, God. "Christianity," he says, "is an exaggeration of the personal, the positive, the ritual. It has dwelt, it dwells, with noxious exaggeration about the *person* of Jesus. *The soul knows no persons.*" What now of the new

trinitarian monism of our day? Of course it is
idealistic to the core. Against the materialism of
Tyndall and Haeckel and others it holds to the
doctrine of the eternal priority of spirit to matter
and to the radical generic difference between them.
Spirit is the *fons et origo* of all material things,
and yet never to be confounded with them. This
view might take a dualistic form. Matter might
be treated as a creation of mind, having a beginning in time, and belonging to an entirely distinct
realm of being. Mind, too, might be regarded as
eternally personal, and as existing only in persons
as personal substances or individuals. Such is the
Biblical theistic dualism. But certainly the fore-
most representatives of the new Trinitarianism are
not dualists. They hold to one eternal spiritual
substance in whatever form it may appear, and it
is on this ground that they assert the true divinity
of man and the true humanity of God. Dr.
Whiton did not speak for himself alone when he
said : "There is but one spiritual nature, and that
may be indifferently spoken of as divine or human.
The universal God is individualized in each personal conscience." That is, personality is but an
accident, or quality of substance, so that impersonal
substance rises higher than personal substance in
the scale of being. The eternal evolution is from
the impersonal to the personal. This surely is
nothing less than a monistic pantheism so far as
the spiritual world is concerned. Whether now a
spiritual monistic philosophy will or can stop here

is the question. At this point dualism might still attempt to assert itself. There are two separate worlds, it might be said, and two separate evolutions, a spiritual evolution and a material one. But can this be true? Are there two evolutionary forces in the so-called universe? Is the universe after all not a *universe*, but a *duality*, with dual forces and laws? We know what science says to this, so far as it can speak. What shall philosophy say? Between the brain and the mind what is there? The end of one form of evolution and the beginning of another? Does a new force here enter that before had no activity or agency, and begin a new order of life? A negative answer of course brings us to the verge of absolute pantheism. And there can be no doubt that this is the logical result of either form of monism, whether materialistic or idealistic. Both reach at last the same pantheistic goal, though by opposite roads, and with opposite views of that original force which by courtesy on both sides is called God. Plainly orthodox theologians are not wholly unaware of the end toward which monism leads and are chary about going too far in that direction. They wish to preserve the form of the old dualism though its substance is taken away. We hear about the " new theism," as if there could be two kinds of theism any more than there can be two kinds of persons, or two kinds of divinity, and as if baptizing anything with the Christian name could alter its pagan nature. For the monism of Augustine and of his theological descendants down to the present day is radically different from the theism of Paul and Athanasius, and is not of Christian, but of pagan New Platonic, ancestry, as the previous chapters have shown.

The same fear of an avowed pantheism is seen in the fine distinctions that are so frequently made between the divine transcendence and the divine immanence. Theologians are trying to hold both and thus play fast and loose with both. For these two terms, in their true philosophical significance, are as opposed to each other as dualism and monism, and can no more be harmonized. Dualism is based on the divine transcendence as monism is based on the divine immanence, and these two principles of explanation of the universe remain in everlasting antithesis, like the two great schools of Greek thought that represent them, the Platonic and the Stoic. Yet men ring the changes on transcendence and immanence, as Coleridge did on "subject and object," as if they could save themselves by such subjective distinctions from the open pit of pantheism, on the precipitous verge of which they stand and into which they are ready any moment to fall. I am well aware how strong is the recoil of man's religious nature from such a result, and there are clear indications of it in our most recent theological literature. But the stream must be as the fountain, and monism, if accepted and followed as a philosophical principle, has but one sure terminus, — the undisguised and complete pantheism of Spinoza and Hegel.

I have protracted this preliminary résumé to what may seem an unnecessary length. But it is absolutely essential to have the foundations of an historical outlook into the future firmly laid. Let it be noted, as we leave this part of our subject, that these three principal tendencies, viz., 1. Sabellian-Patripassianism, 2, man's consubstantiality with God, 3, a monistic philosophy, are organically related and supported, and it is only by a careful analysis that they can be distinguished. They stand or fall together, and really unite what may seem to be different trinitarian positions on essentially common ground.

CHAPTER V

THE TRINITARIAN RESULT

WE are now ready to look around us and ask ourselves the meaning and portent of those phases and changeful attitudes of trinitarian thought which, like a panorama, are passing before our eyes. The survey makes several clear impressions.

One observes at once the vague, fluxive, uncertain, and restless character of present trinitarian speculation. There seems to be no firm footing for theological positions. Trinitarianism, as a theological basis of faith, is like a ship at sea, tempest-tossed, and seeking some new haven of rest. Ask men what Trinitarianism to-day is and they cannot tell you, or if they do, they will disagree at once. Orthodoxy once presented a solid front, known and read of all men. Not so to-day. The definitions of orthodoxy, even by orthodox men, are " as thick as leaves in Vallombrosa." Orthodoxy has at last come to be each man's doxy. The natural result has followed. The ranks of orthodoxy are becoming demoralized. There is no one banner under which all can rally, no real leadership, no common bond of union. The old lines of demarcation between orthodoxy and heterodoxy are fading out in the minds of men, and when the old shibboleths and war-cries are sounded there is no general united response. Moreover the effort to find a new basis of union has hitherto failed. New creeds are being made, but there is no universal acceptance of them. New forms of trinitarian statement are continually being promulgated, but men criticise them or give them no heed. The outcome of it all is that orthodoxy has grown timid and wary, and hides itself. The old bottles of traditional creeds and dogmas are still used and the old labels are suffered to remain, while the new wine of a new Trinitarianism, which is not the old at all, is poured into them. Creeds are now signed for " substance of doctrine," when the substance is the very question at issue.

On so grave a matter I wish to speak within bounds. It is more and more true, as I am ready to affirm, of our younger ministers especially, that they preach honestly and boldly the gospel as they believe it. They are learning to prize their Protestant and Puritan birthright. But it must still be said that the pulpit, and the religious press, largely edited by ministers, have so long borne the yoke of dogmatic bondage that they have to a considerable degree lost the true sense of what bondage and liberty mean. There are exceptions to all rules. No doubt there are not a few splendid exceptions to this one. I have a confident hope that the exceptions will erelong become the rule, and that this sad phase of theological timidity will vanish in the new era of intellectual and moral freedom. But it cannot pass away completely so long as the causes of it continue to work. These causes are connected with the supremacy of the dogmatic spirit; and though this spirit is rapidly yielding to the scientific temper and methods of our day, it is still to be reckoned with, as recent ecclesiastical events show. This spirit lives in the dogmatic theological standards set up as conditions of entrance into the Christian ministry, independently of intellectual and religious fitness, also in the dogmatic creeds imposed on theological instructors in some, if not all, of our seminaries, and still more in the inquisitorial character of councils sometimes called to investigate charges of theological error. The effects of this dogmatism fall with especial weight upon ministers, and it is no wonder that not a few of them, whose daily bread for themselves and their families may depend on a reputation for orthodoxy, are more or less unconsciously governed by a wholesome fear that serves to cramp their intellectual freedom and to breed a timid and craven spirit. This is the explanation in part of the fact that the laity are so much in advance of the clergy in their readiness to accept whatever new light and truth may come from the new science and history, and to lay aside traditional dogmas that are found to be without historical foundation. Of course there are exceptions among the laity, as among the clergy. Some

laymen are still bound in dogmatic fetters, as there
are some clergymen who have broken them utterly.
Let me not here be misunderstood. I am not
dealing with individuals, but with laws of tendency
and their natural results. Some of our most conservative ministers are filled with the spirit of
Christian freedom and tolerance, and so there are
men of the most pronounced radicalism who are as
dogmatic as Calvin himself. But history shows
that, as a rule, the dogmatic spirit develops intol-
erance and spiritual despotism. Conservatism and
dogmatism are not necessarily connected, as examples prove, though they have too often been found
together. The fact remains that causes always
work out their natural effects, and that, while the
reign of dogma is suffered to continue, its baneful
results will inevitably follow.

The situation thus sketched gives a clue to one
of the most remarkable features of it, viz., the
general and combined effort on the part of the ex-
ponents of the new Trinitarianism to make as clear
and wide as possible the difference between Trinitarianism and Unitarianism. It is a curious phenomenon, and well worth a careful study by the
historical observer, for it sheds a bright light on
the anomalous condition into which trinitarian
orthodoxy has fallen. What is the great task now
assumed by trinitarian apologies and polemics?
Not plainly to set forth in all its grand outlines
the ancient dogma of the Trinity, but rather a
"new Trinitarianism," and in doing this to show

that it has no affinity with Unitarianism. But why
the need of showing this? Simply because the
line of difference is becoming so dim that it requires a keen microscopic eye to discern it. In
theological controversy, as in war always, the storm
centre is where the lines of battle run most closely
together. Our previous résumé has shown how all
recent trinitarian tendencies run straight toward a
unitarian result. Monism is unitarianism in essence though it may take on all the colors of the
chameleon. When all the old bottles with their
disguises have been broken and all the mystical
idealistic pantheism has been stripped off, there
remains essential unitarianism. The case is a
strange one. Trinitarians and Unitarians to-day
hold the same philosophical position. Both parties
are monists. In truth, as we have seen, it was
from the Unitarian Emerson that such Trinitarians
as Phillips Brooks and others drew the weapons of
their new philosophic trinitarian gospel. Our preliminary survey also showed how organically connected are all the three fundamental elements of
the trinitarian position. The unity of God, of man,
and of the universe is at its very root. This is
essential unitarianism, to be sure; and wherein is
the Unitarian position different? Let some skilled
logician arise to show. "But," says the trinitarian
apologist, "the Unitarianism against which we
wage Christian war is not the doctrine of the personal unity of God, in which of course we all now
agree, but the Unitarian denial of the Godhood of

Christ." Here indeed is one of the old bottles of the ancient theology. Let us examine the new wine it contains. It may not be so different from the Unitarian wine after all. The doctrine of the Nicene creed concerning the Godhood of Christ was this : There is one only absolute eternal God, the Father Almighty ; and besides there is the Son of God, a second hypostasis or personal being, who is of common nature with the Father, but derived and subordinate, " very God of very God " indeed, but not absolute or self-existent, though timeless by eternal generation ; and further there is a third hypostasis, the Holy Ghost. But what is the new wine that is now being dispensed out of the old flask with its old trinitarian label? This : that God is one only both in person and in essence, but is manifested in different forms, and especially in triune form, and that this triune form has become incarnate in Jesus Christ, who is thus God manifest in the flesh, so that the whole Godhood is in Christ, and there is none other beside him. What, no Father? No, except as in him. No Holy Ghost ? No, not outside of Christ. Christ is the whole God; Fatherhood, Sonhood, and Spirithood are simply forms of Christ's one Godhood. " But we are Trinitarians," they say. " We recite the Nicene creed." Yes, but you do not mean by it what the Nicene Fathers meant. Your Father, Son, and Holy Ghost are but shadows of one real Deity, and that one Deity is summed up and manifested in Jesus Christ. The theism and trinitari-

anism of the creed has departed and in its place
we have the Patripassian monism of to-day. I hear
indeed one voice as if in protest. Dr. Abbott,
with his usual wariness, in the address already
referred to, said: "I never say that Christ is
God, because God is more than the sum of all his
manifestations. Jesus Christ is one of the manifestations of God. Therefore God is more than
Jesus Christ. Jesus Christ is God manifest in the
flesh." This is shrewd, but is it sound? If Christ
is God manifest in the flesh, not in a figure but in
reality, does the manifestation take away from his
full Godhood? Was the incarnation a lessening
of divinity, or not rather an adding of humanity?
The latter, said the orthodox letter of Leo. But
Dr. Abbott makes the incarnation, in which he declared distinctly that he believed, a limiting of
God. God pre-incarnate is so much greater than
God incarnate that the latter should not be called
God at all. Further, if Christ is only one of many
manifestations of God, such as those in man and
in nature and in history, how, but by an utter
subversion of language, can Christ be called God at
all? How is he "God manifest in the flesh" any
more than he is God alone, or than a man or a
mountain is God? Let Dr. Abbott answer for
himself. But what I have to say to all this is
that I commend Dr. Abbott to a re-reading of his
Plymouth Church anniversary address, and to a
harmonizing of the two addresses. And if they
cannot be harmonized, as I suspect is the case,
which of the addresses speaks true?

But to return to the real point at issue, what is the difference between the " new Trinitarianism " and Unitarianism? Here we must note the fact that there are two kinds also of historical Unitarianism, an old and a new. The old Unitarianism was simply monotheism, like the faith of the Old Testament and of Jesus himself. It reappeared in New England in protest against trinitarian orthodoxy in the persons of Channing and Theodore Parker. Much of it, I suppose, exists to-day behind the unitarian christological humanitarianism. The *new* Unitarianism is monistic with all its Emersonian, idealistic, pantheistic features. It makes much of man's divineness and of God's humanness. It is thus ready to exalt Christ to a unique divinity. It goes back to the Nicene creed, and declares its only defect to be one of limitation. The Nicene doctrine of the consubstantiality of Christ with God should have been enlarged to that of the divine consubstantiality of all men. I hold no brief for any of these dogmas, but I venture to affirm that the new Unitarian leaders are quite ready to accept much of the language of their Trinitarian opponents, and even to assert the true Godhood of Jesus of Nazareth in the monistic sense of the term; and if so, what point of philosophical difference is left between the new Trinitarianism and the new Unitarianism? Surely Trinitarianism has been unitarianized or Unitarianism has been trinitarianized. Which? A common monistic philosophy gives the only possible answer. Both sec-

tions of Christian monism agree in these points:
that the supreme Deity is absolute essence, whether
personal or impersonal it is not easy to say; that
Christ's divinity is not different in kind from all
divinity; and that as an incarnate person he is
purely human, with a human birth and a historical
beginning in time.   With such radical agreements,
to talk about differences is to beat the air.   Is it
insisted that there remains a real difference on the
question of Christ's Deity?   Pray show us just
what it is.   Deity, divinity, godhood, are words of
elastic meaning in theology, especially in monistic
theology.   The *real question* at issue, a question,
however, which orthodoxy is continually brushing
aside as irrelevant, is not whether Jesus Christ is
divine, but whether he is *human*.   The old Nicene
orthodoxy begged this question and finally vir-
tually denied it.   The new orthodoxy squarely
affirms it, but arrays Christ's manhood in the
vesture of godhood.   But what is the metaphysical
or historical background of this human-divine
person?   Is it an eternal personal being, or a
human child of Joseph and Mary?   In other
words, was the personal consciousness of Jesus
an eternal divine consciousness of the absolute
God, involving omniscience and other divine attributes, or was it a human consciousness involving
limitation and defect and weakness?   There can
be no doubt as to the answer of the " new Trinitarianism."   It is the same with that of the new
Unitarianism.   The real personal centre of Jesus

is his human consciousness and will, not the
eternal omniscient consciousness and will of a personal God.   Godhood thus becomes but a figure
of speech, or a transcendental universal of Plo-
tinian-Hegelian metaphysics, and one may choose
between them.   The doctrine of divine humanity
and human divinity makes the choice both easy
and non-essential.   The term God has always had
a large and springing meaning in the history of
language.   Even the Bible, with all its stiff monotheism, describes men as gods, and sons of
gods, as in one of the Psalms, "I have said ye
are gods, and all of you are children of the
Most High," and Christ is made in the fourth
Gospel to defend himself against the charge of
blasphemy in calling himself the Son of God, by
quoting this very passage.   Only add now to a
figure of speech a monistic philosophy, and it is
equally easy for a Trinitarian or a Unitarian to
assert Christ's Deity.   And yet this is the curious
historical fact, that these two positions, inexorably
united by common philosophical and theological
principles, are arrayed against each other in solemn
internecine conflict, and the worst heretical charge
that can be brought against any one in the communion of Trinitarian saints to-day is that he is
somehow, one hardly knows how, a Unitarian.   To
such a barren, nay, absurd result has the present
phase of Trinitarianism come!

One cannot refrain from calling attention at
this point in our survey to the illustration here

afforded of a striking fact in the history of theological dogmas, viz., that the shibboleths of orthodoxy are constantly changing with the changing
circumstances of the times. The heresy of one
age is the orthodoxy of another, and *vice versa*.
Only a few years ago the burning question of
theological disputation in New England was the
theory of a new or second probation of certain
classes of men. To assert it became for a while
the very storm centre of heresy. Licensure of
young ministers was made to hang largely on the
answers given to questions concerning this obscure
point of eschatology. Another similar eschatological question was also pushed to the front: that
of the everlastingness of future punishment. On
such points the American Board came near dis-
ruption. It is interesting to observe how rapidly
the whole problem of eschatology, so far as the
final state of men is concerned, is passing out of
sight. If such matters are brought forward in
ministerial examinations, the interest is speculative rather than dogmatic. Licensure is no longer
made to hang on it. In the last generation Calvinism was regnant, and any taint of Arminianism
in the form of asserting free will or contingency
was quickly caught up and vigorously dealt with.
Dr. Emmons, the Corypheus of Hopkinsian Calvinism, came very near being refused licensure
in his youth, because he used rather stronger
language on "natural ability" than the examining ministers were willing to allow, though they

adopted the very same phrase. But at that time "natural ability" was the one great watchword of orthodoxy. To-day such a question would only excite amusement. We are far beyond Calvinism or eschatology. The historical cycle has run out, and we are back once more at the point where Christian history began,—the first stage in the evolution of Christian theology, viz., the question of the man of Nazareth. Who is he? And that question has been evolved to its final answer, that Jesus is God, the only highest God. It is no longer the historical question of his birth, life, character, teaching, and moral power over the men of his own generation, but rather the subtlest philosophical question that human thought can raise, that of the metaphysical relation of the human Jesus to the absolute Deity, and the answer to *this* question is made the test of evangelical faith. The young minister may be at his ease as to his theological system besides, if he can only give as his own the "new trinitarian" version of Christ's true Godhood. Thus history has its revenges.

But what next? we are now ready to ask ourselves; for the historical evolution of dogmas, as of all things else, ever moves on. And here the historical observer finds himself at a point of view where what has seemed confused and perplexing begins to shape itself into order and unity. For one thing grows clear, that the phase of trinitarian evolution which we have been surveying is fast reaching its climax, and cannot move much further on its present line of progress. The old order is ending and a new order must begin. The trinitarian dogma has swung round the whole circle and returned to its initial starting-point, and, further, its philosophical as well as historical evolution has already attained its logical terminus. When Sabellianism has become Patripassianism, and Patripassianism has been metamorphosed into philosophical monism, there remains but one more step to take, juggle with it as one may, and that step is ultimate pantheism. Evolution on this line is forever stopped. The cycle has run out. Let us consider. What step further can the dogma of Christ's Deity take? Already Christ has become the whole Godhead. His very humanity has been completely divinized. For is not man himself consubstantial with God? Another stage of evolution in this direction is impossible. All that can be done is to carry out with logical consistency the monistic principle already accepted, and boldly say that the incarnation is but a metaphor, or applies equally to all men; that miraculous birth is no miracle at all except as all birth is a marvel, as in truth it is; that resurrection and ascension and second coming are but parts of apocalyptic imagery, except so far as it is true that for all men there is to be revival and resurrection to immortal life, and final gathering together to an endless assize and retribution. And all this is being said already. But the evolution must move on, if not in this channel, then in some other.

CHAPTER VI

THE NEW HISTORICAL EVOLUTION

WE have reached a turning-point in our survey of great significance. Little as we may realize it, this age in which we happen to be living is the theatre in which is being enacted the most radical and the greatest epochal movement that history has yet recorded. To read its meaning aright and so be able to forecast in some measure its issues, it is necessary to understand the different ways in which the principle of historical evolution works. It has three distinct, though coöperative, laws of action : 1. The law of development. 2. The law of cycles and of cyclic changes. 3. The law of reaction and revolution. Let me explain, and illustrate, from the history of Christian dogma. "Development" is a term that is often used synonymously with "evolution," but the latter has a wider significance. Development is the primary and ordinary law by which all evolution works. But at certain crises this law is suspended, and a cyclic change occurs, and a new form of evolution begins. This is seen in nature. Its history began with inorganic materials. Then came a change to organic life. The cycle of the azoic ends, and a new cycle of the protozoic begins. The evolutionary movement continues, but under a new form. A new force has entered into nature, producing a new and higher result. So in the passage from the lower to the higher forms of organized life, from vegetable to fish, from fish to reptile, and from reptile to mammal. But in the evolution from mammal to man the cycle of brute life is succeeded by the new cycle of human beings with reason and conscience and free will, and capacity of speech and of religion. All this we may read, as in a book, in the science of geology, where in the different strata of the rocks we may see the new cycles of change that divide one stage of development from another. The same is true of history. The law of development began to work at once in the history of the dogma of Christ. A new cycle began with the introduction of the Greek philosophy with its Logos mediation doctrine. This new cycle continued under the law of development to the Nicene-Athanasian period, and in the Greek Church down through the Middle Ages, and even to the present day. But in the West a new cycle began with Augustine. Augustinian christology was not radically revolutionary. It continued the old Greek trinitarian evolution, but it changed its point of departure, and inverted its whole meaning. A new force entered christology, viz., the New Platonic monism. The history of Christian dogma is as full as the earth's geological surface of such cyclic changes. The last

one in trinitarian evolution is that connected with
the theory of man's consubstantiality with God,
which reminds us of the Augustinian inversion of
Greek christology, being similarly a change of
base rather than the discarding of older views, and
equally the result of a changed philosophy. But
both in nature and in history crises have occurred,
usually after long intervals of quiet development,
when the old line of evolution is not merely de-
flected or changed by cyclic law, but completely
broken by natural or historical convulsions and
revolutions. A new force of tremendous power
has come into play, breaking up utterly all previous
orderly movement, and compelling a completely
new evolutionary beginning. Such were the
mighty catastrophes of the geologic world whose
traces are seen in the vast upheavals and depres-
sions of mountain and valley, and in the rents that
have formed such ravines as the cañons of Colo-
rado. Just such cataclysms have occurred in the
history, not only of political governments, but of
religious and theological dogmas. It is only needful to mention the religious revolution wrought by
the life and teaching of Jesus and the preaching
of his great apostle Paul, and also the Protestant
Reformation in the time of Luther and his com-
peers. In both these cases a complete rent was
made in the old order of faith and thought. Christianity, after centuries of conflict, gave its death-
blow to ancient paganism as a religious system in
the Roman empire, though its hidden leaven still

continued to live and work. The same was true
of the Lutheran movement. First, violent reaction led to radical revolt, and then out of revolution came a new Protestant system of faith, founded
in part indeed on the old Catholic traditions, but
also leavened by the new inductive science with its
cardinal principle of individual freedom. The
Lutheran age thus heralded the dawn of our
modern world. But such radical revolutionary
movements are always the result of deep underlying causes, involving a long historical preparation.
Christianity did not drop into history out of the
clouds of heaven. It was prefaced by a religious
reaction that became widespread throughout the
Græco-Roman world. The old polytheistic and
mythological paganism had lost utterly its hold on
the educated classes. Men had not grown irreligious, — history proves the contrary, — but a
profound skepticism had arisen concerning the
traditional faiths. A new ground of religious belief was sought in philosophy, but here too all was
confusion and doubt, so that even Cicero, after
pleading like a Christian for the immortality of
the soul, was forced to say that he doubted of
all. It was into such a religious vacuum that
Christianity with its " enthusiasm " of faith and
" humanity " came as a new power of spiritual life.
A similar series of causes brought on the Protestant revolt. Roman Catholicism had run its race
of a thousand years, until its cup of superstitions and tyrannies over the souls and bodies of

men was full. The cycle of *faith on authority* had run out, and skepticism under every sort of cover and concealment was honeycombing modern Christendom. Philosophical skepticism, that is, the doctrine that a dogma of faith might be true in theology and yet be false in philosophy, was in vogue everywhere and showed that the end of Catholic church authority was at hand. Scholastic theology had dug its own grave. When Luther appeared, according to the explicit testimony of Erasmus, a man who knew the temper of his age, everything was ready for a complete overturning of religious faith. The hour had struck and the man for the hour had come.

And now how about the situation to-day? The logic of history gives us but one solution. As we have seen, we are at the end of the old lines of development. Even the old bottles with the false labels have become useless. The eyes of men are opened, and no new cycle along some new line of philosophical thought is possible. Metaphysics has tried its hand and miserably failed. Some even who have been active in destroying what " is ready to vanish away " are growing faint-hearted. There are always those who are ready to be caught by the wiles of philosophy, but history has of late been busy with its critical tasks, and its revelations of what philosophy has attempted and failed to do have made even the credulous wary. Meanwhile skepticism is silently doing its work. This is not "an age of doubt" in the true religious

meaning of that word.   It is not an irreligious age,
nor a scoffing age.   It is a serious, earnest, believing age in its whole spirit.   It seeks religious light,
and it glows with the fire of religious love and
freedom.   But as to the old dogmatic traditionalism, that has come down from early Christian days
with all its gathered inheritance of pagan, monk-
ish, mediæval, and popish superstitions and beliefs, this age is intensely skeptical.   Among the
masses of the people it has been thrown aside as a
cast-off garment.   The skeptical spirit, in the sense
of refusal to accept the dogmas of the old orthodoxy, was no more widespread or complete in the
first years of the Christian era, or at the outbreak
of the Lutheran reformation, than it is to-day.
Ask men and women why they have ceased to at-
tend church, and they will tell you that they have
ceased to believe much that is preached, and that
their religious needs are not ministered to.   .I
wonder whether those who assume to sit in Moses'
seat realize with any degree of adequacy the large-
ness and power of this skeptical revolt.   It makes
no noise in the streets, but it permeates the very
atmosphere of social and religious life, like an unseen odor of flowers.   All this simply means that
we are nearing the end of the present theological
era, and are on the verge of radical change.   This
is dimly seen by not a few.   Men who stand on
the watch-towers of our Zion have taken note of
coming events.   We hear much now of " reconstruction."   We are having " new theologies "

and " new Puritanisms ; " but men still fail to realize that the time for superficial cyclic changes is past, and that all " the signs of the times " point to the vastest moral, religious, theological revolution that has yet transpired in history.   It is not an old building rebuttressed and reconstructed in its upper stories that this age demands, but a new building from the very foundations. Yet men are calling for some theological architect and artificer, to lead in reconstruction, as if the time had come for any such action.   Why has no signal theological leader appeared in these latter days?   The reason is simple.   There can be no leadership without *a lead*.   To-day there is no clear lead.   Theological leadership, like eloquence, requires not only the man, but also, and first of all, the subject and the occasion.   The man does not yet appear, because the work is not yet cut out for him.   The times are not yet ripe.   Times of reaction and revolution are first of all destructive.   The old house must be torn down before the new house can be built.   Men are beginning to see some of the steps of this destructive process and are attempting to call a halt.   " The work of destruction has gone far enough," says President Hyde in the " Congregationalist," and that journal takes up and repeats the cry, at the same time, however, making some unusual concessions, and allowing that " our churches, in common with other Christian denominations, have for a quarter of a century been experiencing a disintegration of

doctrine," and urging that the time has come for
" clear, strong discussions and affirmations of great
doctrines in the language which men use to-day and
in the light of the discoveries they have made and
the knowledge they have acquired." All of which
sounds well ; but one cannot help asking whether
the " great doctrines " referred to are not the
dogmas of the old creeds, and whether " the language which men use to-day " means anything
more than a new label for the old bottles, in which
case I submit, as a historical observer, that such
" discussions and affirmations " will be utterly
vain.

But it is time to interrogate our age more directly. We have hitherto studied the course of
historical evolution and seen what must be its logical outcome, viz., an intellectual and religious
revolution. Now let our age speak for itself, and
help us to answer the question, what next ? To
describe at any length the wonderful chapter of
history that the last fifty years have added to human
annals is impossible in our present survey. Most
people of intelligence have some general impression
of it, and have become accustomed to the idea
that we are living in an entirely different world
from that of our fathers. But it is only the historical student who has clearly grasped the law of
historical evolution, and has followed its course
from the earliest historical records down to the
present era, that can fully comprehend its extraordinary character. It has often been said that

the history of an age cannot be intelligently written until a generation or more has elapsed, so that the true perspective may be obtained. No doubt there is much of truth in this. There is danger of over estimation, by reason of closeness of vision, and also equally of under estimation for the very same reason. But it surely is a wrong inference that, when great and striking events occur in the political, intellectual, or religious world, they cannot be seen or estimated at their real value by the men who witness them. First-hand witnesses are after all the best and most reliable in the court of historical appeal. And whatever may be said of other times, certainly the age in which we live is one that he who runs may read. Never was such a deep and radical break and cleavage made between successive evolutionary movements and results in the history of man, as this age of ours is witnessing. Even to enumerate fully the marvelous discoveries in science, in history, in language, in archæology and geography, would be impossible. Take for example the two sciences of astronomy and electricity, and note what a boundless universe previously unimagined, and what tremendous forces previously hid in nature, have been revealed. Human invention has added its quota to human discovery and research until man and nature have seemed almost to be rivals for the tribute of our admiration and astonishment. These achievements of the human mind in scientific and historical fields have stirred the intellectual blood of the age, so that literature and philosophy have felt the impulse and added a new chapter to the history of human thought and feeling, of wonderful power and beauty. Never has the intellect of man had such wide scope of vision and such immeasurable fields of research opened to its activities as now. And such epochs of intellectual stimulus are always accompanied with new movements and agitations in the domains of ethics and religion. It was the golden age of Græco-Roman civilization that introduced a new religion to the world, which has surpassed all others in its ethical and religious purity and loftiness and universality of range. It was the revival of learning with its crowning renaissance of the fifteenth century that paved the way for Erasmus, Luther, and Calvin, and the religious reformation of which they were such distinguished representatives. It is always so. This age of ours is alive beyond all previous times to the appeals, the "categorical imperatives" of man's religious nature. Thus on all sides we find ourselves in the face of an epoch of unparalleled significance, and the impression made by it upon the critical observer, as he scans the evolution of history thus far from start to finish, is indeed profound. Our age surely needs no herald to trumpet its deeds. They are engraved on every re-written and re-edited, as well as newly added page of human annals in every field of man's activity.

And now what answer does it give to our question, What next? Is not the logical answer drawn

from the law of evolution that rules in history also
the answer of the present historical situation?
Can such an epoch pass by and leave no deep trace
of itself in philosophy, in theology, in ethics and
religion? Surely not. The revolution that impends must be as radical and far-reaching as the
movements and changes that will bring it to pass.
What then will be its character and lines of direction? The new revolution will certainly be along
the lines of the deepest and most vital demands of
the times. These demands may be gathered under
three heads: 1, the demand of the *historical* spirit;
2, the demand of the *religious* spirit; 3, the demand
of the *intellectual* spirit.

CHAPTER VII

THE DEMAND OF THE HISTORICAL SPIRIT

It will be seen as we proceed that these three demands are organically related and that the order above given is the logical one, and consequently the one that the historical evolution will naturally take. Every epoch has its own peculiar *Zeitgeist*, or *time* spirit. Some periods are creative and constructive, others are traditional and conservative, others still are reactionary, critical, revolutionary. The different ages of the world have their varied types and characteristics by which they are known to historians. That which characterizes our own age above everything else is *historical criticism*. The historical is the time spirit of the nineteenth century, and every other spirit must yield obedience to it. It had its birth in the scientific inductive method. When that method of research was applied to historical events as well as scientific investigation, a revolution was at once precipitated in the whole range of historical studies. History itself had to be re-written. Myth, legend, miracle, all the marvels of a supernatural realm of beings supposed to hold close relations with mankind were step by step eliminated from the annals of human events. Mythology and the miraculous may have place in a cosmogony or a philosophy of God and the universe, but they are not integral elements of human action, or of history, which is simply a record of such action. The literary revolution caused by this critical movement is already a matter of history. But it is the work of a single century. Distinguished among its pioneers are Gibbon and Niebuhr. Niebuhr's critical reconstruction of Livy's "Roman History" by which the miraculous legends that had grown up around the origins of Rome were separated from the authentic narrative, made an epoch in historical studies. Romulus and Remus and Numa at once ceased to be historical characters, and were transferred to their proper place in the calendar of mythical founders of cities and states. Slowly out of the legendary and semi-historical traditions of a barbarous age the materials of real history began to be gathered, and the foundations were thus laid of a new historical science.

It is not strange that the critical spirit soon began to deal with the Bible itself. That wonderful collection of Hebrew-Jewish literature had been converted into a single sacred volume, and all its mythology, legend, poetry, prophecy, and apocalypse, as well as so-called historical books, had been treated as one historical record from beginning to end. The conversations related in Genesis as occurring between God, Adam, Eve, and the serpent, were held to be as veracious as that

between David and Nathan, or between Christ and
the woman of Samaria.   The results of the higher
criticism in its investigation of the Old Testament
cannot here be told.   Enough to say that its main
conclusions are clearly established, and many a
scriptural story to which we listened in our childhood with a faith that knew no doubting has lost
forever its historical credibility, if not its religious
moral.   To pass from the Old Testament to the
New was a logical necessity.   But the forces of
dogmatic conservatism have here striven to bar
the way, and a conflict is being waged which can
have but one issue.   For the same evolutionary
processes have worked in the development of all
historical literature.   True history has ever and
everywhere been a slow growth out of myth and
legend and prehistoric tradition.   Biblical history
is no exception.   Nor can any line be drawn
between the Old Testament and the New.   Legend
just as plainly plays its part in Matthew, Luke,
and Acts as in Genesis and Kings, though not
perhaps as fully.   It is a mistake to suppose that
legend is confined to prehistoric periods.   It is
ever active, a sort of parasitic growth on every
historical tree.   The life of Washington has its
legends.   Mr. Henry Cabot Lodge, in his excellent biography, has made us acquainted with the
curious manner in which the cherry-tree and
hatchet story was evolved out of the fertile brain
of Weems, an earlier biographer.   Pity that such
a good moral should be spoiled by the critical

historian. But is not the moral just as good even if the story behind it is legendary? Do the lessons of Christ's parables lose any of their moral power because these parables are not historically true? I am sure the tale of George Washington's boyish truthfulness will still be repeated to admiring children for many a day. And if the life of Washington, passed under the noonday light of this modern world, has legendary elements, why should not such legendary tales find their way into the life of Jesus of Nazareth, even more easily, in those uncritical times?

But the work of historical criticism could not stop here. The ancient literature as it was handed down accumulated on its way a mass of interpolations and additions, and of entire writings whose authorship was falsely ascribed to men of renown in earlier periods. The object of this deception, as it would be regarded to-day, was to increase the authority of such writings by the veneration for a great name. The fine moral sense which is felt by us in regard to such deception was evidently foreign to the ancient world. The number of these writings of falsely assumed authorship was legion. Thus the critical examination of texts and dates and authors became an important part of critical work. The Bible, it was found, was especially full of such textual corruptions and of titles of authors that were entirely wanting in critical authority. The traditional dates and authors of by far the largest part of the Biblical writings are of no historical value. The Jews in fact seem to have been sinners above others in this kind of " royal lie." The number of Jewish writings in the centuries immediately preceding and following Christ's birth, whose true authorship was thus hidden under the cover of some great name, is amazing. Enoch, Moses, Solomon, Pythagoras, Plato, Aristotle, are but specimen names among the many that were employed. Is it any wonder, then, that the Bible is found open to the same kind of criticism? It is difficult to realize, or even conceive, how utterly wanting in the critical spirit the early Christian centuries were. The old theory of inspiration by which such literary sins of ignorance were not merely condoned but even denied can no longer be held. Its very foundations have been destroyed by the dissolving force of the new criticism. Who will claim to-day for the writers of the books of the Bible a gift of critical insight which is wholly the result of the modern scientific inductive method? To hide the whole question of authorship, dates, and corrupt texts behind such a preposterous claim is surely vain. To assume, for example, such an inspiration for the author of the Epistle of Jude as to make it possible to believe that the quotation there given from a writing of Enoch, who was supposed to have lived before the flood, is really genuine, is surely beyond the credulity of the average man ; for it involves the astonishing corollary that such a " Book of Enoch " as was extant in the first

century of the Christian era had actually survived
the deluge itself. Such are the shifts to which the
old doctrine of scripture was driven. Similar is
the effort to prove the historicity of the Jonah
story from Christ's quoting it, assuming in him a
critical insight of which his life gives no evidence,
and making that the ground for the historicity of
a narrative which bears on its very face the clear
signs of being merely a parabolic sermon.

The work of historical criticism in connection
with the Bible is not yet complete. This is especially true of the New Testament. Here the battle
of the critics is still being waged. The storm
centre of late has been the question of the Johannine authorship of the fourth Gospel. It is no
wonder that this position is so obstinately con-
tested by the defenders of the old theology, for
with it goes the last refuge of traditional trinitarian dogma. This is fully recognized on all sides.
Mr. R. H. Hutton in his recent " Spectator " essays allows that " if the fourth Gospel could be
relegated to the middle of the second century, it
would have no authority at all, as expounding the
theology of the incarnation." He also quotes Dr.
Liddon as affirming that such a critical result
would " go to the root of the Christian revelation,
at all events as it has been understood by nine
tenths of all existing Christians." [1] That such
men have grounds for their judgment is seen in
the fact that the whole Nicene Trinitarianism was

[1] *Aspects of Religious and Scientific Thought*, p. 225.

made to rest by Athanasias on proof-texts from
the fourth Gospel.   But this suggests to us that
still another duty lay before the Christian historical critic.   On these uncritical and unhistorical
assumptions as to the character of the Bible there
had been built in the course of centuries a system
of Christian dogmas which became the religious
faith of Christendom.   That system of doctrine
was compelled in its turn to submit to critical
examination.   The law of historical evolution has
become the master key to unlock and reveal the
secret of its origin.   Our previous survey contains
the history of the manner in which that key has
been used, and of the results that have been
reached.   " Christian origins " have been the field
of the most intense interest and of the most marvelous historical discoveries during the last few
years.   But " Christian origins " are only a step-
ping stone to the " origins " of other ethnic religions.   Here a new field of research and criticism
was opened, which has thrown a flood of light on
the study of Christian " origins," and given a new
aspect to the whole subject of the origin of religion itself.

Our object in thus summarily sketching the
critical movement is to bring out the fact that it
cannot stop until its work is really finished.   It
is this work that gives our age its true significance.   The " Time Spirit " must " finish the work
that is given it to do," and until that work is done,
no other work of any real and lasting worth can

be made, by any effort of man, to take its place. And that work needs no apology. It is amazing how misunderstood, in some quarters, the mission of historical criticism is. It is charged with being a negative and destructive spirit, as if this were a mark of reproach. It is even more amazing to find historical critics themselves defending and excusing their work as if the reproach was merited. The true answer to all such accusations is that the first work of the historical critic must be destructive in the very nature of things, and that, until that work has been thoroughly done, no other work is in order. The cry now being heard that it is time for the destructive process to cease is simply an anachronism. It implies that the work of destruction is complete, when in fact it is but half done. How can new foundations begin to be laid while men are still contesting inch by inch the removal of stones and timbers from the old mediæval edifice that have nothing but unhistorical tradition and superstition on which to rest? Is it the part of wisdom to attempt to rebuild in such circumstances? It is not only unwise, it is impossible. All such reconstruction is simply wasted labor, a temporary patchwork soon to be cast aside. Much work of this sort is being done. I fully realize how important it is, at a time like this, " to strengthen the things that remain," and I as fully appreciate all such efforts. But the fact nevertheless holds true, that if ever there was a period of theological literature evan-

escent as the passing breeze, it is that which
marks this present time, when the critical spirit
is still earnestly employed in its divinely commis-
sioned destructive labors.   But let it not be forgotten that the real *final* aim of historical criticism
is not destructive but *constructive*.   When the old
false dogmas shall have been radically removed
and the true historical rock-bed shall have been
found, the same spirit of history that has worked
destructively will change its whole manner of operation, and the same law of scientific evolution
that has been engaged in throwing off the worn-
out garments of its childhood will be found as
earnestly at work to weave the new garments of
its manhood, yea, the true wedding garments of the
new Christianity.

CHAPTER VIII

THE DEMAND OF THE RELIGIOUS SPIRIT

WE are now prepared to consider the second demand of our age, — *the demand of faith*, in other words, of man's religious nature. This age has often been described as one of religious doubt and skepticism, as if it were immersed in worldliness and wholly averse to matters of religion. But nothing could be further from the truth. The historical and critical spirit that rules the age has indeed opened the eyes of men to the real character of many of the old traditional dogmas, and they have cast them aside. Such skepticism is necessary and healthful. It is an essential element in all true critical study. Lord Acton has well said that the first attitude of the historical critic towards all supposed facts is "*suspicion.*" Diderot declared that "*doubt*" was the beginning of philosophy. These expressions simply set forth the fundamental principle of the scientific inductive method, viz., that everything claiming to be true must be critically examined and questioned before it is accepted. It was the application of this principle that gave us the new science and the new history; and its further application to-day is

giving us a new Christian' faith. Viewed in its
true historical aspect, what is called the doubting
spirit of this age is its highest title to moral eminence. Skepticism is very different from irre-
ligiousness, and yet is too often confounded with
it. This age is in many ways intensely skeptical,
but at the same time is as intensely religious. No
age since Christ was ever more ready to listen to
a gospel that comes with moral authority to the
soul. But every gospel must show its credentials;
and until these credentials are subjected to scrutiny and are found valid in the highest court of
moral appeal faith holds itself in reserve. In
these days of theological jarring and unrest, when
the old supposed foundations of faith are being
shaken to their centre, such reserve of religious
belief and trust is becoming a common characteristic of thoughtful and self-balanced men and
women, and is really a noble quality, showing a
nature that respects its own moral freedom. Mr.
R. H. Hutton has remarked in one of his "Spectator" essays : "I am not ashamed to feel far more
sympathy with the nobler aspects of unbelief than
with the ignobler and shiftier aspects of so-called
faith;"—a statement that reveals in Mr. Hutton
himself a rare insight into the religious character
of our age, and also the instinct of a noble and
enlarged Christian temper of mind. The *spirit*
of faith in any age may be strong and active,
and yet the *objects* of faith may be vague and
uncertain. Such is the case among us to-day.

Men everywhere are open-eyed to religious things. With the wonderful renaissance of the human intellect brought about by the stimulus of scientific and historical researches, a similar renaissance and awakening of moral consciousness has followed which demands a new revelation of religious truth.

And here we are at a point where we can see how essential it was that historical criticism should first complete its mission, — a mission that was to work toward enlightenment and freedom, having Christ's assurance for its watchword: "If the truth shall make you free, ye *shall be free indeed.*" For the faith of men had been bound hand and foot. A usurped authority had shackled human consciences with creeds and dogmas and "commandments of men." Ignorance is always the mother of superstition. That ignorance had to be dispelled before faith could release itself from its fetters and regain its lost freedom. Such has been the truly divine mission of the new history. Not only the intellects but also the consciences of men have been thereby awakened to a new intelligence and freedom. And it is on these twin pillars that the new faith of men will be built. Such a faith will never go back to the old discarded dogmas of the ages of ignorance and superstition. It will build itself from foundation stone on the new-found truth of the historic Christ and Christian gospel. Here history again becomes its helper. Faith will still have its "ventures," as

Bushnell has suggestively called them, and freely spread its wings to the upper air where the mystical spirit so loves to dwell, but its feet will yet be fixed on solid historical ground.   Myth, legend, and speculative philosophy will be taken at their real value.   Who Christ actually was, what his teachings were, in fact, what the spirit and character of his life and death were, in the light of veritable history, not in the romantic traditions of a later age, — the answers to these questions will be the firm basis on which Christian faith will securely rest, yes, " the faith once delivered " indeed, not as misread and misinterpreted by after times, but as originally experienced in Christ's own disciples; as, for example, in " the woman that was a sinner," whose faith found voice not in creed indeed, but in loving kisses and penitent tears, and was accepted by the Master as true and worthy, when he said to her, " Thy faith hath saved thee, go in peace."

Christ will still be the historical foundation of the new Christianity, " Christ, the same yesterday, to-day, and forever," not the old Christ of Greek philosophical dogma or of mediæval superstition, nor the new Christ of a legendary theory that reduces him to a mere historical shadow, but the real Christ of true flesh and blood, " Jesus of Nazareth, the son of Joseph " and Mary, with a true human biography whose grand lineaments are as clearly defined as those of Cicero or Washington, and shedding forth from that human life an ineffable

moral sweetness and charm which draws men to
him like a magnet, — yet withal true son of God
because so truly son of man, "the image of the invisible God, the first born of all creatures," as Paul
wrote of him, — the very image in which man was
made, by which God and man are united in the
most intimate spiritual union, so that, in a very
true and real sense, man may be said to be consubstantial with God and "partaker of the divine
nature." And it is because of Christ's organic
relationship with man that he was able to reach a
moral headship among his fellows, and wield by
voice and speech and life a moral authority that is
still supreme. For history finds in Christ a moral
consciousness that has surpassed that of all other
men, in its sense of God's true moral fatherhood
and of man's true moral sonship, and in its intimacy of union and communion with his Father and
our Father; and so long as men shall find in
Christ's own moral consciousness of God and religious truth a moral revelation that shall lead them
upward toward Him, so long will Christ remain, as
no other among the sons of men, a divinely sent
Messiah; and from this Christ of history, become
the Christ of faith, the lines of Christian faith will
proceed. The true root of the Christian religious
consciousness, of Christian faith in all its forms of
religious experience and life, is Christ's own religious consciousness, in other words Christ's own
religion. That religion was based upon two fundamental principles: a faith in God as the loving

Father of mankind, and a faith in all men as the common children of God and heirs of his grace and mercy. Hence his proclamation of a divine forgiveness for all sinners, and his call to them all to repent and accept the forgiveness so freely offered. This was his gospel message, the great burden of his preaching. Its essence is contained in the famous parable of the prodigal son. Thus the keynote of Christ's gospel is love, God's love kindling man's love, appealing to his free moral agency as a child of God, and drawing him not by force but winningly and graciously back to God's love. 'So that the note of love involves the note of freedom. It is the loftiest attribute of man as a moral being, made in the image of God, that he has a free will which is the ultimate basis and source of all his moral action. Man as a religious being is a free man, free in his faith and in his whole moral consciousness, and in the direction that consciousness shall take in his whole moral life.

Along these two central lines of Christ's religion the new faith of the age is working. The early Christianity had obscured them both. In their divisions and controversies over questions of dogma men forgot the two essential keynotes of the gospel they were so pertinaciously defending. They ceased to love as brethren, and to respect each other's individual birthright of liberty. The sad consequences of bigotry, hatred, and bitterness, cruelty and outrage, are the staple of church history for a thousand years. Enough to say that historical criticism has broken the yoke of man's moral bondage, and to-day he is free in his faith and religion. And with freedom is fast returning a new recognition of love as the cardinal principle of the gospel of Christ and of all Christian faith. For " He that loveth is born of God and knoweth God." And out of love in freedom what "fruits of the spirit" may not grow !

Thus faith as we have treated it is essentially a free movement of man's moral consciousness, and, as it develops itself in trust and love and kindred moral feelings, is the very heart of religion. The religious life can go no higher. Love to God and to man is the whole moral law. Paul touched the very centre of Christian experience when he said " Love never faileth, the greatest of all things is love." Faith then as such is wholly independent of dogma and may exist without dogma. For dogma is an intellectual *credo* and is based on intellectual processes. The two may be combined, but the one does not necessarily include the other. The sinning woman's grateful love and trust which Christ called faith had no dogmatic background at all, so far as we know, but was a simple free moral movement of her heart. It was a terrible mistake that Christian theologians made, in changing the meaning of faith from a free exercise of the heart and will to a forced submission of the intellect to dogmatic authority. " *Fides precedit intellectum* " was their motto, by which they meant that an intellectual *forced* acceptance of dogmas, based on the

decisions of some ecclesiastical authority, should go
before the use of the individual reason in discovering the truth of such dogmas by free investigation.
Such a dictum, of course, when enforced by power,
enslaved the soul, and put every man's religious
convictions at the mercy of any haphazard spiritual
tribunal. ˙ Still worse, it poisoned the very sources
of the religious life by making the essence of faith,
as the ground of acceptance with God and of the
hope of salvation, consist, not in a right state of
the affections and will, that is, in loving obedience,
but in orthodoxy, or the professed acceptance of
certain dogmas. Of course such a mockery of
religion, such a seed plot of hypocrisy, has no
foundation in Christ's teachings or in man's religious nature. Christ was not a dogmatist. He
gave no theological creed to his disciples. A " pure
heart," not orthodox belief, was the test of entrance
into his kingdom. It is true that he drew from
his wonderful religious consciousness rich and original lessons of faith and love toward God and
man, but as to a theological system, as we call it,
he never attempted to construct one and failed to
indicate that he had any sense of its importance.
His own theology, so far as he had any, was dis-
tinctively Jewish. The reform he instituted was
not along theological lines but wholly moral and
practical. His eschatology was that of his day and
already strongly intrenched in the minds of his
contemporaries. The only new dogma that can be
imputed to him, that of a sacrificial substitutional

atonement, is surely a misunderstanding of his real
teaching, a false construction put on his doctrine
of love for mankind, which he declared had its
highest illustration in the self-sacrifice and surrender that might be carried to the giving up of
life itself. Nor does the history of man as a religious being give any ground for such a false definition of faith. The purest and sweetest and holiest
souls that earth has seen have often lived and died
without any dogmatic bias so far as can be known.
One can be Christlike without holding any definite
creed as to Christ's metaphysical nature, or being
able to answer the question whether or not he was
miraculously born. It is a remarkable fact that
the golden age of theology in the ancient church —
the Nicene and post-Nicene — was one of marked
decline in the religious life of the period, as is vividly illustrated in the records of those œcumenical
councils that formulated the orthodox creeds. And
the same was true of the age which produced the
Protestant dogmatic theology, — the age of Calvin
and Turretin, — a period that has been well described by Charles Beard in the " Hibbert Lectures " of 1883 : " I know no epoch of Christianity
to which I could more confidently point, in illustration of the fact, that where there is most theology
there is often least religion." The spirit of dogmatism and bigotry that has vitiated Christianity
all through its history was born of this confusion
of faith as a principle of religion with intellectual
belief as a principle of dogmatic theology, and if

historical criticism had done nothing else than ex-
pose its unhistorical and vicious character, it would
have amply vindicated its providential mission.

Is it, then, of no consequence in the religious
life what a man believes? Is dogma to be cast
out as of no religious value? Such a result by no
means follows, as will soon be seen. But we are
now dealing with the demand of the age for the
satisfaction of its religious needs, and it is essential
that the radical difference between faith, as the
central element of the religious life, and dogma,
as an intellectual belief, should be sharply discriminated, since it is only by such a discrimination
that the demand of faith can be understood and
met. Even to-day men are insisting that dogmatic beliefs are of the essence of religion and
religious experience, and many are halting between
two opinions, skeptical as to the dogmas of traditional Christianity, and yet earnest to find the
true basis of Christian faith. Before the religious
hunger of the age can be satisfied, the dilemma as
to the relation of faith and dogma must cease to
be a stumbling stone and rock of offense. The
truth, then, must be squarely told, viz., that intellectual belief is not, in any sense, of the essence of
religion or of the religious life. The vital question
of religion is not what a man believes, how much
or how little, but what the disposition of his heart
and will is toward those objects of faith that lie
within the range of his own moral consciousness.
The question of the *content* of that moral conscious-

ness and of the unfolding of it in dogmatic belief
is a wholly distinct and secondary matter. A man
may give very vague and indistinct answers to
such questions as, Who is God? Does He exist in
unity or in trinity? Was Christ human or divine
or was he both human and divine? Was the
atonement sacrificial or moral? and yet be a hum-
bler, more self-sacrificing Christian than another
man who can answer all these questions in the
most orthodox fashion. Yet it goes without saying that intellectual belief has a very close relation
to religious faith, and that clear apprehensions of
truth are of great religious value. But it has its
own distinct place and function in religious experience and comes into it in its own time and way.
As a rule it is a slow development under a process of spiritual illumination and growing insight
into the life and teaching of Christ, together with
other forms of divine revelation in nature and history. But such increase of knowledge and conviction should never be confounded with those Christian graces of faith, hope, and love which are the
essence of religion. Life and the science or philosophy of life are two very different things. Just
as different are religion and its dogmatic or theological expressions in a creed. The one is the
living experience of a human soul, the other is an
abstract, lifeless formula, except so far as it is
made alive by the soul's use of it.

It is a common impression that somehow a theology or philosophy, in other words, a more or less

systematized conception of truth, is necessary for
every preacher of the gospel, not to say for every
Christian believer.   Dr. Lyman Abbott once told
a body of seminary students that every minister
should have a philosophy, but that he should not
preach it; which seems to assume that a set of
dogmas is a vital element of religion, if not of the
preaching of it.   I must take issue with Dr. Abbott if I understand him.   Not only is it true that
ministers should not preach philosophy, but, further, it is not essential that they should have any
definite philosophy at all.   The gospel of Christ
and any human philosophy are as wide apart as
the poles.   Woe would be to many a preacher if it
were not so.   Truly philosophical minds are rare.
A metaphysical system is one of the most difficult
accomplishments of human thought, and at the best
it must be incomplete and even fragmentary; for
a true philosophy of nature, man, and God must
rest on the fullest evidence drawn from all these
sources; and, as yet in fact, the evidence is *not all
in.*   The chances are that a young minister's philosophy would be a very poor one, and a poor one
is worse than none at all.   In truth a man's philosophy is a matter of slow evolution and should be left
to grow of itself.   A manufactured one becomes a
cage for the soul as it advances in religious experience and knowledge.   This is not a merely speculative question.   If it were I should not dwell on
it.   It is one that affects the practical faith of
men.   Many of the articles of the Christian creeds

are metaphysical propositions of the extremest sort, and yet they have been preached in the past as though they were the very essence of the gospel. These metaphysical propositions about God and man may all be true, but, if true, they belong to a philosophy of religion, not to Christ's gospel, which is religion itself. Here again historical criticism is doing its necessary destructive work and thus preparing the way for a new type of preaching as well as of faith.

But this work of the historical critic is not yet complete. So deeply fixed in our religious traditions is the idea that somehow theological belief is an essential and vital point of true religion that even our most liberal leaders are still misleading themselves and others with it, even while pronouncing against it. The employment of the term "faith" in two different senses, as came to be the case with the original Greek term πίστις, has done much to perpetuate this confusion in the minds of men. There is not a word in religious and theological nomenclature that has been so abused in preaching and in Christian literature as this word "faith." The classic Greek word πίστις always meant a purely intellectual act. In Plato, for example, it is used for a lower form of knowledge. Such is sometimes its meaning in the Bible. But Christ and his apostles put the word to a new use. It came to mean a moral and religious act of the heart and will; as when Christ said to the woman, "Thy faith hath saved thee." This is its true

Christian meaning.   But when the classical Greek
intellectualism began to exercise its moulding power
in Christian faith and thought, as it did even from
the time of Paul, the meaning of faith returned
largely to its classic pagan sense, and in Christian
theology came to be an act of the intellect in the
acceptance of dogmas.   This is illustrated in the
ancient creeds, which are declarations of belief in
certain intellectual propositions as to the metaphysical nature of God and of his mediational
work through Christ.   This intellectualizing of
the term " faith " would have done no harm, if its
theological character had been clearly kept in mind
and not been confounded with faith in its Christian evangelical meaning.   But this was prevented
by the intensely dogmatic tendencies of the early
church.   Orthodoxy became the watchword, and
intellectual assent to creeds became the great test,
and from that time down to the present day the
Greek pagan meaning of faith has supplanted the
Christian meaning, or the two meanings have been
inextricably mixed together.   Take for illustration
the phrase " articles of faith " in such common use.
Faith of course here means a set of intellectual
propositions which are to be subscribed to.   Such
faith is essentially *belief*, and is very far from expressing the " faith " of the penitent woman, who
affirmed nothing concerning her beliefs, but simply
showed the state of her heart by her conduct.   If
the term " belief " could be substituted for faith
where the intellectual act is referred to, and the

term "faith" be left to represent the moral act as Christ used it, much confusion and misunderstanding might be avoided.

But there are many who will defend this double use of the term "faith," insisting that Christian faith involves essentially the exercise of the reason as well as of the heart and will, or, in other words, that religion in its very essence is not merely the spirit of obedience and love and sacrifice, but also and equally the assent of the mind to a creed that contains, or is supposed to contain, the essentials of Christian truth. Here at last we come to the issue that is still squarely made by the whole body of traditionalists, even by some who would scarcely wish to be counted in that section of Christian thinkers. *Dogma is of the essence of faith*, they all say, though in varying language, and with more or less modification. Hence it is claimed that faith may properly be used in a double sense, and mean indiscriminately the acceptance of a body of doctrine, or the body of doctrine itself, as well as a Christian experience and life. Let me once more remind my readers that I speak as a historical observer, not as a theologian; but from the historical standpoint I am moved to say that this assumption lies at the very root of the religious skepticism of the age, and that the demand of the age for a new basis of faith and religious life will not be met until its falsity has been thoroughly exposed and the assumption itself cast aside completely from religious language.

In illustration of what has been said, I wish
to call attention to a distinguished writer who in
many ways represents a quite radical phase of religious thought, but who on this point seems to me
to hold an inconsistent and unsatisfactory position.
I refer to Auguste Sabatier, professor of theology
in the University of Paris. "Esquisse d'une Phi-
losophie de la Religion" is a work that is permeated with the historical spirit and is really
written in the interest of a thoroughly scientific
view of religion, in its origin and development.
As a whole the sketch is admirable. Professor
Sabatier's description of Biblical or religious faith
and of its distortion into a synonym for orthodoxy
is well put. "Faith which in the Bible was an act
of confidence in God and of consecration to Him,
has become an intellectual adhesion to a historical
testimony or to a doctrinal formula. A mortal
dualism thus arises in religion. It is admitted that
orthodoxy can exist independently of piety, and
that one can obtain and possess the object of faith
without regard to the conditions which faith pre-
supposes, and even do real service to divine truth
while being at heart a wicked man." Sabatier
also states clearly the radical difference between
faith and dogma. "The affirmation of piety is
essentially different from the scientific explanation
of it." He declares that there can be no conflict
between faith and knowledge, since they belong to
two different orders or planes, viz., the moral and
the intellectual. His definition of dogma is wholly

in accord with this declaration. "Dogma is defined in its strict sense as one or several doctrinal propositions which have been made, by means of decisions of competent authority, an object of faith and rule of belief and life."

But now comes a remarkable change of statement. Sabatier has previously insisted on the essential difference between faith and dogma, and discriminated the two orders to which they belong, but now he undertakes a defense of dogma against those who " wish to suppress the whole doctrinal definition of the Christian faith." A new note is here struck, and it is revealed in the changed use of the term "faith." " The Christian faith " is no longer faith in its subjective sense of piety, but faith objectively considered, in other words, the objects or dogmas of faith. Faith, then, is dogma. There is, he asserts, an organic and necessary connection between faith, or piety, and dogma. "Dogma has three elements, a religious element which proceeds from piety, an intellectual or philosophical element, and an element of authority which comes from the Christ." " Dogma has its first root in religion. In all positive religion there is an internal element and an external element, a soul and a body." Thus Sabatier places himself on the traditional ground that faith and dogma are essentially united, and that the double meaning given to the term " faith " is proper and warranted by history. We are now prepared to hear him say: " Say then no more : Christianity is a life,

therefore it is not a doctrine.   This is to reason
very badly.   One must rather say, Christianity is a
life, therefore it ought to engender doctrine, since
man cannot live his life without a doctrine of it."
Hence his conclusion: "Dogma, therefore, is absolutely necessary to the propagation and upbuilding
of the religious life."

The real explanation of this curious *contretemps*
is that Sabatier is a dogmatic theologian, and intent
on proving that dogmatic theology is an essential
element in the life of Christianity.   His general
premise that dogma is subject to the universal
law of evolution, and so is continually changing,
is of course historical and scientific.   His further
contention that an intellectual acquaintance with
religious truth is of great moral value cannot be
gainsaid.   But when, in the ardor of his advocacy,
he pushes the relation of faith and dogma to the
point of declaring them organically and essentially
united like root and branch, soul and body, so that
each involves the other and is a part of the other,
he is guilty of an inconsistency with his own fundamental historical premise upon which his whole
volume rests.   Faith and dogma, the free volitions
of the heart and the ratiocinative conclusions of
the head, life and the philosophy of life, the concrete and the abstract, cannot be juggled with in
this way.   To be sure soul and body are closely
united.   Body is itself dependent on food and
drink, and so it may be said that the soul is intimately related through the body to these outside

material elements.   But soul is not body nor is
body the food on which it lives, and it is equally
true that " the kingdom of God," which is made
up of pious souls, is not meat and drink or dogma
or philosophy, but " love, peace, and joy in the
Holy Ghost."   The truth is there is a psychological fallacy underlying this whole way of viewing
the relations of faith and dogma.   The soul, though
organically one and having but a single self-consciousness, is yet composed of several completely
distinct faculties, and the action of these faculties
is always clearly distinguishable.   Consciousness
never confounds these different orders of activity.
It never mixes acts of reason or memory or imagination or desire or will heterogeneously together.
An illogical piece of reasoning or a lapse of the
memory is never charged to the account of the
free will and made a burden on the conscience.
These actions belong to different " orders " of the
soul, to use Sabatier's own term.   Faith is a moral
act and condition, it is a movement of the free
will, it belongs to the moral order.   Dogma is an
intellectual process, it belongs wholly to the intellectual order.   To confound them, to say that there
is a dogmatic element in faith, or a faith element
in dogma, is like saying that a mathematical
blunder or a logical fallacy is the same thing as
hatred or disobedience.   Such a psychology is
wholly self-destructive.   To say that these different acts of the soul are all forms of consciousness,
and so essentially one, is to play with words.   Even

bodily actions or injuries all come within the survey of consciousness. Is a hurt to a limb, or a movement of a finger, therefore, the same in nature or order with an act of memory or will? The most radical line of cleavage in the soul is that between the free will with its categorical imperatives of conscience and the intellectual powers, — in other words, between the volitional consenting faculties and the faculties of knowledge and assent. They work in harmony, in all sorts of closest relationship and mutual influence; but they are radically differentiated by the fact that the acts of the moral order are under a law of freedom and responsibility and moral judgment, while the acts of the intellectual faculties, as such, have no moral character and come under no law of moral responsibility, being under laws of a wholly different order. The law under which the mind reaches conclusions through its faculties of abstraction and generalization, or forms its convictions based on evidence, is one of necessity. Given a certain amount of evidence, the mind becomes convinced inevitably. There is no freedom or responsibility attached to it. It is true that the will may interfere with the normal action of the intellect, and, by means of moral presuppositions and prejudices and determinations, may force the mind to a contrary result. So that there is a degree of truth in the adage: "A man convinced against his will is of the same opinion still." But in such a case a violence is done to nature. The laws of

evidence, or of logical premise and conclusion, or
of mathematical axioms, may be tampered with
and nullified for the time, under the stress of moral
passion or determination, but the laws themselves
are fundamental to man's intellectual nature, and
when left to themselves work necessarily to fixed
results.   The will may compel the soul to accept
a historical legend as fact, but when the mind is
left free to act according to its own laws, and the
historical evidence is allowed to come before it,
the result is a necessary one that the legend should
be seen to be a legend.   The moral responsibility
for either result lies not with the purely intellectual powers, but with the free will.

There is great confusion in many minds on this
point.   The acts of the intellect under its own
laws in the pursuit of knowledge are often treated
as morally accountable and sinful.   Men have been
put to death for a conviction to which they were
brought by necessary laws of reasoning or evidence, as if such intellectual convictions were free
and accountable.   Most of the heresies of history
have been of this sort.   The mistake has been in
confounding two distinct orders of the soul's faculties, — the order that works under a law of necessity, and the order that is morally free and therefore accountable.   A historical mistake or an
illogical philosophical tenet is not a sin, since, by
itself, it has no moral quality.   Sin comes in when
the soul in the exercise of its moral freedom abuses
the faculties of knowledge that are under its sway

and turns them to wrong uses, as, for example,
when a man in the interest of a false dogma inten-
tionally distorts history.   A clear understanding
of the psychological laws and facts of human nature is above all things needed in this matter.   It
is certainly strange that such a profound thinker
as Professor Sabatier should be guilty of inconsistency and inaccuracy here.   For he has struck
the keynote of psychological truth, in his doctrine
of the two " orders " of soul activity.   Acts of the
heart and will and those of the intellect are in his
view heterogeneous.   Then of course piety and
knowledge, faith and dogma, are heterogeneous,
and to confound them is to do violence to the
psychological laws of the soul itself.   M. Sabatier
sees this plainly, and he well describes the result
of turning faith, which is an act of the will, into
an intellectual act, that is, a dogma, as " a *mortal
dualism* in religion."   It is just that.   It introduces a moral schism into the soul which is fatal
to all healthy spiritual life.   This is the vital part
of Sabatier's book, and for it I thank him.   As to
the *contretemps* by which he attempts to build a
foundation for dogma in faith itself, it is an antinomy which must be left to the fate that inevitably overtakes all false reasoning.

I wonder whether Dr. Sabatier comprehends
the full force of his own cardinal positions.   He
allows that there may be a barren and morally
worthless orthodoxy without piety or faith, but
does he also see that it is equally true that there

may be a genuine and living faith and piety without orthodoxy? I am not sure. But of course it is so. Two heterogeneous acts and conditions can have no moral relation with each other that shall make the existence of one depend on the existence of the other. There may be faith without orthodoxy, just as easily as there may be orthodoxy without faith; and it is this simple truth based on a sound psychology that our age is feeling after and beginning to realize and insist upon as the starting-point of its new religious faith and life. The power of that word "orthodox" which has been such a spell on the minds of men, is already broken, and it only remains for them, in the exercise of their new freedom, to learn from history and experience and from Christ's own lips and life the fullness of meaning there is in the divine gospel of God's free love to man and of man's free love to God.

I am anticipating a little, but I cannot forbear here to say that it will be a great boon to theological and philosophical speculation, when all questions of dogma shall be wholly separated in the minds of men, as they ought to be, from all questions of practical religion and faith. Theology is a science. It is a work of the mind. Why then should it not be treated as all other sciences are treated, and be allowed the same liberty of investigation. Why should charges of moral heresy and sin and wickedness be brought against a worker in theological science any more than against other scientists. All science is under the same intellectual laws, and these laws, as we have seen, work on the same lines of logical, mathematical, evidential necessity. Why should a moral and religious significance be attached to the labors of one class of scientists rather than to those of another class. There is but one reason to be given for an affirmative answer, viz., that faith and dogma, religion and theology, are radically one, so that a man cannot be pious without being orthodox, even though a man may be orthodox without being pious, as facts prove beyond dispute. But with this false assumption taken out of the way, what remains but that theology as a science should be allowed its full scientific freedom? This is what is certainly coming, and what benefits will accrue to theological investigation I need not say. Freedom of scientific teaching is to be the educational watchword of the future, and out of it will come a new evolution of knowledge and thought that will transcend immensely all previous attainments.

I cannot leave this point without alluding to the peculiar position of history as a science. Unfortunately for the full freedom of historical study and teaching, there is in the traditional creeds and theology of the Christian church a complete heterogeneous mixture of theological speculative propositions and of supposed historical facts. This brings theology within the purview of historical investigation. The miraculous virgin birth of Christ, and the other miraculous or supernatural events that are recorded in connection with it, Christ's own miracles and his miraculous resurrection and ascension, come strictly within the sphere of history and so are subjects of historical and critical scrutiny, and yet they are held as dogmas of Christian belief, and supposed to lie at the very foundation of the Christian religion. Thus the path of the historical student and teacher has been surrounded with great difficulties and even hazards. It is a curious fact that to-day history is more exposed to the attacks of theological dogmatism than theology itself, inasmuch as the last defenses of traditionalism are of a historical and critical rather than philosophical character. The theological teacher may theologize with full freedom, if he keeps safely off historical ground, but the historical teacher has no such option. He cannot retreat behind the clouds of metaphysics, but must come out into the historical open and meet squarely the historical theological problems that arise inevitably in his path, or dodge them utterly and commit hari-kari with his historical conscience. But, happily for historians as well as theologians, the basis for the new faith that history itself has already laid will be their refuge and salvation. The time is at hand when the real heretics will be seen to be, not historical and theological investigators, but men of uncharitable and bitter spirit and of bad lives. It is no wonder that men of the world look with amazement on the theological controversies that still afflict some parts

of Christendom.   A writer in the "Evangelist"
recently stated that Mr. Joseph H. Choate, the
noted lawyer and present ambassador to England,
declared, in reference to the Briggs case in the
Presbyterian church, that "he could not make head
or tail out of it, and could not understand how
rational beings should get into such a tempest over
a matter of purely speculative opinions, with but
the slightest bearing upon life and character."
Thus already our age, in the persons of its most
intelligent laymen, is reaching a correct diagnosis
of dogmatic questions and of the bitter controversies that grow out of them, and sits in moral judgment upon them.

CHAPTER IX

THE DEMAND OF THE INTELLECTUAL SPIRIT

WE are now prepared to consider the *third* demand of our age, that of *the reason* in its more restricted sense of representing all our faculties of gathering and coördinating knowledge. For there is a double meaning of the term " reason " as it is usually employed in theological and philosophical literature. It often stands for the whole moral consciousness, including not only the ratiocinative and logical powers, but also those moral intuitions and principles of determination by means of which the soul is able to sit in judgment on all questions of religious truth and duty. In this larger sense the reason covers the two spheres of religion proper, or faith, and of dogma in the various forms of theology and philosophy. Such was its meaning in the great controversy between Romanist and Protestant as to the question whether faith was before reason or reason before faith. The Romish doctrine was that orthodox religious belief was determined by an ecclesiastical authority set over the individual reason, and not by the reason itself, which must be subjected to such authority and obediently interpret and defend its *ex cathedra* declarations. The Protestant position was that man's private reason or moral consciousness was the primary tribunal before which all questions of religious belief and duty must come for settlement, and that its verdicts must be ultimate and final for the individual soul. It was a sad day for Protestantism when the intensely dogmatic spirit of the seventeenth century led to a retreat from the original ground of protest of the Lutheran reformers back to the very principle of authority which had caused the breach. The only difference then was that, while Catholicism made the church in the person of its ecclesiastical head the ultimate basis of authority, Protestantism put the Bible in place of the pope. But both parties agreed in deposing man's reason or moral consciousness from its throne of final appeal and decision. In such a view reason stands for conscience with all its powers of moral insight and judgment and categorical imperative, to use the very suggestive definition of Kant.

But there is another meaning of reason that is equally common, where it is restricted to the purely intellectual side or order of the soul, and stands for the reflective and reasoning powers of the mind, in other words, the faculty of abstract thought. In this view reason stands over against the conscience and will and moral region of man's consciousness, and should never be confounded with it. I am here compelled, however, to observe that theological literature is permeated with this confusion, and that the term "reason," almost as much as the term "faith," has been sadly abused in the interest of dogmatism and dogmatic authority. It is on this account that I have made the above discrimination. A critical historical dictionary of theological and philosophical terms brought down to date would prove most valuable for present uses. For what is needed now above all things is a clear intelligence of the questions in issue, based on historical and critical knowledge. The time has gone by when either form of the claim of authority can be asserted or listened to; but the murky fogs of theological traditionalism are still dense, and men are left in doubt where the real guideboards of truth are, or what the signals mean. Read almost any one of the recent publications in the theological or religious field, and if the fog grows thicker as you proceed, as will very likely be the case, if I may judge from my own experience, be sure the reason is that such terms as faith, reason, incarnation, divine, trinity, are being juggled with and metamorphosed to such a degree that the very countersigns which ought to lead the reader on into the light only serve to leave him helpless, "in wandering mazes lost."

With the ground thus cleared I proceed to consider the demand of the intellectual or rational time spirit. It is to be noted at once that the intellectual curiosity and inquisitiveness of our age has been largely drawn into the channels of scientific and historical research. The result has been that the tide has turned strongly away from meta-

physical and philosophical studies, and there is
little evidence yet of any reaction. It is true we
hear frequent prophecies of a speedy change.
There are those who are calling loudly for a reju-
venation of philosophical theology. But they are
only voices in the wilderness. So far is this age
from being metaphysical or theological, or even
willing to lend an ear to such discussions, that the
very reverse is true. The prejudice against the
whole metaphysical method of surveying truth is
the one of all most deeply and firmly fixed in the
minds of the masses of intelligent men and women;
and this prejudice is natural and well grounded.
The spirit of the age, as we have seen, is critical
and destructive in all matters of theological tradition, and while the work of destruction is still
going on there can be little interest in any reconstructive process. Men will not build a bridge
over a stream while they are still in doubt whether
it should be crossed at all. Further, historical
criticism has brought to light the fact that the
very foundations of traditional philosophy and
theology are built largely on unhistorical assumptions. Is it any wonder, then, that the age, so
possessed with the critical spirit, should refuse to
accept the results that are derived from such
assumptions? The demand must plainly be for new
foundations built out of new historical material,
and according to a new historical method. The
conservative theologians, who are so averse to have
a single stone or timber removed from the old

structure and are crying continually for a halt, plainly have made a very bad diagnosis of the case. They are striving to save as much of the building as they can, and would begin at once to patch it up for its new uses. But the work of destruction must go on until the last unhistorical tradition has been unearthed and the last *a priori* metaphysical assumption has been pulled out of its hiding-place. How much of the old edifice will be left is no present concern of the historical critic. " Take no thought for the morrow " is as true in historical studies as in everything else. Truth surely is in no danger. God's spiritual kingdom cannot be hurt by the axes laid at the roots of historical trees that have grown out of pagan and mediæval Christian ignorance and superstition and have for too many centuries only cumbered the ground. Thus it grows more and more clear to us why theological reconstruction is so long delayed. Any attempt this way must fail until the ground is ready for it. It is for this reason that the demand of the intellectual spirit of the age is so slow in voicing itself. Each in its own order. The historical demand is as yet only half satisfied; the religious demand still waits on the fulfillment of the historical; the intellectual demand is latest in logical order, and must be equally so in time.

But if the time is not yet, it is surely not far off. For man is, in his fundamental nature, an inquisitive, speculating, metaphysical, mystical be-

ing. His feet must always be planted on the solid
earth, but his form rises upward toward the skies,
and his eyes are ever stretching their gaze away
from the seen and temporal to the unseen and
eternal. The soul is like the body in the evolution of its needs and demands. The purely animal wants of the body are first felt and listened
to. It must be fed and clothed. The myth of
Adam teaches a true historical lesson. But when
these lower wants are supplied, a higher order of
needs begins to find a voice. A less crude diet
and more artistic clothing are demanded. And
so the order of bodily demand rises until human
civilization culminates in the culinary and sartorial
arts of to-day. It is so with the soul. Its earliest
and most imperative wants are those that spring
from the lowest order of its faculties. The child
first uses its five senses, then its imagination, then
its memory, and then its reflective powers. Later
still, self-consciousness emerges into active life.
The will grows moral, and the religious nature
develops apace. Last of all, the eyes of the soul
begin to open toward the wider realms of being
that lie about it. It becomes a questioner.
Whence? Where? Whither? Those old eternal
questions, that have ever stirred the curiosity and
troubled the religious consciousness of men, stimu-
late thought and raise new inquiries. Even at
twelve years of age Christ had entered upon that
path of moral consciousness and inquiry from
which there is no return, and was found by his

anxious parents, oblivious of all things else, among the Jewish rabbis asking questions. As with individuals so is it in the evolution of the human race. First, the stage of imaginative mythologies, then a period of gnomic and ethical poetry, and at last the age of philosophy. Thus, in the Greek world, Homer and Hesiod are followed by Solon and Æschylus, and they in turn by Socrates and Plato. Such always is the order of history. Each age, too, has its order. Ours is no exception. Philosophy has had to wait its time. This epoch of ours has been a workman laying the axe at the foundations of all things human, and patiently seeking the *facts* of things. Thus its eyes have been largely downward looking, like those of Aristotle in Raphael's picture of the School of Athens; but already it is beginning to turn them upward, like those of Plato, whom Raphael painted with hand outstretched toward the skies. This age will and must have its Platonic philosophical period. The same old questions must once more be asked. For with the new light the old answers have become unsatisfactory and obsolete. Not then the old Plato *redivivus*, but a new Plato born. New philosophical wine and new philosophical bottles, a new philosophy and theology even from foundation stone.

But some one will ask with a real concern: " Do you mean that the old metaphysical and theological systems of our own theological fathers, that have been wrought out so conscientiously and have been venerated as the very strongholds of Christian faith, are to become useless and obsolete?" Certainly, yes, must be the frank historical reply. Has it not been already shown that this new age of ours is not merely a new cycle in an old evolution, but one of radical revolution? What is a radical revolution, if not one that works down to the very roots and bases of the old evolution and starts anew? The new theology must be radically new, for it must start and build on *a new principle*. That principle, in one word, is *induction*. Induction is that law and method of discovering truth which proceeds from the particular to the general; in other words, from individual facts ascertained by valid evidence to higher and wider generalizations, as drawn out by valid logical processes. This law and method is the only basis of any sound philosophy. It is what is known as the scientific or historical method, also as the experimental *a posteriori* method, — baptized with the name of Bacon, its great interpreter. According to this law and method, the realities which lie at the basis of all true philosophies or theologies are concrete and individual things, and all abstract thought with its genera, general ideas or universals, are only subjective generalizations and have no real existence except in the minds of men. This method underlies, as we have seen, the new science and the new history. Our whole modern civilization is built upon it. But the philosophy and theology of any age must be in harmony with

its science and history, and must be founded on
the same principles. A deductive *a priori* philosophy cannot be brought into any relationship
with an inductive *a posteriori* science and history.
For they are in radical antagonism. It is this
fact that explains the peculiar condition in which
theology finds itself to-day. Everything else except theology has adjusted itself to the new inductive law and method of investigation. Even
speculative philosophy, outside of its special theological relations, has largely followed in the wake
of scientific and historical criticism, and, planting
itself on the Cartesian premise, "*cogito ergo sum*,"
has essentially accepted the inductive principle. I
do not forget that the Neo-Kantian Hegelianism
still bases itself upon the *a priori* deductive principle, but it cannot be said to hold the field to-day
unchallenged, and its sceptre is passing into other
hands. In the conservative theological camp alone
does the old unscientific metaphysical method still
bear unchallenged sway. Even some men who
accept the new science and history along its evolutionary lines, in all fields of thought except the theological, here fall back on the traditional *a priori*
metaphysics. The reason is they cannot bring
themselves to surrender wholly the old theological
system with its speculative dogmas and assumptions, and thus are compelled to remain on the old
foundations. Traditional orthodoxy is thus forced
into sharp and radical antagonism to the ruling
inductive spirit of the age. For this age demands

that religion and the theological expression of it
be based on the same law and method, and be subjected to the same critical tests, as all other forms
of life and thought.

This antagonism is well illustrated in the attitude that theology has taken toward science. Men
talk about the conflict between science and religion; as if science were by its very nature irreligious and religion were in its nature unscientific.
But no such conflict is possible. What is religion
but the testimony and expression of man's moral
consciousness concerning the existence and character of divine powers above him, and what is
science but the testimony of nature to the same
religious truths? How can there be any conflict
between two different forms of God's self-revela-
tion! Paul builded better than he knew when
he wrote that "the invisible things of God since
the creation of the world are clearly seen, being
perceived by the things that are made, even his
eternal power and divinity." How wonderfully
has science interpreted and illustrated these words,
until "the heavens above and the earth beneath
and the waters under the earth" have been written all over with the evidences of God's moral
perfections. Indeed, the religious aspects of nature are patent to any eye that has the gift of
moral vision. A few evenings since, I happened
to turn my eyes upward to the sky. The air was
unusually clear, and the summer stars glowed with
unusual brightness. Many years had passed since

I first learned to pilot my way from constellation to constellation and study those geometrical configurations that so stirred my boyish imagination. Maturer years have only increased my wonder and admiration, as I have learned through recent discoveries how enormous are the distances of these stars from each other, and how endless are their numbers. But what impressed me that evening was the fact that during all these years not the slightest change of position of a single one of these millions of worlds was discernible. For fifty years not one star has moved a second's point from its original place. Not a circle or square or triangle has in any way altered its shape. And all this, be it noted, when these stars are millions on millions of miles apart, and are millions on millions in number. Is there any geometry on earth like that? The geography of our planet has suffered some changes in its long history, and its maps have needed readjustment. But the map of the heavens needs no revised edition. Now and then peradventure some star scarcely visible at best wholly disappears from sight, or a new one comes into view, but its heavenly sisters march on in changeless procession to one immutable law. The earliest star-gazer of our human race looked out upon exactly the same constellations and geometrical figures that are visible to-day. And has such a scene no religious lessons? Does anything else in the whole range of man's experience teach more impressively " God's power and divinity " ? Is it

any wonder that, as I gazed that night and these
reflections rushed across my mind, a new sense of
man's security under the beneficent care of Him
"who maketh the heavens a curtain and clotheth
himself with light as with a garment" came over
me, and a stronger and more loving faith took
possession of my heart! It was Kepler, the dis-
coverer of those laws of celestial motion that are
called by his name, who said: "I read God's
thoughts after Him." What was it that he read
if not this, that the changeless laws of motion of
the heavenly bodies are the evidences written in
nature itself of God's changeless love and bounty
to his human children?

But suppose that these laws of nature, so stead-
fast and fixed in their operation, were at intervals
subject to change? Suppose that a power behind
and above nature intervened at any unexpected
and unannounced moment to work some miracle
by which the stars should be thrown out of their
orbits, or the earth stopped in full career, or the
elements of air, earth, fire, and water so chemically
changed that fire should freeze and water burn, and
suppose man should realize how uncertain were all
the events and phenomena of nature around him.
What would be the effect on his religious feelings
and faith? Would not his whole religion become one of doubt and distrust and fear? Would
the God of such a universe be a God of love, a
father? Such were the actual ideas of the ancient
world, and such was its religion. No lines were

drawn between the natural and the supernatural in the philosophy of those children of our race. The very air around them was filled with supernatural beings, and their lives were subject continually to their malign power. In such an atmosphere of miracle what must have been religious faith? How could it have been anything else than one of dread and ceaseless anxiety! And such, in fact, is the picture that the history of the ancient religions gives us. Let one study, if he will, that picture, as painted by Lucretius, the Latin poet, in his poem "De Rerum Natura," and let him also note how noble and worthy was the poet's aim to release the men of his time from the slavery of superstition and fear. Lucretius was one of the so-called Epicurean skeptics of his day. But his great work is one of the noblest ethical productions of ancient literature, and its keynote, anticipating our modern scientific revival, is that true science is the firmest basis of true religion.

There is, then, no real conflict between religion and science, and all the suggestions to this effect are simply theological bugbears and will-o-the-wisps to frighten the ignorant and superstitious. All signs of such a conflict are disappearing as science and history continue their work, as are also so many other ghosts of man's conjuring. But there is a conflict still going on, real and radical, — the conflict between science and the scientific critical spirit of this age and traditional theology; and the result is as certain as the law of historical evolution can make it. For the theology that the intellectual spirit of this age demands must be developed wholly along inductive historical lines; while the traditional theology is essentially on deductive and metaphysical lines; and the two can no more mix than oil and water. It is, then, a plain historical corollary that the whole traditional theology, I mean as a concatenated system of religious truth with all its unverifiable assumptions, must go to the wall. It goes without saying, of course, that there is much of religious truth in every system of human thought. The lowest forms of savage paganism contain some glimmerings of such truth. Traditional theology has brought down through the ages and added continually, as it has advanced, many true conceptions of God and his ways with his human creatures. Men of religious genius have built on traditional dogmatic foundations works of literature that the world will not willingly let die. Bunyan's Pilgrim's Progress contains not a little bad theology, but its treasures of religious experience will be a light still for many a Christian wayfarer. But the fact after all remains, that all theological systems that are built on *a priori* metaphysical and unhistorical foundations are surely destined to dusty forgetfulness. There is no help for it. For better or worse the age has made its choice, and the choice must stand. To the historical observer who has emancipated himself, as he ought to, from all dogmatic preconceptions and prejudices, it is one of the strangest phenomena

of our present theological condition that men who
try to be clear-sighted and to "redeem the time"
yet so thoroughly fail to see what is impending.
They still talk about a reconstruction of theology
as if the major premises on which the whole traditional system is built were to remain undisturbed,
and only the minor premises with their conclusions to be superficially modified; whereas it is
these major premises which lie at the very bottom
of the structure that the new inductive method
insists on examining and removing. Theologians
of this class are still busy in readjusting the old
dogmatic modes of syllogistic reasoning and striving to adapt them to modern ideas, building new
outworks of acute speculation on every side, and
seemingly utterly blind to the fact that historical
criticism has already destroyed the metaphysical
foundations themselves around which all their
finely spun works of reasoning hang. The labor
that has been spent on these mediæval air-castles
is indeed vast. What immense tomes of dogmatic
theological literature fill our libraries! It is indeed pathetic to cast the eye over them and reflect
how little that is vital and influential remains of
the mass of these works which are already finding
their own place in the dust-heap of history. It is
only the historical scholar who now thinks of examining them for his own historical ends. To go
back no further, who thinks to-day of reading the
voluminous works of Jonathan Edwards, Samuel
Hopkins, or Nathaniel Emmons? Why are these

writings no longer of any theological value? Simply because they start and carry with them all the way from preface to conclusion a set of speculative metaphysical assumptions that can no longer be accepted by any unbiased historical thinker. This age itself, in its whole method of inquiry and reasoning, has simply dismissed such assumptions as no longer worthy of any attention, and with the assumptions of course goes all that is built on them. Like foundations, like building.

But how about the books of our own time, freshly issued from the press, written from the same standpoint? Take, for example, one of the latest of them, and, I will add, one of the best, — Dr. Samuel Harris's " God the Creator and Lord of All." President George Harris has recently reviewed the work of his uncle with a true filial reverence, and yet with due discrimination. I have no doubt that his avowal of the conviction that Dr. Harris " was the greatest theologian of the nineteenth century" meets the cordial approval of many. I need not say how deep is my personal respect for this noble man, whose portrait, hanging in the library of the theological school where it is my lot to teach, so often meets my eye. But it is not with Dr. Harris himself, but his last and ablest book with which I now have to do, and I choose it as perhaps the best illustration of the radical theological position of conservative thought. I have already shown that the cardinal difference between the vanishing old theology and the coming new theology is that the old theology starts from the ideal and abstract and thence proceeds to the historical and concrete, in other words, from what is unknown by experience to what is known; whereas the new theology starts on inductive lines from the historical and concrete, and thence proceeds to the ideal and abstract as far as valid reasoning may allow, in other words again, from the known by experience to the unknown. This is the precise difference between the deductive method which starts with metaphysical *a priori* assumptions and the inductive scientific historical method which allows no such assumptions at the outset, but starts with a historical survey of all the facts attainable, and then considers whether the philosophical assumptions or hypotheses that may be raised are capable of being verified in accordance with the laws of history or of thought. What now is the starting-point of Dr. Harris's book? Just what we should expect, just what has always been the starting-point of traditional dogmatic theology. Does he start from man and nature and history, in other words, from man's own moral consciousness as a religious being, with his environment of brother men and of nature in all its multiform manifestations? Does he start from what is nearest and best known and then move cautiously out towards the less known and thence on to the mysterious ideal realms of the unknown? Not so. Dr. Harris, on the contrary, reverses this whole inductive process, and begins with the highest and remotest mental abstraction that human thought has ever reached, viz., the idea of God, and around this idea of God he assembles an array of metaphysical speculative conceptions such as few even of the subtlest thinkers can fathom. Let us examine this truly wonderful achievement a little and get a few specimens of its subtle thought.

Dr. Harris begins by saying that "the knowledge of God originates in spontaneous belief." Certainly *some* knowledge of God is spontaneous in man, but *what* knowledge, is the real question. Dr. Harris proceeds at once to define "God." He "is the Absolute Spirit." Whether such a definition is defensible or even conceivable we will soon consider   But, first of all, we ask whether any such idea of God is *spontaneous* in the human consciousness. What does history say about it ? Did the earliest man rise spontaneously into any such height of mental abstraction and think of God as the "Absolute Spirit"? Far from it. The early man was but a child, and "he thought as a child." He pictured God as a larger man or a phenomenon of nature, and he worshiped Him in all these forms as they impressed his imagination by their exhibitions of power or beauty. Not till very late in human history did the thoughts of men rise to any abstract idea of God such as Dr. Harris sets forth. The first thinker in the line of direct historical succession down to ourselves to give such a definition of God was Plato,

and his "idea of ideas," or "idea of the good," the
summum genus or ultimate abstraction of his ideal
theory which was Plato's philosophical definition
of God, is essentially the definition of Dr. Harris:
"God is the Absolute Spirit." To call such an
abstraction, that can be understood only by the
acutest metaphysicians, a "spontaneous belief" of
men is surely one of the most unhistorical or more
truly *anti*-historical assumptions that was ever
hazarded by any theological thinker since Plato
himself. And even Plato never declared such a
definition "spontaneous." His idealism was as far
removed as could be from spontaneous popular ap-
prehension, as he himself proved and illustrated in
several of his dialogues.

It may be said in Dr. Harris's defense that he
was not dealing with the historical development
of the idea of God, but only with its philosophical
implications. Perhaps so. But why then does he
talk about "the knowledge of God as originating
in spontaneous belief"? What connection is there
except by a long process of historical evolution
between the abstract generalization "God is the
Absolute Spirit" and God as spontaneously conceived by men? But I am quite ready to give
Dr. Harris the benefit of the doubt, for this is the
very point that I am seeking to illustrate by Dr.
Harris's own example, viz., how little history has
to do with this whole theological method which
Dr. Harris represents. How the idea of God
started and grew in human history seems to be

no concern of Dr. Harris. What is "spontaneous" and what is the result of reflection and a long speculative evolution is one and the same to him. Dr. Harris is a metaphysician, not a historian, and when he touches historical ground he shows at once his weakness. What I insist upon is that "spontaneous" is the last word in the dictionary to be applied to such a definition of God, or to any definition of Him, in fact, that traditional theology has ever invented. Such definitions are, one and all, the result of a dogmatic assumption unfolded into a highly metaphysical abstract idea. Let us examine Dr. Harris's definition more closely to see if this is not so. "God is the Absolute Spirit." It is noticeable that Dr. Harris begins both the terms "Absolute" and "Spirit" with capital letters, by which he plainly indicates that he is not a pantheist but a theist and holds to the divine personality. But if "Spirit" is used in a personal sense, the question at once arises how can "Absolute" and "Spirit" be joined together, for they are in complete logical opposition. What does "Absolute" mean if not what is unlimited and unconditioned? The Absolute is what is absolved or released by its very nature from all limitation, condition, definition; it is the "Universal of Universals" of Plato, the τὸ ἕν or τὸ ὄν of Plotinus and New Platonism, in short the last and highest generalization of the "Tabula Logica." Plotinus attempts no definition of the first principle of Deity. He is simply the

" I am," or rather, not " I am," which implies personal consciousness, but " the one that is," without positive qualities of any sort. But Dr. Harris makes his " Absolute " a person with personal attributes which he proceeds to name. But personality involves limitation and allows definition. Personal consciousness rests on the distinction between the *Ego* and the *non ego*, between the subjective and the objective ; and this distinction is the basis of definition. The attributes of God are the intellectual and moral powers that are exercised in the realm of self-consciousness and form the divine uni-personality over against the plurality of extra-divine things. Here is a veritable antinomy, a logical contradiction. To define God as " the Absolute Spirit " is as much as to say " God is the unconditioned conditioned," or " the unlimited limited," or " the impersonal personality." Such is the "impotent conclusion " of attempting to define the unknown and consequently undefinable. And yet such an antinomy, in which the very laws of human thought are broken down, Dr. Harris would fain have us regard as a " spontaneous belief."

But, to follow Dr. Harris still further, he goes on to declare that " an absolute beginning of being or power out of nothing is impossible." That is, we cannot conceive such a thing. Hence it follows that we cannot conceive of God as having any cause, of his being, whether outside of himself or within himself. We cannot even say that God is self-

caused.   We can only say that He exists.   And so
Dr. Harris lays it down as a theological axiom :
" That the Absolute Being exists is a self-evident
principle of reason."   This may have been " self-
evident " to such a reason as that of Dr. Harris,
but I am sure that the large majority of men would
sadly stumble over it.   Dr. Harris insists that it is
impossible to conceive of any beginning of being by
any cause proceeding from the being who is supposed not yet to be.   True enough.   But is it any
easier to conceive of the absolute eternal existence
of a being without any cause at all of his existence
either without or within?   One proposition is just
as easy to conceive as the other, and to lay down
either as " a self-evident principle of reason " is to
beg the question at once, and to fall back on a
speculative, unsupported assumption.   The human
mind cannot conceive of existence without a causal
origin.   " Out of nothing nothing can come " is an
axiom as old as philosophical thought.   If anything exists, there must be a cause of its existence
behind or within it.   If anything eternally exists,
there must be an eternal cause of such eternal
existence.   If God exists eternally, He must be
eternally self-caused.   Dr. Harris denies this conclusion, while accepting the premise, declaring it
to be inconceivable.   He holds that, if God is self-
caused, there must be a beginning of his existence
out of nothing, which destroys God's eternity, so
that He is no longer the Absolute Spirit.   I must
disagree with him *in toto*.   If the premise is

allowed, the conclusion, in my view, must follow. But can the premise be accepted? This is the real question. Is it conceivable that God exists *eternally?* Here is another of those speculative assumptions for which there is no basis either in history or nature or man's moral consciousness. What is meant by God's eternal existence? Surely this: that there is no beginning to it and no ending, and that God thus exists by virtue of his own inherent self-existent nature. Now I venture to assert that such a proposition, though it can be put into language, cannot be grasped or even intelligently conceived by the human mind. It is easy to talk about God's timelessness and put Him outside of the categories of time and space, but to conceive God as thus existing is impossible, simply for the reason that *we are so bound by those categories* that we cannot conceive of any one else as existing outside of them. The difficulty lies in the very nature of our minds. The highest flight of imagination has never carried a single human being to the point where he could comprehend God as not under the law of temporal succession. The phrase so frequently used in theology, " *God lives in an eternal now,*" is just one of those nonsensical expressions by which the utter break-down of intelligent thought has so often been concealed. The human reason seeks, by a law of necessity, to find behind all existence, whether mundane or extra-mundane, some cause. As it pushes backward in its inquiries, it puts cause behind cause, until it postulates a first cause, but it never actually finds such a cause. For such a cause must lie at the end of an infinite series of causes, and the mind can never, in any fixed lapse of time, reach the end of such a series. It must pause at last before the first cause is reached. Eternity is really a word that has and can have no meaning to us. The speculative theologian may make a metaphysical jump and think he has compassed it, but his supposed scientific definition will involve another antinomy, like Origen's famous expression, "eternal generation," a theological bubble that Dr. Emmons, to his credit be it said, pricked long ago. Dr. Harris's dogma of God as an eternally existing uncaused Being is not only not a "spontaneous belief," it is one that the very laws of the mind forbid it to attempt to hold.

But I forbear. Enough that I have shown how completely metaphysical Dr. Harris's book is from the very start. It only needs to be added that he resolutely builds his whole theology on these idealistic and speculative foundations. The weakest part of the book is its christology. Here he is obliged to enter directly the field of history, and his ignorance of recent historical and critical investigations is surprisingly revealed. Indeed the whole book is a vivid illustration of the fact that historical studies have made little real impression as yet on dogmatic theologians. There seems to be a fatal incapacity in the mind that remains fixed at the metaphysical standpoint to comprehend the revolutionary character of the new history and criticism. Dr. Harris writes church history just as it was written a hundred years ago. He still accepts the Nicene creed and the Chalcedon definition, with all their unhistorical assumptions. This part of the book is lamentably behind the times in its whole treatment of the critical questions that are concerned with the literary origin of the New Testament books and with the history of the evolution of doctrine in the early church. As we should expect, his trinitarianism and christology are wholly traditional. The Sabellian strain that runs through it is seen in the statement that " Christ as Mediator is not a third person between God and man,"—a statement that is based on the monistic modal theory that there are not three real persons in the Godhead, but that " one God exists in three eternal modes of being." Of course, then, Christ could not be " a third person between God and man." One may well ask what element of mediatorship is left. Has not the mediatorial office of Christ become a docetic farce? Of course Dr. Harris holds to Christ's absolute sinlessness, for he holds him to be Absolute God. No wonder Dr. Harris thinks monotheism is " oppressive." Yet he dislikes pantheism. But, strive as he may, pantheism lurks through his whole philosophy. Whether he realized it or not, he was wearing the old Augustinian-Plotinian mask. He haggles over the term " person " in the same old-fashioned way as his predecessors have done back to Augustine himself. And then, having thus shown himself to be a monistic, modalistic unitarian of the first water, he surprises us, if anything could surprise us now, by declaring that " The Trinity is the only worthy conception of God." But what kind of a Trinity? Why, a unitarian trinity of course, or a trinitarian unity, just as one pleases.

If now it is asked what must be the judgment of the historical critic on this book, the answer must be decided and emphatic. For this new age, with its new science and history, and for the new demand of the intellectual spirit, it has no word. It belongs to the past, not to the present or future. I know not how it may seem to others, but to me there is something sad in noting how many splendid lives have been spent on works of great theological erudition and philosophical acuteness, which by reason of proceeding from false assumptions and along false lines of history and logical reasoning, are seen to have become absolutely valueless to coming times. Such a contemplation reminds one of the last words of Salmasius, one of the illustrious scholars of the seventeenth century : " *Eheu, eheu, meam vitam perdidi laboriose nihil agendo.*"

CHAPTER X

THE NEW THEOLOGICAL METHOD

THUS we are brought to the point towards which all our historical observation has been converging, that the old theology cannot serve us in the construction of the new. However much truth it may contain, its whole method of procedure is wrong. It starts from the wrong point of view; it accepts metaphysical assumptions that cannot be verified by science or history; and, worst of all, it has built its whole structure of Christian dogmas on mythical or legendary unhistorical traditions. Where then must the new theology start and what the course it must follow, if it would satisfy the demand of the intellectual spirit? It has not been the purpose of this historico-critical essay to attempt even to lay the foundations of the new theology. The writer has little faith in such an attempt at present. The new intellectual creation must be, like the physical creation, a slow evolution of time. Theology has its place, but it cannot take the place of religious faith and life, and there may be a very highly developed condition of religion, while a theology of religion may still be in the lowest stages of its formative period. Such

will be the fact in the coming decade, if one may
judge from the present historical outlook. All
signs point to a speedy revival of Christian faith
and religious life along the new line already indicated. Christianity with its gospel of love
and ·brotherhood and sacrifice is entering on its
golden age of achievement and conquest over the
hearts of men. The missionary spirit, starting
from a new motive, is to rise to a new height
of evangelizing power. Christian activities in
every form, which are already adding a new
chapter to political and social as well as religious
history, will widen still further their range.
While the church is thus actively engaged, there
can be little time for the development of a cloistered theology. The outlook for a revival of the
original principles and enthusiasms of Christ's
gospel is indeed inspiring. The Christian church
for ages has like Hagar been "in bondage with
her children," but that bondage is at length broken
and she goes forth free and with the new power
and passion that freedom brings. A new age of
faith is already dawning, — faith, I say, not in its
forced dogmatic sense, but in its true original
Christian sense, a faith of the heart rather than of
the intellect. "The future," wrote Victor Hugo,
"belongs even more to hearts than to minds."
It is to be as true in religion as in other forms of
life. Mind has had the leadership thus far, but
heart henceforth is to take the reins. Not a dead
theological doctrine, but a living gospel is to hold

the field. Neander, the real founder of modern
church history, had more than a glimpse of the
truth when he made the motto of his great work:
" Pectus facit theologum." The heart is to lead
even in theology, and out of its experiences and
affirmations the new theology will draw some of its
highest forms of truth.

The time, however, is certainly coming when the
demand of the intellectual spirit, as well as of the
religious spirit, must be in some measure satisfied,
and, when the needful preparations are finished, the
new theological edifice will begin to rise. But are
the initial preparations yet complete? It cannot be
affirmed. Although the old orthodoxy has long
been trembling to its fall, there still remains deeply
imbedded in the historical background of our age a
body of traditional presuppositions and prepossions and assumptions that stand squarely in the way
of any radical reconstruction; and until this body
of misconceptions is utterly removed, it is vain to
talk of a new theological movement that will be
of any lasting value. The vital trouble with the
foundation and framework of orthodoxy is that
there is mixed all through it, as a sort of cement, a
mass of presuppositions which are opposed to all
the critical results of science and of history and
to the affirmations of man's moral consciousness.
Such, for example, are the assumptions concerning
the supernatural world and its relations to this
world; — concerning miracles as suspensions, if not
violations, of the ordinary laws of nature; — con-

cerning a supernatural or miraculous revelation of
God to man through specially inspired men; — concerning the Bible as a book of divine authorship
and hence perfect and infallible in its religious
teachings and even in its history and science ; —
concerning the historicity of the traditional dates
and authors of the books of Scripture; — concerning the metaphysical being and character of God,
and concerning the account in Genesis of the origin
and fall of man.   These are a few of the most striking presuppositions of orthodoxy, and it can be
seen at a glance that they are utterly inconsistent
with all the discoveries of science and all the latest
results of historical scholarship.   But it will be
asked : Are they not already discarded by all intelligent evangelical Christians ? By no means. Take
any latest theological book, even of the most liberal
evangelical sort, and one will find one or more at
least of these traditional presuppositions, half
concealed, perhaps, but still assumed throughout.
There is but one way of eliminating such assumptions, viz., by a radically new method of procedure.

The first question, then, in considering how a
new theology shall be formed, is one of *method*.
Propædeutics or methodology is the first necessary
stage in a new theological movement. Methodology
has to do with *the way* in which matters of religious truth are approached and examined.   The
materials of theology are not here in question.
As I have already suggested, much material of the
old theology will enter into the new.   Let me not

be misunderstood on this point.   It is not the *material* of the old theology, but *the way* in which that material is handled, the method of systemization employed, and the unscientific and unhistorical mixture of true and false materials, that render it useless for the new theological builder.   What has continued the old theology so long in existence is the fact that it has preserved and defended so many of the vital truths of religion.   Such are the truths of man's free moral nature and responsibility, of sin and sinfulness and its moral effects, of man's capacity for repentance and a new spiritual life, of the religious sense of God and of his moral supremacy, of man's instinctive hope of immortality, of conscience that commands to duty and stirs the conviction of moral reward and punishment, and of the revelations of God's goodness and love in nature and providence, and especially in the gospel of Christ.   But while such truths have been held, theological presuppositions and assumptions have been put behind them that have entirely changed their character in a theological system, so that they have become repugnant to the moral consciousness and reason, as well as inconsistent with sound historical and philosophical criteria.   It is not these great and essential religious truths themselves, but the way in which they have been shaped and distorted in a system, and mixed with all sorts of errors, mythological, legendary, Jewish, pagan, that makes the old orthodoxy, as a system of truth, a thing to be rejected and cast away.

Let me give an example. Take the fact of *sin*. History is full of illustrations of it. There can be no true theology in which sin does not play a central part. But what is the doctrine of sin in the old theology? It starts with a myth that had floated down through primeval tradition and had become incorporated into the Hebrew Scriptures. This myth is treated as veritable history. It runs in this wise, as theologically interpreted, that a serpent tempts the first man and woman to break the commandment of God by eating the fruit of a tree. This act of disobedience results in the total fall of our first parents into a moral depravity that becomes a necessitated second nature which is communicated to the whole human race, so that all men are by nature totally depraved and as moral beings commit evil, only evil, and that continually. Such is the tremendous theological result of the single act of two inexperienced children. This myth with all its absurdities I need not dwell upon. But the old theology did not stop with the myth itself. It added a figment of Greek philosophy. Plato had made universal ideas the true realities, and individual phenomena only concrete expressions of such realities. Augustine applied the Platonic idealism to his doctrine of sin. When Adam sinned, it was not merely Adam the individual, but the universal in Adam, that is, human nature, that sinned; consequently when Adam sinned all his descendants sinned in him and fell with him. Therefore, on metaphysical as well as supposed historical grounds, it is held that the whole human race, without a single exception, is sinful, guilty, and punishable eternally. Note that this terrible dogma of "original sin" which has hung like a nightmare over the Christian faith of these long centuries is the simple result of the distortion of the truth about sin by means of the falsifying of history and the introduction of a piece of purely speculative philosophy. Is it any wonder that all men of intelligence to-day reject it with scorn?

I am tempted to illustrate this point by another example, — the old theological dogma of *Hell*. This dogma, which held so large a place in the Middle Ages, as is witnessed by the paintings on the walls of churches and by the great poem of Dante, had its birth in the religious, materialistic imaginations of barbarous and pre-Christian peoples. The realistic descriptions of the "Inferno" and of "Paradise Lost" are anticipated and rivaled by those in Plutarch, and Plato, and Josephus. The Jews obtained their doctrine apparently from the Persians. Christ's references to it are few and apocalyptic, and simply reflect the Jewish faith of his day. One of the saddest effects of this dogma of a place of material suffering, in which fire was made the chief instrument, was the practice of burning heretics which formed such a horrible chapter in the history of Christianity. How a dogma that gives such stimulus to the development of the most cruel sentiments of human nature

could have been retained so long in Christian theology can only be accounted for by the tenacity
with which the dogma of the plenary inspiration of
the Bible has been held.   Strange to say it has not
yet wholly passed out of Christian belief.   That sin
will find in some way its punishment is surely a
truth of revelation in many forms, but the old
dogma of a local, material Hell as a place of torment of the bodies and souls of men is as surely a
relic of pagan superstition as it is contradicted by
all science and history.   The Copernican theory
gave it its real death-blow.   There is no hell save
in the sinner's own remorseful soul.   Such was the
truth put by Milton into the lips of Satan : —

> "Me miserable !   Which way shall I fly
> Infinite wrath and infinite despair ?
> Which way I fly is hell ; *myself am hell.*"

If any one doubts whether this dogma still lives in
the old theology, let him consult Dr. A. A. Hodge's
" Outlines of Theology," in which it is declared that
" the material body of Christ rose from the dead,"
and that " our resurrection is to be because of and
like to that of Christ, which was of his identical
body."   On this assumption is based the further
doctrine of a definite, local, material heaven and
hell, and of a material punishment, involving " the
punitive infliction of torment, — God's wrath descending upon both the moral and physical nature
of its objects."   How, after all this, Dr. Hodge
should hold that " the terms used in scripture to
describe these sufferings are evidently figurative "

is surely surprising.   I would also refer the reader
to Dr. Shedd, who in his "Dogmatic Theology"
devotes two pages to "Heaven" and about fifty
pages to "Hell," showing at least the deep interest
he took in the subject.   He defends at length the
traditional view and bases it on Christ's own teaching, whom he makes "responsible for the doctrine
of Eternal Perdition," and whom he calls "that
omniscient Being who made the statements respect-
ing the day of judgment and the final sentence."
Plainly Dr. Shedd remained wholly unaffected by
the new history and criticism.   But if he was ignorant of modern science, he was certainly learned
in the old traditionalism.   His acquaintance with
"Hell" is as direct and personal as that of Ulysses
or Æneas.   He knows not only where it is, but
also the exact condition of its lost inhabitants.
"Hell is only a corner of the universe.   The Gothic
etymon (Hohle, Hölle) denotes a covered-up hole.
It is bottomless but not boundless."   And, as to
its inhabitants, "there is not a single throb of
godly sorrow, or a single pulsation of holy desire in
the lost spirit."   How has Dr. Shedd learned all
this? one may well ask.   Certainly Christ pictures
Dives in Hades as having some "pulsation of holy
desire," since he begged Abraham to send Lazarus
to his brethren, "lest they also come into this place
of torment."   Surely here is an altruistic state of
moral feeling that is far removed from Dr. Shedd's
description of lost souls.   Would Christ have
spoken such a parable had he regarded such souls

as lost to all right moral emotion or desire? If
Dr. Shedd held Christ to be "omniscient" and
"responsible" for the orthodox eschatology, why
was not his testimony accepted on so vital a question as the moral state of souls who leave this
world impenitent! The truth is that we here
touch one of those metaphysical assumptions that
underlie Dr. Shedd's whole theology.

These illustrations are enough to show that the
rejection of such dogmas of the old theology is a
very different thing from rejecting the truth itself
concerning sin and its consequences. It has been
the task of historical criticism, as we have seen, to
clear up the confusion that has so long existed of
religious truth with its dogmatic disfigurements.
Theology has so long masqueraded as the very
"holy of holies" of truth itself that men have forgotten that it is only a sartorial dressing up of it.
What is a theological system? Only the philosophical or theological way in which some man
looks at truth. So we have Calvin's theology, or
that of Edwards or that of Emmons. The number
of theologies is legion. But truth we know is one,
though the forms or aspects of it may be as numerous as are the observers. Here lies the great
benefit of free theological inquiry, that it allows
truth to be studied on every side, so that all its infinitely various aspects may be brought more clearly
to view and become the common property of all.
The more theological systems the better for our
knowledge of truth if they are made undogmatic

and free, just as the more telescopes there are
raised to the skies, the better for our knowledge of
astronomy.   Theology is simply a science among
sciences.   It is a science of religion, as astronomy
is a science of the physical heavens.   Scientists
may make mistakes, by means of wrong observa-
tions or hypotheses.   The Ptolemaic astronomy as
a system is false, because based on a wrong hypothesis.   The Copernican is true for the reverse
reason.   So there are false and true theologies or
philosophies of religious truth, as a result of the
different philosophical or historical assumptions
that lie behind them.   But the truths of astronomy
and of religion do not stand or fall with any man's
science or philosophy.   A man may hold the truth
as it is in Jesus and yet reject half of the theologies extant, yea all of them; for truth is independent of all theological form, as a rose blooms and
sweetens the air regardless of botany.   It is the
arrant dogmatism of the old theology that has discredited it utterly with this scientific age.   It has
not only claimed to be the whole and the only
truth, but has also set itself up as the sovereign
arbiter of all questions concerning truth in its
every form.   The theologians of this school make
theology the fountain head of every other science,
" *scientia scientiarum*," in the sense that all other
sciences are to be determined in their principles
and results by the dicta of theology, that is to say,
of these same theologians.   This assumption forms
the very warp and woof of the old theology, and

yet it seems so preposterous to our modern ears
that it can scarcely be believed that one should be
found to squarely avow it.   But the old theology
still boasts of stout defenders, and certainly President Hartranft of Hartford Theological Seminary
may be reckoned among the stoutest of them.   His
inaugural address delivered only a decade ago was
a sort of theological *ultimatum,* and displayed the
defiant air of a man who has put his back against
the wall.   It is an indictment of all sciences in
their claim of independence and equality with theological science.   His main proposition is "that
theology is the absolute head of all sciences," "the
starting-point and goal of all genuine knowledge
as a whole, and of all classified knowledges."   This
proposition is made to rest on the major premise
from which everything starts, viz.: "The absolute
supremacy of Christ's views of God and the universe, man and the world."   Of course behind this
premise lies the implicit assumption that Christ is
the Absolute God, in the full exercise of the divine
omniscience, in virtue of which his utterances on
every question, not only of religion but also of history, science, politics, philosophy, art, literature,
are absolutely true and therefore of supreme authority.   This involves the corollary that Christ's
church, which is the repository of his truth, "must
have her own canons of art, literature, philosophy,
science, based on her Lord's supreme doctrine and
ethics."   Thus the dogmatic foundations are laid
for his indictment against modern science and phi-

losophy which is that "all divisions of human learning," instead of remaining as "branches of theology," have become "estranged and independent," and so "have become helpful to doubt and darkness and have made themselves aliens from the commonwealth of which they ought to be the worthiest citizens." And then follows a diatribe against this anti-Christian position of the sciences and also against "the greater body of the church to-day" who are "meekly acquiescing" in it, closing with the remarkable declaration that the effort to "reconcile science and religion" is "all bosh and very unmanly bosh at that." And why "all bosh"? Because there is no such thing as science apart from religion, that is theology, since "all the knowledges are theology, not science, not ethics, but theology, sublime, tranquil, eternal." And what does all this rodomontade mean, when we get down from the sublimities and tranquillities, etc., to plain English? Just this, that for all our history and science and methods of scientific historical criticism we must go to the Bible. Christ exercises "absolute supremacy" in this whole business. He indorsed the Old Testament, therefore its myths and legends are real history, and are to be accepted as such by all Christian scholars. Therefore Moses is to be accepted as the author of the Pentateuch, whether he really wrote it or not. Did not Christ plainly speak of him as the author? Therefore the parable of Jonah and the big fish is to be accepted as a historical narrative of what really occurred. Did not Christ speak of Jonah as being three days in the whale's belly? Of course the first chapter of Genesis is good geology, and the world was created in just six days, and the sun standing still at Joshua's command is good astronomy at least for *that day* when the command was uttered. I am not doing Dr. Hartranft any injustice. What else does he mean by asking: "Is not the scientist's view of the universe deemed of higher moment than Christ's view?" Of course Dr. Hartranft here means that in his view Christ was a perfect scientist and that his gospel should be accepted as the scientific grammar and text-book of all Christian scientists. So of "chemistry, geology, astronomy." What is the matter with our geology according to Dr. Hartranft? Plainly the fact that it does not tie itself to the first chapter of Genesis. Of course there is no arguing with such a position; for there is no common ground on which the disputants can stand. All these amazing theological assumptions historical criticism dismisses at once as unworthy of the slightest attention. They belong to a *method* that has "had its day and ceased to be" to all true scholars. The intellectual spirit of the age utters its demand in vain in the presence of such dogmatic pessimism, and passes it contemptuously by, regarding it with a curiosity such as a scientist feels toward some specimen of an extinct species, fit only to be classified for its proper place in a museum of antiquities.

Enough surely has been said in illustration of

the false method of the old theology and its underlying metaphysical assumptions. But there is one assumption which has a place by itself, and perhaps should be specially considered, because it claims to rest on historical grounds that cannot be impeached. I refer to the argument so often pressed triumphantly in proof of the traditional miraculous origin of Christianity and its dogmas, viz., that its very history shows it. The trouble with this argument is that it proves too much. Not everything that outlives persecution and the mightiest efforts of human powers is therefore divine and morally perfect. The counsel of Gamaliel in the Jewish Sanhedrim, based on the theory that "if this work be of men it will be overthrown, but if it is of God ye will not be able to overthrow them," no doubt was discreet and wise, but the theory behind it has had a very imperfect realization in history. Other religions beside the Christian have survived every effort to destroy them, and have rivaled Christianity itself in their long and wonderful hold on the faith of men; for example, Buddhism and Mohammedanism. The Roman Papacy uses the same argument in support of its claims. No other institution in history has such historic ground on which to stand. Slavery might be defended in the same way. The truth is, Christianity has lived and evolved itself by the same historic laws as other religions and religious institutions and beliefs. The old theology, in pressing this point, has shown the same lack of historical insight and perspective that has characterized it everywhere. It has idealized Christian history, as if the church were a sort of heaven on earth; whereas, in fact, Christendom has never been free from the corruptions and wickednesses and awful crimes that beset our poor humanity everywhere and always. The time has gone by for such idealized pictures of Christian history as the old historians used to paint. The great œcumenical councils that formulated the old theology were the scene of unchristian antagonisms, and bitter strife and fightings that were never rivaled in the history of any other religion, and no religion of which history has a record was ever guilty of such cruel persecutions as Christianity, whose founder was the meek and lowly Jesus of Nazareth. Whether the Christian religion is a religion from God, in a sense in which no other religion is, or not, the history of its so-called disciples, from the fourth century down to recent times, has been one to make men often blush, and the story of many of the practical fruits of the old theology is one of the saddest chapters in human annals. I submit, then, that this assumption must go with the rest.

So much for the question of *method* and the reasons growing out of it for the rejection of the old theology as a basis for the construction of the new. The next question is that of *material*. From what materials shall the new theology be constructed?

CHAPTER XI

THE MATERIALS OF THE NEW THEOLOGY

EVERY science has its material to work upon, its own field of operation in which its scientific principles and laws can be freely and independently exercised. So theology as a science has its own materials and field of working. And if theology be, as it surely is, the philosophical account which religion and the religious sphere gives of itself, then the materials of the new theology must be derived from that sphere. What then in the sphere of religion and religious experience are the sources or media of religious truth in the various forms of divine revelation? The answer of course must be determined by the new inductive method, and hence we must dismiss at once the old theological assumption that a miraculous revelation was communicated directly by God to a few specially inspired prophets, and by them, or by others inspired like them, incorporated in a book; for there is no valid evidence of such a divine procedure, and it is, moreover, in violation of all God's other methods of communicating with men. Religious truth can come to the soul only through its own laws and faculties of receiving knowledge, and hence man's

own moral consciousness is the only direct and ultimate avenue of moral light and inspiration from
God.

But the divine providence employs other media
through which to reveal itself indirectly. One
such medium is *nature* in all its material forms.
Of nature or science as a religious teacher I have
already spoken, and need only to add here that
too little has hitherto been made of this source of
religious truth. The prejudice raised by the old
theology against all natural science has prevented
its light from clearly shining upon many religious
minds. It is certainly remarkable how little appreciation theological writers of the old school
have had of the religious aspects of nature. John
Calvin lived in Geneva surrounded by some of the
grandest and most beautiful scenery in Europe.
Mt. Blanc was in full view from his windows;
yet there is not a single allusion, so far as I know,
to those " wonderful works of God" in all his
voluminous writings. To him this world was
simply a place to stay in, not a temple illumined
with the Shekinah of God's presence. But as this
theological prejudice disappears and gives place to
right views, the religious revelations of nature will
grow more and more luminous. Already our
noblest forms of literature are being inspired by
these revelations. Modern poetry since Wordsworth has been pervaded with a deep sense of the
divine presence in natural scenes. One cannot
walk over the Lake district, where Wordsworth

lived so many years, without realizing how close was his sympathy with Nature in all her moods, and how full of the elements of religious thought and feeling were the fountains around him from which he drew. If one has never withdrawn himself from the haunts of men, for a considerable period, into the retirement of mountains and forests, he knows little of the real companionship with God that may be enjoyed in such solitudes, where nature speaks to man face to face.

Another medium of divine revelation is *history*, or the record of human events and lives. Through history man is helped to read himself and his religious relations and duties in the lives and conduct of his fellow men. The history of the human race becomes as if an enlarged moral consciousness in which, as in a glass, every faculty and aspect of man's moral life is displayed in every possible form of human working and development. Hence history has a vital religious function, — one that has hitherto been sadly neglected. Nature and history together, embracing everything outside of man's own subjective moral consciousness, are the two great avenues of the revelation of God himself, — that infinite and unknown being "whom no man hath seen or can see." But there is one unique illustration of moral consciousness in history that bespeaks our special attention. I mean that of Jesus Christ, as being the loftiest and divinest form of such consciousness that has yet been seen among men. I have already dwelt

upon it in the chapter on the demand of the religious spirit.   But we now approach it from the
intellectual rather than religious side, inquiring as
to the degree and character of the religious light
shed by the moral consciousness of Christ on our
own paths in life, not only as religious but also
as intellectual beings.   We ask ourselves, then, as
to the qualifications of Christ to be a teacher of
moral truth.   The basis of such qualifications
must have been the peculiar character of his own
moral consciousness.   'It may be asked what I
mean by Christ's moral consciousness.   I mean
that faculty of his moral nature through which he
realized God's personal fatherhood and relationship, and also that moral kingdom of which God
is the head-spring.   It was this consciousness that
gave Christ the two cardinal foci of his gospel, —
divine sonship and human brotherhood.

Now as to Christ's moral consciousness, the *first*
thing to be noted is that it was a completely human one.   Born in the natural line of a human
genealogy, Christ had a complete human nature.
Such a nature involved a complete human consciousness, one, I mean, wholly like that of all
other men.   There is nothing in the three Synoptic
gospels, which give us the earliest and least idealized picture of Christ, to indicate that he ever
rose into any form of religious consciousness that
was superhuman or unnatural.   Everywhere and
always he was a man speaking to brother men.
In his highest and sublimest flights of thought he

never lost sight of his real humanity. He is ever the same simple, unpretending, meek and lowly Jesus of Nazareth, the son of Joseph and Mary, with brothers and sisters who are continually moving in and out of the circle of his daily life.

But, *secondly*, it is clear that Christ's consciousness was eminent in its whole religious movement above all who were around him. Hence it was that he spoke with a new kind of moral authority. "No man ever spoke like this man." So like others was he and yet so unlike. Naturally and humanly like, morally and religiously unlike. The difference was not in kind but in degree. His religious consciousness not only rose higher, but began to develop itself earlier than that of other men. What is most remarkable in his conversation with the rabbis at twelve years of age is not the fact that his questions and answers were so wonderful in themselves, as that his mind was occupied with them so early. That a child of twelve should be able to meet rabbis of mature years on equal footing was indeed a marvel of religious precocity.

There is a *third* feature of Christ's moral consciousness that is perhaps the most wonderful of all, — the clear and steady sense he had from first to last of *its limitations*. That Christ should have confined his teaching so closely to purely religious themes grows the more remarkable the more one considers it. What temptations beset him, as beset all teachers, to include in his communications other subjects of thought and interest? But what a wonderful reserve characterized him, even when questions put to him seemed to be providential opportunities to enlarge his sphere of instruction! Yet never once did he yield to such temptations. He never set himself up as a philosophic theologian, or scientist, or critic, or politician, or historian. " My kingdom is not of this world," he said, when men sought to learn something of his views on purely temporal and earthly things. His sphere was moral and religious, the sphere of his own religious consciousness, " the kingdom of God within " him. It is indeed amazing that men like President Hartranft can make Christ "absolutely supreme" in the whole realm of knowledge, when he so carefully guarded himself against all danger of such an interpretation of his mission among men. What shred of science or history or philosophy or art can be found in any of his words? He professed only to be, just what he was, a plain unlettered Galilean peasant, learned only in the Holy Scriptures of his own Jewish people, and using these Scriptures only to enforce and illustrate the religious intuitions that absorbed his soul. What stronger proof can be found of what surely needs no proof, that Christ was our true fellow man, than the steadiness with which he kept himself within the limitations of his human nature and historical surroundings? In all matters of earthly science and learning Christ was no authority, and never claimed to be. Only in the region of man's moral nature did he speak " as one having authority, and not as the scribes." But in that realm his words come with the same authority to-day, because they were spoken out of a consciousness of intimate relationship with God and his kingdom of moral truth that is still unrivaled, in its heavenly intuitions, among men.

It will be asked, Is the *Bible* not to be reckoned among the media of divine revelation? Certainly; but not in the way in which the old theology would reckon it. Its presuppositions of a divine miraculous origin and character, differentiating the Bible from all other religious literature, can no longer be admitted. Historically considered, the Bible is simply a literary product of the Hebrew and Jewish nation. Yet its place in religious literature is unique, and in the New Testament especially we have those precious sayings and biographical notices of Christ which place it above all similar productions. The Bible thus becomes a very important part of history as an interpreter of the moral consciousness of the race. The accounts of Abraham, Moses, David, Elijah, Paul, and Jesus himself, and the history of the whole Jewish people, furnish a chapter in the universal history of mankind that could not be omitted without irreparable loss to the world. It is the high form of religious consciousness manifesting itself in the whole Bible, as in Christ, that gives it such a unique place in religious history. It is worthless indeed for purposes of science or even of philosophy, but it remains still the Book of books for religious faith and devotion, and is thus preëminently essential as a medium of God's revelation of himself to man.

It may be expected that the *Church*, as a religious institution, should be included in this account of the materials of the new theology. The Church, as an expression for the united people of God, has already been described under the term "history"; but as to the Church, in the sense of a corporation claiming to be the recipient of authority from Christ to lord it over the religious faith and doctrines of men, as is claimed by the Papal Church or by High Church Protestants of any kind, the inductive historical method knows nothing of it, and gives it no special place in the media of revelation. Christ's kingdom of the truth is not an outward institution of any kind, but "is within," in the religious consciousness of all godly souls.

CHAPTER XII

THE CONSTRUCTION OF THE NEW THEOLOGY

THE *method* of the new theology and the *materials* out of which it is to be constructed having been determined, the ground is clear for the construction itself. The path thus opened is truly alluring to any constructive thinker. But such a theological evolution is not within the purpose and plan of this historical essay. It is possible only to break ground a little in this direction, and that, not by any effort to build up a theological system, for which, as I have before indicated, the time is not yet ripe, but merely by way of hints and illustrations of the method of procedure with the materials in hand. And in doing this I shall confine myself to the special subject of which this book is a history, viz., the doctrine of God and of the revelation of Him as made in Jesus Christ.

The doctrine of God has become so completely metaphysical and speculative throughout the whole history of Christianity that it is exceedingly difficult to treat it inductively without disturbing considerably traditional ideas. The old definitions of God have been made and accepted as if He were as well known as the most conspicuous character of history. The process, as we have seen, was a curious one. Philosophy slowly reached the conception of the most abstract universal idea that logical laws could evolve. This ultimate abstraction, unlimited and indefinable, was then made synonymous with God. But God, to be an object of religious belief and trust, must be a person. So the abstract God was turned into a concrete God, with personal attributes and definitions. And it is this philosophical deity that has been for ages the God of Christian theology, and largely of Christian faith and worship. I have already brought out the irreconcilable contradictions that are involved in this traditional dogma. But it is deeply intrenched in the minds of men, and many will no doubt continue to think of God as everywhere and yet nowhere; as always existent and yet under no laws of time; as incomprehensible and yet as possessing attributes that are wholly comprehensible, else they could not be defined; as a God of love and yet as a Being above all passion or affection of any kind; as having no form or place of existence and yet as tabernacled in the effulgence and glory of the heavenly places. Now, as to all this view of God, it is here to be said that the new inductive theology can make no use of it. All true induction proceeds from the known to the unknown, not from the unknown to the known. The metaphysical view of God, therefore, cannot be accepted by the inductive method, and so it must proceed by a new path of its own to form its conception of the Father of all souls that man's religious nature instinctively intuits and craves. It starts with a concrete personal being, an intuition of the moral consciousness which is as fixed and radical as its own nature. For a moral nature involves personality and cannot exist without it, and such likewise must be its conception of God. Here lies the very basis of the whole doctrine of God. The moral consciousness of man can never accept a pantheistic God, or a God evolved from the concrete into the abstract, in other words, "the absolute" of philosophy. As man's moral and religious nature develops, and the light of nature and history reveals to him more and more of the divine wisdom and power and goodness, his idea of God's perfections gains in breadth and height, but never can lose itself in any transcendental speculation that removes God from the horizon of personal faith into some region of unknowable abstraction. *A priori* philosophy may predicate a First Cause, uncaused or self-caused, as God, but no inductive facts carry the mind thither, and the religious consciousness remains steadfastly within the limits of its primary intuitions and refuses to embark on a speculative sea that has no shore. Induction finds God inconceivably great and wise and good, but further it cannot go, and at this point leaves Him in the mystery that must eternally surround Him. The new theology will have its mysticism as well as the old, but while it will be ready to acknowledge the fact which all the media of revelation unite in declaring, as Plato did, that " God is hard to find, and when found is difficult to make known to others," it will nevertheless agree with Paul that "God is not far from every one of us, for we are also his offspring," and that men therefore "should seek God, if haply they might feel after Him and find Him." The mysticism of the old theology was irrational, for it attempted by reason to transcend reason. But the mysticism of religious faith which through love believes and trusts God, and is able thus to look beyond the things that are seen and temporal to the things that are not seen and eternal, — such a mysticism was that of Christ himself when he said, " The kingdom of God cometh not with observation ; " " it is within you." The mysticism that " walks by faith and not by sight " is that of Paul ; but the mysticism that is built on the Platonic philosophy of the supreme reality of universal ideas is that of all pantheists from Plotinus to John Scotus Erigena and Eckhart and Hegel. Nature is mystical when it points to something behind itself of which it is the material expression. History is mystical when it reveals the movements of a divine providence. The moral consciousness of man grows mystical when it begins to say, as Christ said at twelve years of age, " Wist ye not that I must be about my Father's business ? " But it is the mysticism of personality and of theism, not of pantheism. The new theology, whatever else it may be, will not be pantheistic. All the true media of divine revelation — nature, history, man's moral consciousness, the Bible, Christ — speak the same word about God, and that word is *theism*, in its monotheistic, not in its pantheistic form.

We are here brought face to face with that evolution of the doctrine of God which forms the most remarkable chapter in the history of the old theology, — the dogma of the Trinity. This dogma is not peculiar to Christianity. It had a long history in the Ethnic religions before Christ was born, and the philosophical presuppositions that lie behind the Christian form of it lie equally behind all the Ethnic trinities. The idea of a trinity in the Godhead, or of trinities in the pantheon of divine beings, is one of the most original and widely spread religious notions of the human race, and seems based on many trinitarian analogies in nature and the human soul, and in the structure of family and social life. The theological assumption that the Christian dogma is a new revealed truth, dating from the Christian era, is an unhistorical tradition that like so many others has been shown by historical criticism to be utterly without foundation. The earlier chapters of this book have given the history of the stages of evolution through which the trinitarian dogma passed before it reached its complete form in the Nicene and pseudo-Athanasian creeds. It has also been shown that the dogma had its philosophical origin in the mediation ideas of the Platonic dualism. The history of the Ethnic trinities, moreover, brings out the fact that the mediation principle had much to do with the development of the Ethnic trinitarianism. In truth, nothing is historically clearer than that the trinitarian ideas out of which the various Trinities grew, whether Ethnic or Christian, have a common origin in man's religious consciousness. But the Christian Trinity, as fully developed, has a character of its own, and two radically opposite forms of it, as the history has shown, are distinctly revealed, — the tritheistic and the monistic or Sabellian. The point to which I wish to call special attention here is the fact that neither of these forms of trinitarian dogma are reconcilable with monotheism. Tritheistic Trinitarianism makes three divine Beings, Father, Son, and Holy Ghost, form in some metaphysical way one God. Such a doctrine cannot be made monotheistic. *Three* personal Gods cannot by any logical twist be made to equal *one* personal God. We know how Origen and Athanasius attempted to unite a monotheistic doctrine with Trinitarianism. Subordinationism was the magic word. But if there are three divine Beings, though subordinate to each other, how can it be said that God is one? Such a trinitarianism must involve tritheism. As to the Sabellian or monistic Trinitarianism, it is really no trinitarianism at all, but simply a pantheistic cloak under which theologians have striven to hide their unitarian tendencies. To speak of Father, Son, and

Holy Ghost as a Trinity, and to mean by them only three modes of operation of the one personal God, is simply to play hide and seek with language.

What now has the new inductive theology to say to such trinitarian orthodoxy? Simply this: that it is unhistorical and irrational, and further, a dogma to which the religious consciousness does not respond; for, as we have seen, the new theology is bound to be monotheistic. Dogmatic Trinitarianism is either polytheistic or pantheistic in its very nature and must be classed philosophically in one or the other of these positions, however hard theologians may struggle against it. But the true voices through which God speaks to men, the voices of nature and history and man's own moral being, the voices of Scripture and Christ, are in a different strain. They speak only of God as a single personal holy and loving being. It may be, as some think, that there is no such God at all; but one thing is certain, that the media of divine revelation all point that way, and such a Being is the only one that man's moral nature can grasp and love and worship.

Thus the old feud between the Trinitarian and Unitarian has lost it vigor, simply because the theological springs that fed it have dried up. The very terms "trinitarian" and "unitarian" have no longer any other than a historical antiquarian significance. The one was the correlate of the other. Neither has any meaning without the other. His-

tory with its potent dissolving force has destroyed
the very weapons with which the old combatants
fought. The theological assumptions on which
Stuart and Channing stood together, while disa-
greeing as to the conclusions to be drawn from
them, have utterly perished, and there is no ground
left on which the battle may proceed. The very
watchwords and signals of orthodoxy or heterodoxy
have lost their old significance. "Trinitarian" and
"Unitarian" have no place in the vocabulary of
the new theology. Of the two terms, "Unitarian"
etymologically contains the most of truth, for on
one side, at least, it stands squarely for the single
personality of God. But it suffers, as does its
counterpart "Trinitarian," from the history that
lies behind it, and cannot easily be disconnected
from it, and therefore is not a word to interpret
the new theology. "Theism," or more strictly
"monotheism," is the only word that is free from
the danger of misunderstanding or reproach.

CHAPTER XIII

THE NEW CHRISTOLOGY

THERE remains the christology of the old theology, or the doctrine of Christ's person. This has always been made an adjunct of the doctrine of God, and thus becomes an appendix of the dogma of the Trinity. The doctrine of Christ's true deity having been settled, there arose the question of his humanity. Hence the Chalcedon definition, by which the dogma of the God-man was set forth as one Person subsisting in two distinct natures. The attempt was thus made to bridge the chasm between the divine and the human by the incarnation of God in human nature in such a way that all the divine attributes were preserved, while the human attributes of a man were assumed. Jesus Christ was therefore wholly God and wholly man, that is, the God-man. How such a bald antinomy could have been adopted by theologians who were adepts in the Aristotelian and Platonic philosophies is truly a marvel. The real explanation is that it was forced upon them by the exigencies of the political as well as the theological situation. Two great parties were opposed to each other, one defending the unity of Christ's person, the other its duality. The Chalcedon definition cut the Gordian knot by its dogma of one person in two natures. I have already explained the theological contradiction here involved. To say that God as a personal divine being is so united by a miraculous incarnation and birth with a human being or nature that the two are henceforth personally one, and are equally both God and man, is equivalent to saying that $1=2$, or, to put it psychologically, that there is in Christ a complete human nature with all the attributes and qualities of such a nature, and yet with no distinct human personality, or, still again, to show on another side its contradictory character, that the God-man, Jesus Christ, is both omniscient and ignorant, omnipotent and not omnipotent, eternal and temporal, eternally begotten and begotten in time, a Son of God and a son of man, having God as his Father in one way, and Joseph as his father, or at least Mary as his mother, in another way. Now what was the object of all this unhistorical and unscientific violation of logical and psychological laws? Simply to sustain the dogma of Christ's deity, and that also of the Trinity which had grown up around it.

And now we see why the doctrine of Christ's person has always been connected with *theology* in its more contracted sense, or the doctrine of God, and not with *anthropology*, or the doctrine of man. It is the divine side that is the essential side, and the human side is wholly sacrificed to it.

Christ is essential God, not essential man. It is the divine personality that rules him, not the human. All human traits are seeming, not real. His ignorance is only a seeming ignorance. All through the history of orthodoxy, Christ's humanity has been only a cloak to hide the reality of his deity. The recent theory of "Kenosis" is only a metaphysical makeshift to cover the real contradiction which in the older view stands out visibly to every intelligent eye.

How completely unhistorical all this is, the preceding chapters have shown, and it is scarcely needful to raise the question, what the new theology will say to it. With the old theology of the Trinity goes also the old christology, both resting upon the same speculative foundations. The inductive historical method brings Christ back to us as a true member of the human race, and turns christology into a branch of anthropology. But while he is thus historically a true man under human conditions, his moral eminence is not thereby at all endangered, nor his unique place among the media of divine revelation lost. It was not necessary that the moral consciousness of Christ should be divinized in order that he might become a true channel of God's gospel of love and grace. Rather would such a deifying of him have unfitted him for such a mission. Only through a human consciousness could God reveal himself to human beings. The most direct revelation of God's love to us is through a human love. If it were true that

God, in order to open a way of redemption to man, must become flesh and dwell among us, the only method would be to enter the human race in the natural ordinary way, and so completely ally himself with human conditions ; *not* by an unnatural miraculous act which would thereby separate him from the beings he came to save. Strange indeed that God, to become truly man, must come in such a way as to make men doubt whether he could be the man of true flesh and blood he was proclaiming himself to be, and, in doing it, break the very laws of his own creation ! Christ then, because human, does not cease to be the moral and religious leader of the race; and, though the old christology is reduced from theology to anthropology, there is left large scope for a new christology based on the scientific and historical facts connected with the evolution of human nature, especially on its moral and religious side. There is no limit that can be set to the growth of man's moral consciousness. Compare the unclothed savage of the cave-dwellers with the enlightened and cultured man of to-day; "and it doth not yet appear what we shall be." Why may not a man have appeared, in advance of his age and surroundings, so exceptional in moral development and consciousness as to become and remain a guide and example to his fellow men in all religious faith and conduct ? Such is a true inductive christology. All this talk of which the air to-day is so full, about the divineness of man, is really caught from the scientific law of evolution which shows man to be a progressive being, of unlimited capacity. Whittier only turned science into poetry when he wrote : —

> "And step by step since time began
> I see the steady gain of man."

No wonder, as he turned his gaze from the past and present to the future, that his prophetic vision gathered more and more of hope and cheer, and that he sang on : —

> "Through the harsh voices of our day
> A low sweet prelude finds its way.
> Through clouds of doubt and creeds of fear
> A light is breaking calm and clear."

Surely it is no mere poet's dream, that man is moving ever forward to higher and higher stages of intellectual and moral attainment. It is the last word of science itself, that what is best and divinest in our conceptions of God — his moral attributes of righteousness, truth, justice, love, mercy, and compassion — is within the reach of every son and daughter of our human race. The idea of Christ's divineness is but the prefigurement, in one illustrious supreme example, of the ultimate divinization of humanity itself. Nay, what does the daring hypothesis of Phillips Brooks — that there is an eternal humanity in God — mean, if not just this, that the divine Fatherhood, which man's moral consciousness feels intuitively and strives to bring within the ranges of his faith and love, is only the transcendent background and

picture eternally stamped in the nature of things
of man's own inextinguishable sense of sonship, —
a truth which Paul only echoed from Christ's
teaching when he called men " sons of God, and
if sons then heirs, heirs of God and joint heirs
with Christ." What is the difference between the
christology of Paul, when accurately measured,
and that of the new inductive theology? The
doctrine, supposed to be so original in theological
thought, of the consubstantiality of man with God,
is merely a metaphysical exposition from a monistic point of view of an old truth, and when reduced to its lowest terms means simply that man
was created in the divine image, and is capable of
rising by unending stages of progress towards God
himself. On such a basis metaphysics and science
may meet and " kiss each other," — the only difference being that while metaphysical theology proceeds in a pantheistic way from the divineness of
God to the divineness of man, the new inductive
theology proceeds from man as under a law of historical evolution that involves a continuous upward
moral progress to God as the end of that progress.
Those words which Athanasius uttered from the
standpoint of the Platonic dualism, " Christ was
made man that man might be made divine,"´the
new theology may accept from the standpoint of
scientific evolution. Dr. Lyman Abbott, in his
Lowell lectures on the " Evolution of Christianity," expressly excepted Christ from the law of
evolution which he made universal in its range

outside of him. But this is to destroy the very order of history and the world. There can be no exception to this order. Nor is it needed. That Christ may be a moral leader of the race, he must be under the law of race evolution, and so a member of it. But this is not to take away with one hand what is given by the other. Moral leadership and supremacy does not involve or necessitate a metaphysical chasm between such a leader and those he leads. From the standpoint of man's generic relationship with God, bearing in mind also that law of evolution by which individuals of the race may rise above their fellows in moral and intellectual advance, as we may speak of all men as having in them an element of divinity, so we may speak of Christ as diviner than other men and more closely related to God, and so the Son of God in a peculiar sense, without however differentiating him from other men, as if he did not belong with them to a common human species. The old dualism which drew a hard-and-fast line of separation between the divine and the human is certainly put out of court by scientific monism as the result of the law of natural evolution. The moral nature and attributes of God and man are essentially one. The moral divineness of man is a natural corollary. The peculiar divineness of Christ follows as a matter of course, if his moral consciousness was more complete, and rose to higher and clearer spheres of vision. The truth is that the new science and history, with their

common law of evolution, have given the religious
thinker an entirely new point of view from which
to behold God and his relations to men, together
with the mediatorial function of Christ. The
chasm which Athanasius fixed between God and
his moral creatures is gone. The true dualistic
chasm is not between God and man, but between
man and the material world. For between God
and matter there can be no moral relationship or
unity. But if human beings are created in the
divine image, as all the media of revelation prove,
then there is a scientifically and historically true
sense in which they are generically divine. They
are indeed " partakers of the divine nature ; " and
if the degree and measure of moral consciousness
be the true standard, as it must be, of that " par-
taking," then Christ surely must be in the highest
sense divine. But this does not separate him from
us. Rather is the closeness of his moral relationship with us increased. No bond is so close as
love. But " he loved us," as no other has, " and
gave himself for us." Not in kind, but in degree
only, is he differentiated from us. Dr. Abbott, in
asserting this, was on firm historical ground.

It is interesting to note, in passing, how a cycle
of theological thought that is in process of dissolu-
tion connects itself with a new cycle that begins as
the result of a radical revolution. The consubstantiality of man with God as a metaphysical conception belongs to an old and outworn theology,
but, in the new form of the scientific doctrine of

evolution, the divineness of man becomes a vital truth, and out of it arises a christology that removes Jesus of Nazareth indeed from the order of Absolute Deity, but at the same time exalts him to a place of moral eminence that is secure and supreme.

CHAPTER XIV

THE NEW CHRISTIAN ATONEMENT

THERE is one other doctrine of the old theology that is directly connected with its christology, and in fact is built upon it, which cannot here be left unnoticed, since it is made practically the central note of that theology as a whole. I refer to the doctrine of the atonement. Perhaps there is no better example of the law of historical evolution, when once it begins to work, than this one of the evolution of the old orthodox doctrine of the atonement. There are three distinct stages of growth of the doctrine in the New Testament writings. The first stage is the teaching of Christ himself; the second is that of Paul; the third is found in the Epistle to the Hebrews. It should be said at the outset that the term "atonement" in its traditional orthodox meaning of a propitiatory sacrifice occurs once only in the King James version, while in the new revised version it gives place to the word "*reconciliation*," which is the right translation of καταλλαγή. This word, with its corresponding verb, καταλλάσσω, is used nine times by Paul, but appears nowhere else in the New Testament. The Greek term properly means a change from

enmity to friendship, as when Paul wrote : " Let
the wife remain unmarried or be *reconciled* to her
husband." This is the plain meaning, also, in all
the other uses of it by Paul. Moreover, in Paul's
view the reconciliation was to proceed from man
to God, not from God to man, as is shown in the
passage in 2 Corinthians v. 18, 19, where Paul
speaks of God as " reconciling men to himself,
not imputing their trespasses unto them." Paul
regards the whole redemptive process as starting
from God, who through Christ gave his ministers
" the ministry of reconciliation." According to
this doctrine, God needed no mediatorial expiatory
sacrifice or offering in order to his reconcilement
with man, but initiated a movement to bring about
the reconcilement of man to himself. This of
course is not the old orthodox doctrine of atonement at all. Paul's view of reconciliation is essentially that of Christ, though he adds a new
feature, as we shall see.

As to Christ's own view, he had no conception
of an atonement in its sacrificial sense as a blood
offering for sin. He protested against the bloody
sacrifices of the Mosaic law, as having in themselves any efficacy in taking away sin. He made
little of the temple rites that were still continued
in his day. " One greater than the temple is
here," he said in protest against the Pharisaic
traditions of his day, by which the letter of the
law had been raised above its spirit, adding " but
if ye had known what this meaneth, ' I desire

mercy and not sacrifice,' ye would not have condemned the guiltless." His own doctrine of sacrifice was that of the later prophets and psalmists,
the sacrifice of the heart, the self-sacrifice of love.
This was to him the meaning of the cross. It
was the emblem of a sacrifice of self for others
even unto death. Such sacrifice was the highest
form of righteous living, it was salvation. " He
that loseth his life shall save it." Later literalistic
interpretation has seized on the term " ransom "
which Christ once casually used, and has made it
to mean a propitiatory vicarious sacrifice.[1] But
this is to strain its real significance, as the context
shows, and as all Christ's other teachings also
show. Christ was declaring that his true mission
" was not to be ministered unto but to minister."
It was a mission of service for others even to the
point of giving his life, and the power of such a
service in his view was its moral effect on men,
not its sacrificial effect on God, as if there could
be any remission of sin by the shedding of blood.
Christ never taught such a doctrine. It was as
far as possible from his own point of view. " I,
if I be lifted up from the earth, will draw all men
unto me." The effect of his death was to move
men's hearts by the spectacle of love, not to propitiate and satisfy the divine wrath or law. His
doctrine of God's attitude to man was that of a
Father ready to forgive every penitent, not that

[1] See appendix C. on Prof. Pfleiderer's article in the *New World*.

of an offended Being who demanded a ransom in
the way of a bloody sacrifice. Such a view of God
was repugnant to him. The later doctrine of a
mediator who comes between two parties that are
estranged in order to reconcile them by the shedding of his blood seems never to have occurred to
him. His parable of the prodigal son, which contains the very essence of his whole gospel, has no
mediation element. No third person comes in between the father and his prodigal child, and none
is needed. How would the whole significance and
pathos of the story have been destroyed, had a
third person been introduced to make peace between them. What Christ taught in this parable
was not a substitutional atonement, but immediate
at-one-ment. The father and his wayward son
were made one directly and without any go-between.
How clearly and touchingly is this fact brought
out in the story! The prodigal, already penitent,
is on the way to his father's house. What now
does the father do? Does he send a messenger to
state the terms on which he will allow his son's
return? Not so. "While he was yet a great way
off his father saw him and was moved with compassion and ran and fell on his neck and kissed
him." Such is the gospel method of reconciliation.
What a travesty upon it was the later doctrine of
atonement that usurped its place! That doctrine
is not Christian, but Jewish and Pagan. It rests
on one of the earliest superstitions of the race,
viz., that God may be appeased or propitiated by

offerings, especially by such as involve the death
of the victim.   The more costly and precious the
sacrifice, the more efficacious it would be.   Hence
human sacrifices were common on extraordinary
occasions.   With growing civilization and enlightenment, the practice of offering human victims
became obsolete, and generally libations and cakes
took the place of the more bloody forms of animal
sacrifice.   It is one of the astonishing facts of history that Christian theology should have seized on
such a relic of barbarism, and should have incorporated it, in its grossest form of a human victim,
into its doctrine of redemption.   Plainly pagan as
this whole atonement doctrine is, it was the more
readily accepted as an article of Christian belief
by the uncritical use of passages of Scripture
which were interpreted, on the principle of " an-
alogy of faith," as representing Christ's own doctrine.   But historical criticism has demolished this
principle of interpretation, and with it go the doctrines built upon it.   Critical scholars no longer
regard Christ as thinking or declaring himself
" the lamb of God " in any sacrificial sense, because
the author of the fourth Gospel makes John the
Baptist call him so, or because the Revelation,
once ascribed to John the Apostle, employs the
same term so frequently.   Both of these writings
represent a later stage of evolution of doctrine,
when there was a falling back on Jewish conceptions of sacrifice, and when anticipations of Christian ideas were sought in the Old Testament.   But

behind all such exegetical perversions there still come clearly to view Christ's own original teachings. The story of the prodigal son can never be blotted out of man's heart, and on it will rise the new theology of man's at-one-ment with God.

The *second* stage of evolution began with Paul. While holding to Christ's teaching of at-one-ment rather than atonement, Paul introduced a new element which practically changed the point of view of the whole doctrine. This element he derived from Greek philosophy, viz., the mediation doctrine of the Platonic dualism, which in Philo was developed into the Logos doctrine and afterward in this form made such a figure in Christian trinitarian theology. The Greek term μεσίτης (mediator) as a New Testament expression first appears in Paul. It had already been employed in Philo to designate the mediating character of the Logos. Jewish theology had no such dualistic theory, and never developed a Logos mediation doctrine. Hence its entire absence from Christ's teaching. In this, as in many other respects, Paul was the real founder of dogmatic Christian theology. He introduced into it elements of Greek speculative thought and created for it a new philosophical basis. Christ became to him a sort of middle being between God and man, like the Logos of Philo, and hence a new feature was introduced into his view of the reconciliation of man with God, that, namely, of a go-between or mediator. It was through Christ, as such a go-between, that God reconciled man to himself.

But Paul went no further. The character of the
mode of reconciliation was not essentially changed.
God's love is still behind all.   It is true that Paul
occasionally employs the sacrificial language of the
Old Testament in setting forth the gospel doctrine
of redemption.   This is not surprising when we
consider his rabbinical education.   His mind was
steeped in Old Testament ideas and imagery, and
he constantly recurs to them in his explanations of
the new gospel that he had received.   But to take
such language literally is to mistake Paul's whole
meaning.   Take, for example, the term " righteousness," and observe in the Romans how he gives to
it an entirely new gospel meaning.   The gospel
righteousness is not the old righteousness of law
and wrath, but the newly revealed righteousness of
love and mercy.   Hence Paul opposed the Jewish
legalism in which he had been brought up, and
proclaimed the new doctrine of a righteousness or
ground of acceptance with God, which was not
of works but of faith.   Just so in his use of the
terms " wrath," " propitiation," " redeem," " justify."   They formed a part of the old sacrificial
language, but a new sense was given them.   A
crucial passage is that in Romans v.   Here, as
elsewhere, God himself is made the ultimate source
of the redemptive process.   " God commended his
own love toward us, in that, while we were yet sinners, Christ died for us.   Much more then, being
justified by his blood, shall we be saved from the
wrath (of God) through him.   For if, while we

were enemies, we were reconciled to God through the death of his Son, much more, being reconciled, shall we be saved by his life." Here Paul plainly sets forth the doctrine of a mediatorial sacrifice as the way of reconciliation between man and God. So far he was still a Jew. But does he here hold that Christ's death had for its object to change God's attitude from one of enmity and anger to reconcilement and love? Surely not. God's own love was behind Christ's death, and the object of that death was to change man's attitude from one of enmity, as the result of sin, to one of reconcilement and restored sonship. The key of the true interpretation is lost, if it is not noted that Paul employs the old sacrificial language in a new Christian sense, — a key that Paul himself has given in the previous chapters of the Epistle. "Wrath," for example, is no longer a divine anger that demands a bloody expiation and atonement, but is changed by the gospel into a new revelation of divine love shining through Christ's sacrifice and seeking man's salvation. Thus interpreted, the passage is in complete harmony with Paul's other statements concerning the ground and process of reconciliation between man and God. His doctrine everywhere is that God's own love is the procuring cause of Christ's mission, and that its object was not to propitiate the divine feeling, but to reconcile mankind to God, by the display of the divine mercy in the sacrifice of Calvary.

But while Paul thus introduced an entirely new

element into Christ's teaching, viz., that of a mediator and of a mediatorial sacrifice, his doctrine
must be carefully distinguished from the *third*
stage in the evolution of the traditional dogma of
the atonement, which first appears in the Epistle
to the Hebrews.   Here for the first and only time
in the New Testament Christ is made not merely a
μεσίτης or mediating principle, but *a sacrificial
victim to propitiate God*.   The whole Jewish and
Pagan theory of bloody offerings to expiate sin is
squarely affirmed and applied.   All the Old Testament sacrifices are made antitypes of the one
great sacrifice made by Christ himself.   "Without
the shedding of blood," it is declared, "there is no
remission."   "Christ hath been manifested to put
away sin by the sacrifice of himself."   "For it is
impossible that the blood of bulls and goats should
take away sin."   But the blood of Christ does thus
avail.   "We have been sanctified through the offering of the body of Jesus Christ once for all."
Here then appears in fully developed form the
new Christian version of the old Jewish and Pagan
doctrine of the efficacy of a blood offering to God
to take away sin, and make God propitious to men.
Note how Paul's mediation theory is changed.   The
"mediator" no longer represents God's love and
mercy in the effort to reconcile men to God, but
becomes a representative of men to intercede with
God, who is offended and wrathful and needs to be
appeased.   The reconciliation is not manward, as
Paul always puts it, but Godward.   It is not man

who is to be reconciled, but God. It is to the Epistle to the Hebrews, then, that we owe the traditional orthodox doctrine of the atonement. Its adoption was helped by the tradition that the Epistle was written by Paul and so expressed his own view. So uncritical were those times in the matter of external as well as internal evidence.

It is impossible here to give any extended survey of the further evolution of this doctrine. Little attention was paid to it in the early church. Irenæus, however, struck the keynote of the Epistle to the Hebrews in declaring that "God was offended with us," and in making this the ground of Christ's work of atonement. Anselm's "Cur Deus Homo" laid the foundations of the mediæval doctrine of the atonement. He held to the Godward view, though he made it the divine law and justice that demanded a satisfaction or full equivalent for man's violation of that law, rather than the divine offended feeling. But in the later Catholic doctrine the divine wrath became prominent. Thomas Aquinas, the great Catholic theologian, held that Christ's sufferings were "penal," — Christ taking the place of sinful men and suffering punishment in their stead. Calvin, whose theology has had such prevailing influence in New England, held extreme views on the subject of the atonement. Christ "was destined to appease the wrath of God by his sacrifice." "God was our enemy, until He was reconciled to us by Christ." "He took the punishment on himself, and bore what by the just

judgment of God was impending over sinners;
with his own blood expiated the sins which rendered them hateful to God." The later Protestant reaction to the so-called "governmental" or
"moral" theories is in the line of a return to Paul,
and the at-one-ment or manward view. But this
is to be said about all such modern views that they
are still based on the mediation doctrine which
Paul introduced from Greek dualistic philosophy,
and stop short of Christ's own teaching.

What now the new theology will do with the
Greek metaphysical theory of the necessity of a
semi-divine μεσίτης or mediator between God and
man, who must offer his life as a sacrifice to atone
for human sin, may be easily determined. The
inductive historical method immediately raises
such questions as these : Did Christ authentically
teach any such doctrine ? Is any sacrificial atonement necessary to enable God to forgive every
penitent soul ? Is not forgiveness a moral act
that spontaneously follows, by a law of moral
nature and necessity, every act of repentance ?
Does not the petition in the Lord's prayer, " Forgive us our trespasses, as we forgive them that
trespass against us," rest on this assumption ?
Further, is not man's moral relationship to God so
close and complete as to render such a metaphysical mediation needless ? And if it is such a theological necessity, why did not Christ teach it in
his parable of the prodigal son ? Such questions
show what the central point of difference between

the old theology and the new must be.   It is as to
the *character* of the mediation required in the
relation of man to God and of God to man, and
especially in the matter of the moral separation
brought about by sin.   The old theology insists on
the necessity of a *metaphysical* mediatorship, and
declares that Christ as a sufficient mediator must
be a divine being.   The new theology dismisses at
once the metaphysical speculations of Greek philosophy and its dualistic mediation theory, but
allows a *moral* or spiritual mediation principle as
running through the moral kingdom.   The spiritual relationship of all moral beings involves a
mediation element.   Motherhood is the earliest
illustration to every child.   Souls are always mediating between other souls.   Christ above all
others was such a messianic mediator.   His teaching was full of mediating elements.   The parable
of the prodigal son has been the mediating bridge
over which many a soul has crossed to find itself
at home in the Father's house.   Such a mediation
doctrine is true to nature and history and human
experience.   At-one-ment is often brought about
by the intervention of a third person.   But this is
not traditional orthodoxy, which claims that the
only available mediation between sinful man and
God is through a Divine Person who becomes
incarnate, and makes atonement for sin by a bloody
death.   History declares such a view to be essentially Pagan and Jewish and a product of speculative thought, not of historical fact.   The historical

account of Christ's death contains no visible element of a propitiatory atoning sacrifice. He was executed as a criminal, with two other criminals, by Roman soldiers at the command of a Roman governor. How utterly unhistorical is it to turn such a death into an expiatory sacrifice for human sin to satisfy a broken law or propitiate an offended Deity! Such a sacrifice demands an altar, a priest, a rite of worship, as in the story of Abraham's attempted sacrifice of Isaac. Of course the answer of the defender of the traditional doctrine is that under the veil of the outward history of Christ's death there is a revelation of God's method of redemption of man, by which Christ's death was made essential, in the form of a propitiatory sacrifice. But history shows that this whole doctrine of a substitutional propitiatory sacrifice in man's behalf in order to satisfy or appease an offended or angry God, or to enable God to exercise and manifest his disposition of love and forgiveness, is not the teaching of Christ himself, or deducible at all from the facts of his death, but part of a historical inheritance from primitive barbarous times. The sacrificial system of the Old Testament is simply an illustration of practices that were well-nigh universal in the ancient world. The theory of the Jewish sacrifices was that of the peoples around them, viz., that God needed to be propitiated by bloody offerings in order to appease his anger or secure his favor. The character of Jehovah, as indicated by the Jewish sacrificial rites, was like that of a human being, subject to passion and affected by gifts. Hence all those anthropomorphic expressions so frequent in the Old Testament, in which God is described as repenting, becoming angry, etc., and moved by prayers. All this anthropomorphism is a relic of the primitive religious conceptions of the race. Plato in the " Republic " quotes from some earlier writer a saying that well illustrates this anthropomorphic view: " Gifts persuade the gods, and reverend kings." It is true that the Hebrew system of sacrifices put into prominence the sinfulness of the people, and thus introduced an ethical element that was fruitful in later times. But a like element had its place in all the ethnic religions and sacrificial cults. What made the gods objects of fear in part, though not wholly, was the sense of sin and of consequent need of atonement by way of substitutional offerings. The sacrificial rites in all the religions of the ancient world were the direct results of the development of the moral consciousness of men. The account of the sacrifices offered by Cain and Abel in the beginning of Genesis shows how quickly the sacrificial idea took shape in the traditions of the human race. It was one of the most remarkable facts concerning Christ's teaching that he so completely spiritualized the whole Mosaic law of sacrifice and thus showed how thoroughly he had imbibed the spirit of the great prophets before him. As we have seen, his only doctrine of sacrifice was that of a self-sacrificing heart which led one to give himself wholly for others. But Paul, as we have seen, fell back on the Jewish sacrificial tradition, and he was followed in this by the writer of the Epistle to the Hebrews. Thus it is plain that the Christian dogma of the atonement is a direct historical evolution of Jewish and Ethnic sacrificial rites and ideas.

As to the moral effect of such ideas and rites, the history of all religions gives terrible and conclusive evidence. Principal Fairbairn, in his recent address before the International Congregational Council in Boston on " The Influence of Other Religions on Christian Theology," fresh as he was from the study of the ethnic religions, well said: " The rites of appeasement or propitiation are in all religions the focus of the forces that materialize and deprave." The history of mankind justifies this statement ; and Dr. Fairbairn scarcely needed to add: "This is no rash generalization ; it is simple, stern, indubitable fact." I would say, further, that the history of the Christian dogma of the atonement forms no exception. There is no dogma of Christian theology that has had so baneful an influence on the character of Christendom, or that has led to such terrible results. The view of God, involved in that dogma, as a Being that was propitiated by a bloody sacrifice, that delighted in material expiations and punishments, and that was angry and revengeful toward the objects of his displeasure, had the effect to develop in Christian believers the same traits of character. When we have examined the pictures of God, and even of Christ, in those horrible representations of hell and of the torments of the lost, on the walls of the mediæval churches, it is easy to understand how Christians could persecute each other so cruelly, and believe that in doing it they were doing God service.

But it may be insisted that the Christian doctrine of the atonement differs essentially from all previous sacrificial conceptions. Dr. Fairbairn seems to be of this opinion, for he proceeds to draw the contrast between the sacrifice of Christ and all other sacrifices. But it is noticeable that his points of contrast do not affect the radical relationship of the Christian dogma to ethnic sacrificial ideas. His *first* point is that Christ's sacrifice was essentially a divine, not a human sacrifice. " God takes it out of the hands of man and offers it himself. Its qualities are all ethical, for they are all of Him." But of course Dr. Fairbairn holds that Christ's sacrifice was made in a true human nature and through a true human shedding of blood and death. " Its qualities " then were *not* "all ethical," any more than those of other human or material sacrifices. The whole dogma of propitiatory sacrifices involves and necessitates a material element. So the Epistle to the Hebrews declares that " without the shedding of blood there is no remission," and makes the contrast between the Old Testament sacrifices of bulls

and goats and that of Christ on the cross to consist in this, that Christ was a higher being, and
therefore a more precious and acceptable offering
to God, than animals, which were only types and
symbols of the true sacrifice on Calvary. The
contrast then lies in the character of the victim,
not in the form and character of the sacrifice,
which in both cases requires a real bloody offering.
Now it is precisely this feature of the necessity of
a bloody sacrifice, involving a violent death, that
makes all such propitiatory rites, as Dr. Fairbairn
himself declares, "the focus of the forces that
materialize and deprave," and it is this very feature which forms the essence of all the ethnic
sacrifices that became the vital characteristic of
the orthodox dogma of the atonement. According
to that dogma God could not bring about a reconciliation between himself and mankind without a
human sacrifice and death which was the only basis
of such a reconciliation. It was also equally necessary that the victim should be divine as well as
human. Hence the incarnation of God in the
person of his Son, who entered human nature by a
miraculous birth and so was able to give up a true
human life on the cross as a sacrificial offering for
sin. What now is the peculiarity of the Christian
dogma as compared with all ethnic ideas? Simply
this, that the sacrifice on Calvary was precious
beyond all comparison with any sacrifice of a mere
human being. Christ's death was both a human
sacrifice and a divine sacrifice, whereas all other

sacrifices, even the most precious, are only human. Is then the radical character of the offering changed? Not at all. That view which rests at the bottom of those degrading human sacrifices which a later civilization cast away is also the very basis of the old Christian orthodoxy.

But Dr. Fairbairn will attempt to meet this by his *second* point of contrast, viz., that God in Christ offered atonement " once for all." " It can never be repeated: man can never share in it." But if Jesus was a real man, certainly man *did* " share in it" once at least. Of course Dr. Fairbairn gets this point from the Epistle to the Hebrews. If Christ was God himself, surely no repetition of such a sacrifice was needed. Is this really Dr. Fairbairn's own christology? However that may be, the fact that no repetition of Christ's propitiatory sacrifice is needed does not at all affect the question as to the character of the *one* sacrifice on Calvary, or remove it from its historical place in the category of bloody offerings. Nor is it true that there has been no repetition of Christ's sacrifice in the history of the church dogma of atonement. The theory of a *repeated* sacrifice of Christ as taking place whenever the Lord's Supper was celebrated came in very early in Christian faith, and culminated in the dogma of the Mass, in which it was believed that the very body and blood of Christ were present in the bread and wine and sacrificed afresh for the saving of souls. It required the Protestant Reformation to

break that superstition, and that movement was
only partial, and how many Protestants as well as
Catholics there are to-day who piously believe that
in some supernatural mystical way the Lord's Supper involves a true repetition of the one sacrifice
of the cross! And can all this be "the truth as it
is in Jesus"? How clear is the answer of history,
and also of the moral consciousness of mankind?
The simple picture of the death of Christ is indeed
infinitely tragic and pathetic, and it has made him
the unique martyr of history. But the essence of
every true human martyrdom is the same. What
then is the secret of the peculiar tragicalness of
the death on Calvary? Not surely the external
circumstances of suffering, pathetic as they were.
Such dying experiences have been repeated again
and again, with severer and more prolonged ago-
nies. Christ paid the debt of nature as all of
human kind have done or must do. What makes
that death so supremely impressive is the manner
in which it was brought about. The crucifixion
on Calvary was the tragic end of a career that has
moved the world's heart by its complete devotion
to others and to the truth of God, and by the new
gospel of divine love that was proclaimed to men,
so that as we gaze upon the cross of martyrdom,
we are compelled to say: "No man ever lived or
died like this man." The spectacle of such a life
and death draws on human sympathy and love and
gratitude as nothing else can. It is indeed what
Paul declared it to be, "the power of God unto

salvation." But change the picture, and substitute for it the picture of orthodox tradition, viz., of a divine propitiation offered to God in the guise of a human sacrificial death, and how irresistibly are we carried back to the rude and superstitious materialism of the ancient world, from which mankind has been slowly rising through these long centuries. How difficult and slow the moral and religious progress of the world has been history amply illustrates. Even to-day materialism and superstition are large factors in religious faith. But true religion is a purely moral condition and experience. At-one-ment and mediation are moral events. They belong to the realm of spiritual realities, not to the order of material things. Bloodshedding and death cannot in themselves have any moral meaning. It was Christ's spirit of sacrifice, his gift of himself, that made his death on the cross an event of the highest moral significance. It was his life rather than his death that has given him his moral supremacy in the world. Nor did the power of that life end with his death. His work was no transient spectacle, but one that has entered vitally and permanently into human history, regenerating and sanctifying it. His at-one-ment and mediation in their most blessed forms are going on still in the persons of his true disciples of every age, in whom his spirit is exhibited, and from whom it flows as a lifegiving stream into humanity.

CHAPTER XV

THE LEADING FEATURES AND BENEFITS OF THE NEW THEOLOGY

WE have thus sketched a few of the lines along which the new theology will advance towards its historical completion. Further it is not permitted us to go. But looking backward over the way we have gone, it is easy to see what the leading features of the new theology will be, and what special religious benefits it will confer on thinking men. *First*, it will serve to stay the pantheistic current of thought that now threatens to engulf us. The real conflict to-day is not between the Trinitarian and the Unitarian, as some theologians would still have us believe, but between the Theist and the Pantheist. Philosophical monism cannot stop short of religious pantheism. Nor can the reason, on its intellectual side, here help us. Metaphysic only plunges us the more deeply into the abyss we dread. Witness the abortive efforts of theological thinkers who walk the metaphysical path to save themselves from the pantheistic consequences of their own philosophical premises. Help here can come only from man's moral consciousness. That consciousness intuitively testifies to the eternal reality of theism. The personal soul distinguishes itself with irresistible energy from the world around, and even from its own bodily environment. History, which gathers up the total individual experience of the human race, speaks in clear tones for the theistic doctrine, and it is history that forms the bone and sinew of the new theology. It will be more fully recognized some day what a blessing history has wrought for this age, in breaking the reign of metaphysic, and dissolving the pantheistic mists and vapors that have gathered around it, as about some mountain peak.

Secondly, the new theology will also help to stay the tide of materialism which is setting so strongly, and to build the foundation of a true spiritual philosophy. Materialism is only another phase of monistic pantheism, but deserves special consideration. If monism be scientifically and philosophically accepted, there can be but one result, resist it as you will. If there is but one original substance in the universe, and that either mind or matter, and mind is evolved from matter or matter from mind, if, I say, one horn of this dilemma must be chosen, there is no doubt what the choice must be. The universal law of scientific and historic evolution is ever from lower to higher, from matter to mind, and materialism is our only refuge. But here again man's moral consciousness utters its fixed ineradicable protest against such a philosophical result. It declares itself not only individual and personal, but, in

doing this, also declares itself a spiritual, and not
a material, being. Theism is spiritualism; pantheism is bound to be materialism at last. The
new theology will stand on the affirmations of
man's moral consciousness, and of history which is
its great interpreter. In doing this, it takes issue
not only with philosophic monism in any of its
forms, but also with the inherent tendencies of the
old theology, which has always reduced to a mini-
mum the spiritual elements of religion. A cursory
glance at it shows at once what a thoroughly
materialistic shaping is given to most of its dogmas. Its doctrine of God is materialistic, making
Him a God of wrath and vengeance and readiness
to inflict material suffering on the objects of his
displeasure. Its doctrine of man and of sin is
materialistic, treating sin as a hereditary taint of
fallen human nature, in which all the descendants
of Adam are involved. So with its doctrine of
atonement, which is accomplished by a human-
divine sacrifice to propitiate an offended God.
And so with its eschatological doctrines, — the
personal second coming of Christ in the clouds of
heaven, the bodily resurrection of mankind, a
local material heaven and hell. If any one doubts
this, let him read a few of the sermons of John
Wesley and of Jonathan Edwards. By such terrible descriptions of God's dealings with sinners the
moral sense is shocked, and cries out against them.
All these materialistic forms of dogma the new
theology dismisses at once. They are wholly in-

consistent with the moral character of God, as revealed in man's own moral consciousness, and with the moral laws which govern his kingdom.

Thirdly, the new theology will draw the line sharply between *faith as a religious act* and *belief as an intellectual act*. The day when creeds are treated as articles and expressions of religious faith is passing by. The idea so deeply rooted in the old theology that there is salvation in a creed received its death-blow when the history of the creeds of the church and of the manner of their formation was truly written. The law of historical evolution has also destroyed the closely allied idea that the church of the early centuries was competent to decide and fix the dogmas of religious belief for all time. Do we go to the third and fourth centuries of the Christian era for our science, our astronomy, our geology, our philosophy, our history? Why then should we go to them for our religious dogmas? The ancient creeds are like the fossiliferous strata of the earth's surface, which contain rather the records of decay and death than living beings. A creed is mostly a like record of dead issues, not a living gospel. Hence the new theology must reject all creeds as religious tests, and can accept them only as historical testimonials of the religious beliefs of earlier times. It sharply distinguishes religious faith from religious knowledge, love for Christ and truth from opinions about Christ and truth. Its only religious *Credo* is one of the heart, not of the speculative reason, and Paul's words would well state it : " But now abideth faith, hope, love, these three, and the greatest of these is love." *In the new theology the old unadjusted antagonism between faith and reason ceases forever.*

It is pleasant, as we conclude this chapter, to turn away from the past, and catch a glimpse of what is to come. For there is surely a bright future for theology as a science of religion. Like other sciences it must ever remain incomplete, even more so than its sisters, because its materials are less available and less easily concatenated into systematic form, and because new materials from larger horizons are continually being added. But when wholly freed from its traditional fetters and based on the inductive method, it will become the noblest department of philosophy. For philosophy theology essentially is. Examine any history of philosophy, and see how intertwined the two terms are. Philosophy may be the more extensive of the two, if theology is limited to the more specific doctrine of God. But if anthropology and the doctrine of creation be included in theology, as they usually are, what radical difference is there between them? For nature, man, and God exhaust the materials of philosophy as well as theology. There is no object of thought beyond. Practically, however, philosophy deals more with speculative metaphysics, and theology more with vital Christian beliefs. But theology may become as speculative as philosophy, and this was true in fact all through the dogmatic period of Christian history.   But when the dogmatic yoke has been completely broken, and theology shall have found its true place as a form of philosophic thought, its golden age will begin.   Even in the past, in spite of persecution and dogmatic bitterness, human thought has achieved noble results in its efforts to find the secret of the universe, of man, and of God.   Such illustrious thinkers as Socrates, Plato, Aristotle, Origen, Plotinus, Athanasius, Augustine, John Scotus Erigena, Abelard, Francis Bacon, are immortal.   What names the future has in store its unrolling scroll of history only will tell.   But that they will be even greater and more illustrious we are as sure as that light and knowledge will increase with more and more rapid strides, and that philosophy will attain more and more of grasp and certainty.

CHAPTER XVI

CONCLUSION

THE historical situation, as thus surveyed, leaves us on the verge of a limitless future of progress toward still higher and better historical results. History itself, we are coming to see, is perhaps, beyond all other modes of divine revelation, the grand interpreter of God and his ways with man. And as its principles and processes are better understood, and its spirit of prophecy gets surer footing, the outlook to the historical observer becomes more and more realistic and inspiring. How vast and wonderful is the outlook to-day compared with that of ancient or even mediæval times! How contracted their view of nature and its phenomena as compared with ours! What worlds upon worlds have come within our gaze into the heavens of which they never even dreamed! Just so with our *historical* outlook as compared with theirs. For them no law of evolution explained, as it does for us, the intimate relations of the past and the future so clearly that they could become true seers of events still far off and invisible. Pessimism is a false note of the historic spirit. Progress in ever-ascending stages is the last word

of historical as well as scientific evolution. There
may be reactions and revolutions, but they are
only the convulsions that are needed to prepare
the way for new eras of higher and fuller life.
The final cause and end is good, and step by step
that end is kept in view. The seed is before the
plant, the bud before the flower, the instinct of
the brute before the reason of man, man himself
before the angels. But that man shall "be as the
angels" is the final end. What heights of intellectual and moral life have been reached that to
the early savage were utterly inconceivable! But
humanity is not yet at the end of its career. The
evolution must go on. There is no room for pessimism in such a view. The real pessimists of
to-day are those who cling to the past with all its
unhistorical and traditional rubbish, and bewail
the resistless advance of the critical Time Spirit.
No wonder there are birds of ill omen in the air.
For coming historical events are casting their
shadows before, and the handwriting on the wall
can already be read by any clear-sighted observer.
That handwriting is the voice of history itself. It
pronounces the doom of what is "old and ready to
vanish away," but it also heralds a new dispensation of God's eternally fresh and progressive
revelation of truth. History, indeed, is our true
idealist. Its idealism, however, is not that of a
Platonic or Hegelian metaphysic, but that of a
historical Baconian induction.

But while historical methods and studies are

thus optimistic and idealistic in their entire outlook, the historical scholar cannot hide from his view the fact that such a mighty revolution as we have been surveying is fraught with momentous trials and perils both intellectual and religious. As political revolutions involve temporary civil and social disorders, and even ruin to many individuals, although their occurrence is a necessity and their results are beneficent, so must it always be with intellectual and moral revolutions. When one realizes that this age is passing through the most radical revolution that the intellectual history of the race has ever recorded, it is idle to expect that it can be accomplished without tragic accompaniments of individual mental and moral suffering. Surely the divine revelations in history are often sharp and bitter teachers. We are living in times when many " men's hearts are failing for fear " of what impends. Nothing is so timid as theological tradition. It requires a serene and courageous soul to stand firm and undaunted in the midst of a death struggle between the powers of a venerated tradition that has held unbroken sway over the minds and consciences of men for nearly two thousand years, and the powers of the *Zeitgeist*, armed with its fatal weapons of history and science and criticism. Christ prophesied of such a time as anticipating his own spiritual advent, and added the needed exhortation, " In patience possess your souls." Courage and patience are indeed the watchwords of the hour. God is

working out his own purposes. It is for man to
"be still." In all the present stress and tumult
of destructive and reconstructive forces, we may
hear above the din of human voices the "still
small voice" of the divine providence, repeating
its word of nineteen centuries ago, and saying once
more: "*Behold, I make all things new.*"

APPENDIX

A. THE JOHANNINE PROBLEM

A HISTORICAL investigation of the question whether
the Apostle John wrote the fourth Gospel naturally
falls under three distinct heads.

I. What are the historically accredited facts concerning John?

II. What is the character of the fourth Gospel as
compared with the Synoptic gospels, and what is the
earliest date of its appearance in history?

III. When and how did the tradition that John was
its author come into vogue?

I. The historical facts concerning John. In the
Synoptic gospels John appears as one of the original
Galilean disciples. He was the son of a fisherman and
himself followed that calling when Jesus invited him
to enter his service. Like the other Galilean disciples
he was "unlearned," which means that he had no rabbinic or Greek culture. His vernacular was Galilean
Aramaic, — a dialect distinguished for its barbaric pro-
vincialisms, — Galilee being a comparatively uncultured
district. It was this which led to the amazement of the
Jews at Jerusalem when Jesus, who had been reared in
Nazareth, appeared as a teacher and showed himself
able to meet the rabbis on their own ground. The
same surprise was shown by the Jewish Sanhedrim, on
hearing the defense of Peter and John, "perceiving
that they were unlearned and ignorant men," and their

explanation of the marvel was the natural one, "that they had been with Jesus." There is no evidence that Jesus himself or any of his Galilean disciples had any education beyond that which had been gained in the peasant surroundings of their childhood and youth. The great objection continually employed by the religious teachers and leaders of the Jews against Christ was that he assumed to teach without having passed through their rabbinical schools. He did not teach "as the scribes." The same objection applied equally to his disciples. They were "unlearned men" and hence unfitted to teach. It is not surprising, therefore, that there is no hint in the gospel records that either Jesus or any of his original Galilean disciples committed his teachings to writing. The first Epistle of Peter, if genuine, is the only really authentic written document that has come down from their hands. Christ and his disciples were intent on the oral proclamation of the gospel. The reduction of that gospel to a written form was to be the work of a time when the original witnesses of Christ's ministry were passing away, and when the spread of the gospel beyond Palestine and the increased number of churches made it expedient.

It is remarkable, in view of the later reputation of John, how small a part he plays in the New Testament narratives. He is always secondary to his brother James, and, in the trio of Peter, James, and John, he is usually last. There is no hint in the Synoptic gospels of any peculiar intimacy between John and Christ. Remarkable, too, is the fact that John never is introduced as a speaker. There is not a saying of his recorded. On the two only occasions in which he specially figures, his brother James is joined with him, and, as James's name is first, the natural inference is that he was the chief mover in both affairs. It is also notable that both occasions reveal defects of disposition and character which called forth from Christ the language of disapproval and even of rebuke. Their sensualistic view of the Messianic kingdom and their own personal ambitions were exhibited in their request, made through their mother, that they might sit nearest to Christ in his kingdom. Christ's answer was: "Ye know not what ye ask." In the second instance their carnal anger against the Samaritans led them to ask permission to call down fire from heaven to consume them. But "Christ turned and rebuked them." Very far was John *then* from that mellowed sanctification which caused him in post-apostolic tradition to be known as the Apostle of Love. Passing to the Book of Acts, John's name appears in the list of disciples who awaited the day of Pentecost. A few days after he is joined with Peter in the affair which resulted in their appearance before the Sanhedrim, when Peter is the chief speaker. But from this early point in the narrative he disappears from the scene. After this, other disciples, such as Peter, Philip, James, and especially Paul, occupy the stage, but John is not once mentioned. At the gathering in Jerusalem, recorded in the fifteenth chapter, where all the leaders of the church were assembled, there is a significant silence concerning him. Paul indeed refers to him, in the Epistle to the Galatians, as being at Jerusalem about this time, but this is the last clear glimpse of him in authentic apostolic history. The rest of his life is left entirely in shadow, and the place and date of his death are unrecorded. It is notable that Paul in his later epistles makes no further allusion to him. A recently discovered fragment of Papias preserved in excerpts from the "Church History" of Philip Sidetes, if authentic, as it seems to be, gives us what may be regarded as the most natural and probable account of the manner of his death : " Papias in his second book says that John the divine and James his brother were slain by the Jews."   This would accord with the words of Christ as given in Mark, in answer to the request of the two brothers that they might sit one on his right hand and one on his left in his kingdom : " The cup that I drink ye shall drink, and with the baptism that I am baptized withal shall ye be baptized : " which plainly implies that they both would die a martyr's death, and certainly this must have been the tradition when the present Mark was written or edited.   The Acts informs us that "James the brother of John" was put to death by Herod, and that " when he saw that it pleased the Jews he proceeded to seize Peter also." It may be that John too fell a victim to Herod's desire to please the Jews, and that the tradition in the form related by Papias may be thus explained.   There is a Syriac martyrology, also, that unites James and John as martyrs.

The change from the comparative reticence of the New Testament concerning John to the mass of traditions which gathered around his name in subsequent years is truly marvelous.   He became the centre of a legendary growth which far surpasses that which was formed around any other apostolic personage except Christ himself.   What were the precise causes of such a growth it is vain to seek, in an age when the historical critical spirit was still unborn, and when all historical and biographical events speedily became mingled with legendary additions.   There were indeed special reasons why the early Christians should have been easily led to accept for truth the legendary stories that rapidly grew up concerning Christ and his immediate disciples.   Christianity had its very birth in the air of marvel' and miracle.   Messianism prepared men for

the expectation of immediate wonderful events. Jesus
himself, as the Christ, quickly became the centre of a
whole legendary cycle in which, as we have seen, his
mother Mary played a prominent part. The same was
true of the original Apostles. In the Acts they are still
in Judea and Galilee and the immediate vicinity preaching the gospel in the only language with which they
were acquainted. Paul gives no hint in his epistles
that any of them went far from Palestine. When he
met the three "who seemed to be pillars," "James,
Peter, and John," at Jerusalem, it was arranged between them that Paul and Barnabas should go to the
Gentiles and "they unto the circumcision." Thus Paul
became a foreign missionary, while the Galilean disciples remained at home among their own Jewish people.
The only exception is Peter's visit to Antioch, and
afterwards to Babylon, among the Jews of the disper-
sion, according to the natural interpretation of the
closing verses of the first Epistle of Peter, if that Epistle be genuine.

But when the historical ground of the New Testament is left, the whole scene changes. Later tradition
sends them into all parts of the known world, Thomas
to Parthia and India, Andrew to Scythia, Bartholomew
to Arabia, Thaddeus to Edessa, Matthew to Ethiopia,
James to Spain, Peter to Rome. So John is sent to
Ephesus, where he lives to a great age, becoming the
centre of a Johannine circle or school and writing the
Gospel which has made him the most famous apostle
after Paul himself. It was once the custom to accept
many of these legends as containing substantial truth,
but such acceptance is no longer possible. Critical
scholarship has completely destroyed their historical
credibility and has transferred them, almost if not
quite *en masse*, to the realm of fable. It is not a

grateful task to play the part of iconoclast with so
many creations of Christian fancy and devotion. But
here the plain truth must be told. As soon as the historical inquirer has stepped off the historical ground of
the New Testament and entered the post-apostolic age,
he finds it impossible to retain any secure historical
footing concerning John or his fellow disciples. When
at length, a hundred years or so after the close of the
Acts, he first meets with the traditions that begin to
gather, it is true that they rapidly increase in number
and also in wonderfulness, and reach a widespread
unanimity, but the fatal defect with them all is that no
clear historical *nexus* can be found which may connect
them with the historical ground that has been left
behind. Not only is there a gap of a century, but the
traditions themselves bear the clear marks of legend,
and these marks grow clearer and clearer as the evolution goes on, until at last all trace of anything historical
is lost in romance and miracle. It may be expected
that historical criticism should distinguish between what
is historical and what is legendary. But this will be
found impossible. Professor Plumptre, the writer of
the article on John in Smith's Bible Dictionary, truly
says: "The picture which tradition fills up for us has
the merit of being full and vivid, but it blends together,
without much regard to harmony, things probable and
improbable." What can the historical critic do with
the story which Tertullian records as historical fact
concerning John's being plunged unhurt at Rome into
boiling oil, and afterwards being sent into exile ; or the
relation of Apollonius, given by Eusebius, without a
hint against its veracity, that "a dead man was raised
to life by the divine power through John at Ephesus,"
or the "current report" recorded by Augustine as
"found in certain apocryphal scriptures" "that John,

when in good health, ordered a sepulchre to be made for him, and that when it was dug and prepared with all possible care, he laid himself down there as in a bed, and became immediately defunct, yet not really defunct, and while accounted dead was actually buried while asleep, and that he will so remain till the coming of Christ, the fact of his continued life being made known by the bubbling up of the dust, caused by the breathing of the sleeper." Augustine does not decide as to the truth of this report, but informs us that he " has heard it from those who were not altogether unreliable witnesses." This wonderful story reaches its climax in a Greek ecclesiastical historian of the fourteenth century, in the addition that " when the tomb was subsequently opened it was found empty " ! I have selected these items especially because they are vouched for by such writers as Tertullian, Eusebius, and Augustine. The verdict of Professor Plumptre is the only one that can be accepted by historical criticism, viz., that " these traditions, for the most part, indicate little else than the uncritical character of the age in which they passed current." It may still be urged that the wheat of historical truth ought to be sifted out of this mass of legendary chaff. But Professor Plumptre well says : " We strain our sight in vain to distinguish between the false and the true, between the shadows with which the gloom is peopled and the living forms of which we are in search." The defender of tradition may fall back on the position that *all* historical traditions, though they gather legendary accretions with years, yet always have a historical *substratum*, and that it is the function of criticism to separate the real facts from such legendary accretions. The implied premise on which this assumption rests is that a legend never grows without a historical *nucleus* as its root; but this cannot be allowed.

History furnishes not a few examples of such legends.[1] It may be claimed that the events recorded in the New Testament concerning the Apostles are the nuclei of the later traditions, and that if the New Testament accounts are accepted as historical, the later ones cannot be treated as wholly legendary. But the difference between the New Testament narratives and the post-apostolic traditions is radical. In the Synoptic gospels, the Acts, and Paul's epistles, we are at least on historical ground. Jesus and his chief disciples and Paul are historical characters as indubitably as Augustus or Herod. That legend crept into the New Testament narrative is no more surprising than that it should have filled the opening pages of Livy, or disfigured the gossiping biographies of Suetonius. Here the task of the critic is plain, viz., to separate as far as possible the historical truth from unhistorical legend, — a work now going on, though not yet completed. But the case with post-apostolic legendary tradition is entirely different. Here there is wanting the very basis of history itself. There is no clear historical ground on which the critic can work.

Take, for example, the case of Peter. He disap-

[1] A good illustration is the legend of St. Christopher which had such a wonderful popularity through the Middle Ages, and was made the subject of such poetic and artistic elaboration. This legend has recently been critically investigated by a German scholar, and his work is reviewed in the last number (November-December, 1899) of the *Revue de l'Histoire des Religions*. The reviewer concludes, in full agreement with the author, that the legend rests on "no initial historical fact," and must be regarded as "only the fruit of pure religious imagination." "The giant Christopher is mythical ; we can affirm no more" Yet St. Christopher has a special day set for him in the Calendar of the Greek and Latin churches (May 6, July 25), as if he were a historical person.

pears from authentic history about A. D. 50. Some
years later, we know not how many, he may have gone
to Babylon to preach the gospel to his Jewish countrymen sojourning there in large numbers. This is the
end of our historical knowledge. Tradition more than
a generation after begins by alluding to Peter as a
martyr. We wait for the next step of evolution nearly
a hundred years, when his martyrdom is made to occur
at Rome. From this point the tradition grows more
and more widespread and unanimous. In the third
century the manner of his death is added, viz., crucifixion, and then the crowning touch is given, that, at his
own request, he was crucified with his head downward.
From this point tradition branches out into the varied
forms of which perhaps the legend found in Ambrose is
most touching : that, when persuaded by his friends to
flee from the death that threatened him, he met Christ
at the gate of the city, who, on Peter's asking him
whither he was going, replied: "I go to Rome once
more to be crucified." This rebuke revived Peter's
courage and he returned to his death. To this account
it should be added that by the beginning of the third
century it was believed that Peter's tomb could be
shown in Rome. The further tradition which the
Roman church started, making Peter the founder and
first bishop of that church, on which was afterwards
built the papal claim of supreme ecclesiastical authority, I need not dwell on.

Now the only real historical basis of all this legendary growth is simply the account in the Acts of Peter's
meeting with Simon Magus in Samaria. This meeting
was made the foundation of the legendary romance of
the Clementine Homilies in which Peter is made to follow Simon through Syria and finally to Rome. This
romance is full of the most flagrant distortions of his-

torical fact, — Peter being made to descend to the lowest
arts of magic and miracle.   But how should this purely
legendary meeting between Peter and Simon have been
accepted by the early church as historical?   The story
is a curious one.   The basis of it is found in Justin
Martyr about the middle of the second century.   He
lived for a considerable period at Rome.   There he saw
a statue, in an island of the Tiber, dedicated to *Semo
Sancus*, a Sabine divinity.   The name was plainly confounded by Justin with that of Simon the magician of
the Acts, whose fame was spread in Samaria, where
Justin was born.   Hence in his Apology, which he
wrote at Rome to the Emperor, he referred to Simon as
having visited Rome and been honored with a statue
bearing the inscription *Simoni Deo Sancto*.   It was on
such a plain mistake that was raised one of the most
colossal legends that was ever fabricated.   But Justin
made no allusion to Peter.   Neither did Irenæus, who
continued the Simon Magus tradition, apparently making Justin his authority, yet connect Peter with it.   But
the germ in the Acts could not fail finally of coming to
fruitage.   Passing by the Clementine Homilies and Re-
cognitions and the Apostolic Constitutions, the dates of
which are uncertain, we come to Eusebius, who gives us,
in the fourth century, the fully developed tradition, viz.,
that Peter followed Simon to Rome, where he overcame
him by supernatural power.   The account in Eusebius
bears plain marks of resting on the testimony of Justin
Martyr concerning Simon's going to Rome, for he quotes
Justin Martyr's account, following it with his own account of Peter.   Further, he alludes to the statue to
Simon at Rome, and gives, as the date of Peter's going
to Rome, *the same date* which Justin Martyr had assigned to the visit of Simon Magus.   Where Justin got
his date or his account of Simon Magus he does not

tell us. If it were historically verifiable, it would not make the Peter legend any the more true. But the fact is that Justin's date, viz., "In the reign of Claudius," afterwards attached to the growing Peter legend, is the foundation stone on which the Roman papal claim really rests.

Whether Peter ever visited Rome has been one of the much mooted questions of history. It began to be disputed in the fourteenth century. But even later Protestant historians have, some of them, like Neander, allowed to their Romanist opponents that so unanimous a tradition had an air of probability. Such a concession cannot be made to-day. Historical criticism finds no ground even of probability that Peter ever left Palestine for Italy. The whole story rests on the visit to Rome of Simon Magus, which is a complete fiction, born, we must believe, in the brain of Justin, as he mused over the inscription on the statue of a Sabine god which he misread or mistranslated. The discovery, in the sixteenth century, of the pedestal of such a statue, with the inscription *Semoni Sanco Deo*, has solved the riddle.[1] Much has been made of the unanimous character of the later Peter legend. But such proof would establish the historicity of many of the absurdest traditions extant. All tradition becomes unanimous when once fixed. Peter's supposed tomb, over which St. Peter's church was afterwards built, has no doubt settled many a wavering mind in favor of Peter's martyrdom at Rome. But there was scarcely an illustrious saint or martyr in the apostolic or post-apostolic church whose bones were not discovered, if we may believe tradition, in the fourth and fifth centuries. Jerome was the greatest scholar of his age. Yet he believed that the

[1] Schaff's *History of the Apostolic Church*, p. 371; Fowler's *Roman Festivals*, p. 136.

bones of Andrew, of Luke, of Timothy, and even of Samuel, had been exhumed and brought by the Emperor Constantius to Constantinople. So Augustine gravely informs us that the bones of the first martyr Stephen had been discovered by a miracle, and distributed over North Africa, and he relates that some seventy persons had within his knowledge been healed by their sacred touch. How much historical value can attach to the reputed tomb of Peter or of any other saint in such grossly uncritical times, when men like Jerome and Augustine were ready to accept on the merest hearsay every such marvel! The whole Peter tradition, then, must be dismissed as a pure legend from beginning to end. No sifting process is possible.

Now what is true of the Petrine legend is equally true of the Johannine. In fact the balance between them leans in favor of the Petrine, for behind the Petrine legend is a basis of historical fact, to wit, the historical Simon of the Acts, and his meeting with Peter in Samaria. But no such fact lies behind the Johannine tradition. It starts out of the completest historical darkness, we know not how or when or where. It may be suggested that Christ's words to Peter concerning John, as given at the end of the fourth Gospel, is a historical basis for the tradition of his long life. But the date and historicity of the fourth Gospel is the very question at issue, and it cannot therefore be used in evidence. Are not the reputed expressions of Christ concerning John rather evidence that the Gospel was written at a time when the tradition of John's great longevity was already spread abroad? The testimony given at the beginning of the Apocalypse concerning the seer of Patmos, whose name is given as John, cannot be accepted as bearing on the question at issue. The Apocalypse is not history and does not pretend to be.

Whether the name of John was assumed by some unknown writer, as was so frequently the case in that period, or if a real John, what John it was, — for there were Johns many in those days, as there have been ever since, — is wholly uncertain. There is nothing in the passage to identify the seer of Patmos with John the Apostle. A later tradition identifies him with John the Elder of Ephesus. The whole story of John's exile to Patmos is late, and is attached to other stories that are historically impossible, such as the effort to put him to death by immersing him in a caldron of boiling oil. The first allusion to it is at the very end of the second century, when the way had already been prepared for it. It is true the Apocalypse in some form had already seen the light, for Justin Martyr alludes to it, but he says nothing about the exile to Patmos. When the proem was prefixed is unknown. Thus all historical basis for the Johannine tradition seems to be wholly wanting.

But I do not forget the protest that will at once be raised by the defenders of the Johannine authorship of the fourth Gospel. Their last rallying point is the testimony of Irenæus, and to this I now turn my attention. It is noticeable that a change has come over the method of defense of the Johannine authorship within the last generation. Formerly it was usual to rely on the growing unanimity of tradition. Thus Dean Alford in his New Testament commentary holds the ground that tradition as a whole is completely trustworthy, and that the different parts support each other. But as the progress of critical investigation has demonstrated more and more clearly the untenableness of such a position, there has been a tendency to fall back upon Irenæus as the main historical support of the conservative side. This is well illustrated in the writings of Professor G. P.

Fisher, which on the whole contain, in my view, the clearest and most forcible statement of the arguments in favor of the Johannine authorship within my knowledge. In his earlier book, " Essays on the Supernatural Origin of Christianity," Professor Fisher makes general tradition his main support, and goes carefully over the whole ground. Irenæus of course has his place in this consensus of tradition, but it is not specially magnified. Professor Fisher, too, with Alford, relies on the mutually supporting character of the traditional chain of events, concluding his survey with these words: " Not all these separate items of evidence are of equal strength. Together they constitute an irrefragable argument," and he concludes that " it is morally impossible to discredit the tradition of the early church." But it is plain at once that such a line of argument cannot be sustained in the light of the most recent researches. As we have shown, every "separate item" of traditional evidence fatally fails of any clear historical basis and support. "Out of nothing nothing can come" is an axiom as true in history as in nature. A hundred weak arguments cannot make one strong argument. A dozen broken cisterns hold no more water than one. If every link of the chain is weak, the whole chain is weak, however long you may make it. No wonder, then, that in Professor Fisher's later "Beginnings of Christianity" he puts Irenæus immediately at the front, declaring that "the strongest consideration, as far as external proof is concerned, centres in Polycarp, and in the relations of Irenæus to this Father." Professor Fisher proceeds to quote Irenæus at length, and makes his testimony the very chief corner-stone of the external evidence. In taking this new position, Professor Fisher shows his clear historical insight. He realizes that tradition is worthless and fades at once into pure legend unless it rests on some trustworthy historical foundations. If Irenæus' writings have come down to us *in authentic form, and his testimony can be accepted as trustworthy and authoritative*, we find ourselves on firm historical ground. Here then we are brought face to face with the question that is practically decisive. Does the evidence of Irenæus stand the test of historical criticism, and is its author left unscathed as a credible historical witness?

In considering this point there is, to begin with, a preliminary question of textual criticism. The original Greek of Irenæus' work, "Against Heresies," is lost. Only a Latin version remains to us, with the exception of copious quotations from the Greek by Epiphanius and Hippolytus. The learned editors of the "Ante-Nicene Christian Library" affirm that "the text, both Greek and Latin, is most uncertain." "Irenæus, even in the original Greek, is often a very obscure writer; and the Latin version adds to these difficulties of the original by being itself of the most barbarous character. In fact it is often necessary to make a conjectural retranslation of it into Greek, in order to obtain some inkling of what the author wrote." "The author of the Latin version is unknown, but he was certainly little qualified for his task." Of the lost writings of Irenæus a few fragments are preserved, especially one which contains a passage of great importance in its relation to our subject. The genuineness of this fragment rests wholly on the authority of Eusebius, who wrote his "Ecclesiastical History" a century and a half later. With these textual facts before him the historical critic is obliged to confess that the very basis of a just critical review and estimate of Irenæus' character as a credible witness seems ready to slip away from under his feet, and one cannot help raising at once the question whether the

testimony of Irenæus, in view of the uncertain character
and purity of the original text and of the Latin version,
can be allowed any credibility at all, except so far as
it is sustained by other credible evidence.   In fact, on
the special points in question, where his testimony has
most importance, it stands alone.   But we must accept
the text of the Greek quotations and Latin version as
we have it, and deal with it as best we may.

At the outset it is to be noted that Irenæus has suffered recently in a general way, with all the early Fathers, in the matter of historical and critical reliability
and veraciousness.   All alike were utterly wanting in
the scientific and critical temper.   Irenæus was perhaps
no worse than the rest, but he displays again and again
a wonderfully childish innocence and credulity.   For
example, he accepts without hesitation a legendary tradition that had grown up among the Alexandrian Jews
concerning the miraculous origin of the Greek Septuagint version of the Old Testament, to the effect that
King Ptolemy separated the seventy translators from
each other, and that when their translations were compared they agreed "word for word from beginning to
end."   Irenæus was the first to defend the canonicity
of our four present gospels against the claims of other
gospels then extant as urged by the Gnostics.   His
argument is a curious illustration of his utter want of
critical sagacity.   He begins by asserting that it is not
possible that the gospels can be either more or fewer in
number than they are, and the reason given is that
"there are four zones of the earth, and four principal
winds."   "The cherubim too were fourfold, and their
faces were images of the dispensation of the Son of
God."   So the Gospel of John is like a lion, that of
Luke is symbolized by a calf, Matthew by a man, and
Mark by the eagle.   "For the living creatures are

quadriform, and the gospel is quadriform." "That these gospels alone are true and reliable, and admit neither increase nor diminution of the aforesaid number, I have thus proved!" Further argument Irenæus deems unnecessary. Against persons who had gathered from the Synoptics that Christ's public ministry extended only a year, Irenæus quotes the answer of the Jews, as given in the fourth Gospel, "Thou art not yet fifty years old, and hast thou seen Abraham?" and argues hence that Christ's ministry must have continued from ten to twenty years. If these illustrations are not enough, I will add one more which shows how ready he was to accept as authentic any tradition that came to him. Oral sayings ascribed to Christ were prevalent in this period. Irenæus quotes one such saying which he declares that John the Apostle heard from Christ's own lips and communicated to "the elders," concerning the millennial times: "The days will come in which vines shall grow, each having ten thousand branches, and in each branch ten thousand twigs, and in each twig ten thousand shoots, and on each shoot ten thousand clusters, and on each cluster ten thousand grapes, and each grape when pressed will yield five and twenty measures of wine." This remarkable *logion*, so out of character on the lips of Jesus, appears in its earliest form in the Jewish Apocalypse of Baruch. Irenæus makes Papias his voucher for it, calling him "a hearer of John." But Papias, as we shall see, was not a hearer of John the Apostle but of another John, "the Elder." Still, Papias might have given currency to this reputed saying of Christ. Eusebius refers to certain "other accounts of Papias which had been received by him from unwritten tradition," which Eusebius himself regarded as "rather too fabulous," declaring that Papias "was very limited in his comprehension,"—a statement which would seem equally applicable to Irenæus, at least so far as historical matters are concerned.

What now is the inference which the historical critic must draw from such illustrations as these concerning Irenæus as a historical witness. Certainly but one answer is possible, to wit, that he can be credited only in cases where critical skill is not called for, and where he is dealing with matters that have come so recently under his observation that there can be no room for failure or inaccuracy of memory. This verdict on the historical credibility of Irenæus is essentially the same that must be passed on all the early Fathers. Even such great lights as Origen, Jerome, and Eusebius are utterly unreliable on all historical questions where the exercise of a scientific or critical faculty is required, or when the event in issue is quite removed from present cognizance. To each and all alike the power to distinguish fact and legend by means of historical criticism is wholly wanting. The history of the Peter legend amply illustrates this. To the want of critical tact must also be added an entire want of historical candor. The bigotry and uncharitableness of the early Fathers, shown in their treatment of their theological opponents, is so strong as to throw discredit on all their statements concerning those who disagree with them. It was the discovery of the historical untrustworthiness of these early Fathers that has stimulated recent critical studies in Christian origins, and the result has been to remove much of the halo of veneration and sacredness with which tradition had invested them. The idealized legendary histories of the early church that used to be written are practically useless to-day.

But to return to Irenæus. The testimony to which such prominence has been given by Professor Fisher and others is as follows: Irenæus relates that in his childhood and youth in Asia he heard Polycarp discourse and "speak of his familiar intercourse with John and with the rest of those who had seen the Lord." These reminiscences were written when Irenæus was a bishop in Gaul and quite advanced in years, as late as A. D. 185. Polycarp had died a generation earlier, and it must have been nearly if not quite a generation earlier still when Irenæus as a youth saw and heard him. There is no evidence that Irenæus had met Polycarp afterwards. The question at once arises as to the accuracy and credibility of one's memory of events so early in life, in the case of a man, quite old, recalling the scenes of his youth. The treachery of memory in such cases is proverbial. The broad lines of events in one's youth are usually quite indelible, but the particular incidental facts that are connected with the general current of events are, as a rule, quite beyond the power of recovery. Mr. Leslie Stephen, the editor of the new "Dictionary of Biography," in a recent article in the "National Review," draws out of his personal experience as an editor some vivid illustrations of the fallacious character of memory concerning the events of one's past life, and concludes that letters written when the events were fresh in the memory, "in the main, are the one essential to a thoroughly satisfactory life." He refers to an experience in his own life concerning an old letter which he had burnt, and the contents of which in later life he had entirely forgotten, the result being that "I now only know that my own account of my life is somehow altogether wrong." He multiplies such cases and concludes: "Such incidents represent the ease with which the common legend of a life grows up, and the sole correction for good or for bad is the contemporary document." Now this is just the trouble with the account given by Irenæus in his old age of a transaction

of his youth. There is no "contemporary document"
to sustain its accuracy. I dwell on this feature of the
case, because it will be found to be at the very root of our
whole judgment concerning the credibility of Irenæus'
testimony. The whole question at last is resolved into
this: Can the memory of Irenæus be relied upon for
the exact particular facts related a half century or so
after, concerning what transpired in his youth? For not
only is there no "contemporary document" to validate
Irenæus' accuracy of information or memory, but what
testimony we have is of a directly contrary character.
I refer to that of Papias, a contemporary of Polycarp.
Irenæus declares that Papias was also a "hearer of
John." But Papias himself in the fragments preserved
in Eusebius gives evidence that Irenæus was mistaken.
For Papias distinguishes two Johns, "John the disciple
of the Lord" and "John the Elder," putting the first
John in the number of Christ's immediate disciples,
and the second among "the followers" of the Apostles.
Papias does not pretend to have heard John the Apostle
or any other of the first generation of Christ's disciples.
But he declares that he gathered what he could orally
from the followers of John and his fellow Apostles, and
among them he mentions "John the Elder." Papias
thus distinguishes three generations of disciples, — the
original Apostles, the followers of those Apostles, and
those who, like himself, learned from these followers at
second hand what the disciples of the first generation
said. Eusebius draws special attention to this mistake
of Irenæus and corrects it, saying that "Papias by no
means asserts that he was a hearer and eyewitness of
the holy Apostles, but informs us that he received the
doctrine of faith from their intimate friends." He also
adds that Papias elsewhere says expressly that he was
"a hearer of John the Elder," and quotes a tradition

concerning Mark which he heard from him. Thus the testimony of Papias himself proves that he had never seen John the Apostle and that Irenæus was mistaken in his assertion that Papias was a "hearer of John." Plainly Irenæus had somehow confounded the two Johns, as Eusebius suggests.

The query naturally arises, whether Irenæus was not guilty of the same confusion in the case of Polycarp. For Polycarp was contemporary with Papias, as Irenæus himself declared. The truth seems to be that Irenæus had confounded two generations of disciples or elders, and so placed Polycarp and Papias together in the second generation, instead of distinguishing them from the "followers" of the Apostles and so putting them in the third generation of disciples where they really belonged, on the testimony of Papias himself. This view of the matter is also in harmony with all we know concerning Polycarp. In his Epistle to the Philippians, which seems to be genuine, there is no reference to any personal relation with John the Apostle. John's name is not even mentioned. This is the more remarkable since Polycarp refers to Paul again and again, and frequently quotes from his epistles. Especially on one occasion he speaks of "Paul himself and the rest of the Apostles." If he had held such "familiar intercourse with John" the Apostle as Irenæus represents, how natural would it have been to make some personal reference to him in this connection. There was a special reason, to be sure, for his frequent reference to Paul, since Paul had visited Philippi and had afterwards written an epistle to the church there. But is it not strange that in Polycarp's own Epistle, which is full of quotations from some Synoptic form of the gospel, either oral or written, and from Paul's epistles, there should not be a single quotation from that

Gospel which he must have so greatly prized, or even a hint of its existence! It is also a fact of no little significance that Polycarp should have repeatedly set forth his doctrine of God the Father and of Christ the Son, and yet made no allusion at all to the Holy Spirit, if the fourth Gospel was in his hands. For that Gospel has a clear trinitarian character and really completes the evolution of the dogma of the Trinity by its doctrine of the Paraclete. But the term Paraclete does not appear in the Epistle, nor does Polycarp give any evidence in it that he held the full trinitarian dogma. How could that have been, if Polycarp was acquainted with the fourth Gospel? Further, the chief peculiarity of the fourth Gospel is its Logos doctrine. Defenders of the Johannine authorship hold that John's Gospel introduced the Logos doctrine into christology. If this be true, and if Polycarp was a hearer of John, and acquainted with his Gospel, how can it be explained that Polycarp's christology knows nothing of the Logos?

Polycarp's death occurred in A. D. 155 or later, and even allowing the truth of the tradition of his great age, he cannot be made contemporary with John except by assuming the truth of the unhistorical tradition that John also lived to an equally great age. Such is the slender thread of historical assumption on which the Johannine problem really hangs. But even the tradition of Polycarp's extreme longevity cannot be regarded as authentic history. It depends wholly on the "Martyrdom of Polycarp," which bears such clear traces of interpolation and is so filled with miraculous and legendary elements that it is impossible to sift out of it the grains, if there be any, of historical fact. Thus we are thrown back on the single testimony of Irenæus, which is unconfirmed by Polycarp himself, and is opposed to the indirect counter testimony of Papias. So that the case stands thus: Irenæus in his old age gives a reminiscence of his youth in regard to which clear evidence shows that he must have confounded two generations of disciples together and in this way confounded a John of the first generation with a John of the second. Thus only can all the known facts be harmonized. So that the conclusion is forced upon us that Irenæus, either by failure of memory or want of sufficient information, was mistaken. It is my firm conviction that no other conclusion is possible, and my only wonder is that any scholars are still found to take exception to it, or to defend the credibility of Irenæus' testimony. When one considers how treacherous the memory becomes in the course of a long life, how utterly uncritical Irenæus was concerning all historical events, and how easy it was for him to confound two persons of the same name as he wandered back in memory among the uncertain and darkening shadows of his youthful days, it is certainly much easier to believe that he was mistaken as to Polycarp's true relation to John the Apostle than to believe that he was right, when corroborating evidence is wholly wanting, and especially when we remember that in making a similar assertion concerning Papias he was certainly wrong.

I have dwelt thus fully on this first division of the subject, because I regard the result at which we have arrived concerning the real facts of the life of John as practically settling the whole question as to the Johannine authorship of the fourth Gospel. Remove the legendary traditions concerning John's sojourn in Ephesus, and his extreme longevity reaching to the reign of Trajan, and acknowledge, as we must, it seems to me, the complete unreliability of the testimony of Irenæus, and little ground is left on which to base the Johannine authorship. Whether any such ground is to be found in the two following divisions of the subject, we now proceed to consider.

II. We next have to deal with the character of the fourth Gospel as compared with the Synoptic gospels, and the earliest known date of its appearance in history. No one can read the fourth Gospel, even in the most cursory way, without realizing at once that its whole intellectual and religious atmosphere and tone of thought is in complete contrast with that of the Synoptics. Its very introduction, with its sharply defined Logos doctrine, removes us entirely from Jewish Palestinian ideas, and transfers us to Greek Alexandrian philosophic thought. The whole christology of the fourth Gospel is radically different from that of the Synoptics, and indicates a long process of evolution. As we have seen, the Synoptic gospels hold the view of Christ's Messianic character. He is the promised anointed one of David's royal line. There is no hint of a superhuman preëxistence, or of a Logos doctrine. But the fourth Gospel at once goes back of Christ's human birth into the eternity of the divine existence, and out of God himself by a divine incarnation makes Christ proceed; and this divine nature of Christ, as the eternal Logos of God, is the keynote of the whole Gospel. Christ is no longer a human Messiah with a divine commission, but is a divine being, metaphysically united to God himself, and thus able to mediate in a cosmological rather than a soteriological way between God and man. We have explained the relation of the Pauline christology to that of the Synoptics. Paul advanced from the Jewish Messianism to the Greek Philonic mediatorship dogma borrowed from paganism. But the fourth Gospel proceeded a step further, raising Christ above the Pauline position of a $\mu\epsilon\sigma\iota\tau\eta s$ or middle being between God and man, to that of the $\lambda\acute{o}\gamma os$ of

God, God of God, derived indeed, but essentially divine. There are close resemblances, with some sharp differences, as we have noted, between the Logos doctrine of the fourth Gospel and that of Justin Martyr, indicating a common chronological stage of evolution. But to attempt to coördinate the christology of the fourth Gospel with that of the primitive Synoptics involves an anachronism of nearly a century.

In the *second* place, the fourth Gospel differs radically from the Synoptic gospels in its doctrine of the essential ground and character of the Christian life. In the Synoptics Christ is represented as making the essence of his religion to consist in a life of Christian trust and love and obedience. There is no marked dogmatic element in his teaching. No creed concerning his own metaphysical relation to God is made the basis of discipleship. Repent, accept my gospel of the new kingdom, and "follow me" as your anointed leader, is his constant message. But how different is the teaching of the fourth Gospel! It begins with setting forth in theological form the dogma of Christ's complete divinity, and to accept that dogma as an article of faith is made all through the Gospel the sole condition of Christian discipleship. "Believe in me" takes the place of "Follow me." To enforce the acceptance of this dogma is declared by the author of the Gospel to be his purpose in writing it. "But these things are written that ye may believe that Jesus is the Christ, the Son of God, and that believing ye may have life in his name." In the Synoptics Christ's teaching is practical and experimental, inculcating a change of life by a new law of love to God and to one's fellow men. In the fourth Gospel the whole point of view is changed. Love still remains the central element of manifestation of the Christian spirit; but how may love spring up in the heart? Dogmatic belief is now made the root of all true religious experience. In Christ's long discussions with the Jews, his position is continually reiterated: "Except ye believe that I am he, ye shall die in your sins," and the special dogma on which he insists is that he is the divine Son of God, — a point emphasized so strongly that the Jews charged him with blasphemy in "making himself God." Not only is the very nature of faith changed from the hearty acceptance of Christ as the promised Messiah, involving the following of him in loving discipleship, to the intellectual acceptance of a metaphysical dogma, but the character of the object of faith is radically changed from God the common Father of Jesus and of all men to Christ himself, who, as the Son of God, the divine Logos, is the true mediatorial object of faith and of worship. How different is the whole theory of the root of personal religion in the Synoptics, as compared with the fourth Gospel, is shown in the different way in which Christ treats those who come to him. Compare his treatment of the sinning woman in Luke with that of the man blind from his birth in John. The woman's love and devotion shown in her actions brings to her Christ's words: "Thy faith hath saved thee." But when Christ finds the blind man now restored to sight, he asks him, "Dost thou believe on the Son of God?" and the reply is, "Lord, I believe," and the record adds, "and he worshiped him." True religion in the case of the woman of Luke consisted in works of grateful love; in the case of the restored blind man of John, it consisted in reciting after Christ an article of metaphysical belief. Thus the whole focus of the Christian life is changed from "the way," as it came to be termed in the primitive tradition, involving the following of the Master in a discipleship of loving sacrifice, to a form of belief, involving assent to a christological dogma. Here, again, an evolution of doctrine, requiring considerable time, is plainly discernible. There is no evidence of any such change in the Synoptic gospels or in the Acts. For the Credo recited by the eunuch to Philip in the eighth chapter of the Acts is a later interpolation, indicating the growing evolution. Paul gives us the first step towards it. But with him dogma is still secondary, and faith and love are primary. Paul, however, introduces us to the Greek metaphysical conception of religion as a kind of philosophy, and by his dogma of a $\mu\epsilon\sigma\iota\tau\eta\varsigma$ prepares us for the later Logos doctrine. It was after the rise of the Gnostic systems and controversies that the speculative metaphysical spirit fully entered Christian thought and led to the development of philosophical theology. The Logos doctrine marks this great change. So that the history of the christological evolution points directly to a time as late at least as the middle of the second century for the date of the fourth Gospel. In fact, as we have seen, it was just about this time that the Logos doctrine first appears in christology, in the writings of Justin Martyr. So that all attempts to bring the Synoptic gospels into doctrinal harmony with the Fourth, we again perceive, involves a flagrant anachronism.

Thirdly, it is merely an enlargement of the two points of difference already noted, to say that the whole philosophical character of the fourth Gospel is radically different from that of the Synoptic gospels. This is so patent that it needs no further illustration, especially as I have already in the first chapter remarked on the evidences in the fourth Gospel of Philonic and Gnostic influence. There is no evidence that the Greek writings of Philo had spread from Alexandria to Aramaic Palestine in Christ's day, or that their influence was felt.

Paul shows some traces of such influence. So too does the Epistle to the Hebrews. But the fourth Gospel gives clear evidence of it, not only in its Logos doctrine, but in its metaphysical conceptions and modes of thought. The influence of Gnosticism is equally apparent in its vocabulary, and especially in its dualistic ideas. But Gnosticism did not appear till the second quarter of the second century, and the influence of Philo is not clearly marked among the early Fathers till the third century, except so far as it represented Greek philosophy in general. So that the fundamental metaphysical conceptions of the fourth Gospel point directly to a period considerably later than the Apostolic age.

There is *another* characteristic of the fourth Gospel which quite distinguishes it from the Synoptics. I refer to its mysticism and transcendentalism. The more deeply one studies this Gospel the more strongly is one impressed by these features of it. All religion has its side of other-worldliness and of mystical thought and feeling,— its tendency to rise above the seen and known into the transcendent mysteries of Absolute Being. In the Synoptics occasional glimpses of such mystical flights of Christ's moral consciousness are revealed to us. Still, as a whole these gospels are ethical and practical and experimental, dealing with questions related to this present life. The kingdom of heaven which the synoptic Christ proclaimed as at hand was essentially of this world, though it shaded off into the retributions and rewards of a world to come. But how different is the whole point of view of the fourth Gospel. It is the transcendent eternal world that comes into full view from the outset. The reader is carried at once into the invisible and transcendent state of being. Christ is essentially a heavenly personage. Even while on earth he is still "in heaven." The whole atmosphere of the

Gospel is unearthly and supernatural. Christ everywhere walks among men as if separated from them by
some supernal relationship. "He that cometh from
above is above all." His miracles partake of this highly
unnatural, mystical character. He turns water into
wine; he raises Lazarus from a four days' death and decay. His conversations are all keyed to the same super-
earthly and heavenly strain. No man hath seen the
Father, but Christ himself has. "Ye are from beneath,
I am from above. Ye are of this world, I am not of
this world." Even "before Abraham was I am." "I
and the Father are one." For "the Father is in me
and I am in the Father." And Christ seeks to draw
his own disciples into the same mystical union with one
another, with himself, and with God. For them the
true religious life is "the eternal life," and that eternal
life consists in "knowing the only true God." This
"eternal life" thus realized already in the present state
is the true resurrection life. "I am the resurrection
and the life. Whosoever liveth and believeth on me
shall never die." Thus time and eternity are mystically
united together, and that great eschatological event
called the resurrection, which in the Synoptics is only
referred to as occurring at the end of the world, is
represented as a present experience. Such is the lofty
mysticism of the fourth Gospel. How different is the
picture of Christ here given from that of the Synoptic
gospels. How different its picture of the world, of man,
and of the heavenly kingdom! The human, anointed
master of the Synoptics preaching the sermon on the
mount, and speaking parables full of practical wisdom,
and thanking God that the mysteries of his kingdom
were revealed unto babes, has become in the fourth
Gospel a heavenly descended Logos, never forgetful of
his divine origin, distinguishing himself from those

among whom for the while he dwelt, and seeking to gather his own out of the world into the celestial society from which he came and to which he was soon to return. Could such a transcendent mystical gospel have been written by one of those Galilean fishermen who, as history tells, were Christ's closest disciples and from whom came to us the primitive synoptic tradition?

There is *still another* point of contrast between the first three gospels and the fourth: the remarkable want of harmony, and, in some instances, the irreconcilability of the historical narratives. I do not propose to enter into a minute examination of this point, for it is unnecessary. So radical is the difference that it forces itself at once on the reader. The old explanation has been that John, the assumed author, wrote his Gospel as a mere supplement to the Synoptics. But such an explanation wholly fails to explain. It bristles with historical difficulties. The two accounts are completely inconsistent with each other, for example, as to the length of Christ's public ministry, his labors in Jerusalem, the substance of his discourses, the date of his death, the circumstances of his crucifixion and resurrection. Surely if this Gospel is a veracious history of Christ's life, though supplemental to other gospels, the broad outlines of it would harmonize with them. But, in the fourth Gospel, not only are events unrecorded which are made prominent in the Synoptics, such as Christ's baptism, his temptation, the institution of his Supper, the scene in Gethsemane, but events are related which we should expect would have been also recorded in the other gospels, if they had actually happened. Take, for instance, the raising of Lazarus, — the most extraordinary and conspicuous miracle of which we have an account in any of the gospels. When we consider the peculiar circumstances under which it took place, its nearness to Jerusalem, its publicity, the sensation made among the crowds that were attending the Passover, the eager curiosity of the "common people" to see Jesus and "Lazarus also whom he had raised from the dead," the fear felt by the Jewish leaders that such a miracle would increase Christ's popularity, and their consequent efforts to secure his arrest, which led to his betrayal by Judas; and when we also consider that the other immediate events with which the raising of Lazarus was closely connected are fully related by the Synoptics without the slightest hint that such a remarkable miracle was ever wrought, it is exceedingly difficult to accept its historicity. How could so startling an event, which directly caused Christ's death and which must have been known to all the disciples, have failed to be recorded in all the Synoptic gospels, and have disappeared utterly from the earliest Apostolic traditions? Surely a miracle which helped to precipitate the tragedy of Calvary would not have been left by the disciples who saw it to be picked up and written down a generation after by one of their number in his old age. A strange bit of supplementary matter surely! The truth is that such an explanation of the origin and character of the fourth Gospel would never have been thought of except for the assumption that John was the author of it. But when that assumption is dismissed and the Gospel itself is consulted, we find the writer clearly explaining the object he had in view: "These things are written that ye may believe that Jesus is the Christ, the Son of God." The motive, then, is dogmatic, not biographical or historical. The events described are only the setting of the dogma, which is the real theme. When the Gospel is read in the light of this squarely avowed aim in writing it, much becomes plain that before was obscure and inexplicable. It is not the earthly career

of Jesus that is set forth so much as the incarnate life
of the heavenly Logos, and the historical events that are
introduced are wholly subordinate to and illustrative of
his divine character and mission. Thus the earthly
events of Christ's life are idealized and their real historicity becomes doubtful. There is a transcendent element everywhere transfiguring and divinizing the human
and historical. Such is the verdict which the historical
critic must pass on the historicity of the fourth Gospel
when it is compared with the Synoptics. It is plain
that in some way we are no longer on the same historical ground. The author is not writing a human life,
but is expounding his thesis of a divine incarnation in
mortal form, and from this point of view every event
assumes a supernatural and quasi-unhistorical character.
It is remarkable how little history there is in the Gospel.
A few events are referred to simply to give opportunity
for transcendental and mystical discourses whose whole
strain and character is utterly unlike the familiar, practical, parabolic utterances of the Synoptic gospels. The
very miracles have a dogmatic purpose and prepare the
way for mystical utterances. In fact, the Gospel as a
whole is not so much a biography of Christ, or even a
collection of Christ's sayings, as a series of long conversations and discourses connected together and reduced
to a spiritual unity by certain sporadic events whose
sole aim seems to be to afford the opportunity to teach
the spiritual truth desired. How much of a historical
character can be allowed to such a gospel it is difficult
to say. But certainly when marvelous events are introduced, like the miracle of Cana or that of Lazarus,
where the dogmatic motive is so plainly visible, it can
hardly be expected that they should be accepted as having any historical basis, unless they are supported by
other testimony. The difficulty with several of these

accounts is that they stand alone, and have no historical vouchers.

But my object in this critical comparison is not to break down the general historicity of the fourth Gospel, but to show how impossible it is to harmonize its historical accounts with those of the Synoptics, and thus to make clear the inference which must be drawn, that the author of the fourth Gospel cannot have been one of the original Galilean circle of disciples. It is true that the writer must have been well acquainted with the Jews and their country. But if a Jew himself, he is no longer in sympathy with his countrymen. He writes as a foreigner, as belonging to a different world. If he was personally acquainted with Jesus and his sojourn of thirty-three years on earth, he takes little interest in it. He gives us no glimpses of his birth or early home in Nazareth. His mind is wholly intent on portraying those manifestations of divinity which should prove him to be the incarnate Son of God. Hence he dwells so fully on the circumstances of Christ's last night in the flesh, his arrest, his trial, his death and resurrection. These events are the precursors of the end of the earthly life, under which the eternal Logos had for a brief period veiled himself, and of the return to that heavenly condition from which he came. The deviations here from the Synoptic gospels are peculiar and suggestive. The Synoptics represent Christ as refusing to enter into a defense of himself before Pilate. "He answered nothing, so that the governor marveled." But in the fourth Gospel we have a full account of a remarkable conversation between them, in which Christ is made to utter some of his most idealistic and mystical sayings. "My kingdom is not of this world." "To this end am I come into the world that I should bear witness unto the truth. Every one that is of the truth

heareth my voice." There is an equally notable difference between the dying words of Jesus as given in the
Synoptics and as given in the fourth Gospel. Matthew
and Mark make him cry, "My God, my God, why hast
thou forsaken me?" Luke puts into his lips the prayer,
"Into thy hands I commend my spirit." But our
fourth Gospel author makes him close his work on
earth with the words so full of mystic meaning, "It is
finished." In fact, the more closely the four gospels are
studied in their relation to each other, the more radical
and complete grows the difference between the fourth
and the others. The fourth Gospel bears all the marks
of belonging to a later age and to a wholly different
philosophical environment. The Synoptic gospels represent early oral traditions which gradually were reduced
to writing by many different hands, and which, after
various recensions and supplementary additions, became
fixed in the form in which they have come down to us.
The fourth Gospel, on the contrary, was plainly the
work, in the main, of a single writer, whose aim was
not to gather together the oral traditions that passed
current in his day concerning Christ and his teachings,
but to set forth his own philosophic views of Christ's
metaphysical nature, and to enforce them by means of
the literary use of certain historical events. The thoroughly philosophical and mystical character of the Gospel must always throw a cloud of doubt over the evidence
of its complete historical veraciousness. The author of
this Gospel was not alone in making history the vehicle
of philosophical ideas. It was quite the fashion of his
day.

Certainly, whatever view be taken of the authorship
of the fourth Gospel, one cannot finish the comparison
between it and the Synoptics without doing full justice
to its unique religious idealism. Whoever the author

was, he had drunk deeply of that spring of spiritual truth which he believed had been opened to man by a being no less exalted than the divine Son of God, — the metaphysical mediating Logos between the unseen supreme Being and this visible world. No wonder his Gospel has been sanctified and made holy, beyond all other gospels, in the eyes of the Christian church, or that the Apostle whom tradition made its author became the centre of the most hallowed legends. But the historical and critical spirit cannot suspend its work in deference to any religious sentimentalism. Were the external evidence for the Johannine authorship much less weak than it is, the character of the internal testimony furnished by the study of the fourth Gospel itself is so overwhelmingly strong against it, that it would seem impossible to resist the conclusion that is forced upon the mind. Much has been made in past times of the deep spiritual character of the fourth Gospel as evidence of its having been written by an inspired Apostle who had drunk in the living truth from the lips of Christ himself. How, it has been argued, could the author of such a gospel have remained unknown? Such an argument may prove too much. Is not the authorship of some of the noblest creations of human genius unknown: for example, the books of Job and Ecclesiastes, the second Isaiah, the Epistle to the Hebrews, the Synoptic gospels, the Iliad and the Odyssey? No historical valid proof of authorship can be built on such *a priori* assumptions.

The result to which the study of the fourth Gospel thus leads us is supported by its external history. It first clearly appears as a distinct gospel in the latter part of the second century. Theophilus, who was bishop of Antioch from 168 to 188, is the first post-apostolic writer to refer to it as a "holy writing" by an "inspired" man, and quote from it. Tatian, a contemporary of Theophilus, gives apparent quotations from it, but does not state whence the quotations are derived. If the "Diatessaron," ascribed by tradition to Tatian, be genuine, a point, however, not wholly free from doubt, it would furnish additional proof of Tatian's use of the fourth Gospel. But this fact would not be so significant as some have argued, for it does not push back at all the date already furnished by Theophilus. A strong effort has been made to prove that Justin Martyr, whose writings belong to the third quarter of the second century, antedating a few years those of Tatian and Theophilus, was acquainted with this Gospel. This effort has been the more persistent, since Justin has been regarded as the real key to the whole conservative position. But too much importance, in my view, has been given to Justin and his relation to the Johannine problem. It has been supposed that if the date of the fourth Gospel could be put as early as Justin, "his proximity to the Apostles" would give good ground for the claim of Johannine authorship. But the real point at issue is not whether the date of the fourth Gospel can be carried back a few years more or less earlier, but whether the traditions concerning John's later sojourn in Ephesus and his death as late as the reign of Trajan are history or legend. If they are unhistorical and legendary, the whole effort to push back the date of the fourth Gospel is surely of little account. Allow that not only Justin Martyr, but even the Gnostics, Valentinus and Basilides, were acquainted with it, there still remains a space of half a century or more to be spanned in order to connect the Gospel with John as its author. Much learned ingenuity has been spent in this effort, and, as I think, wholly in vain. Dr. Ezra Abbot's essay is a conspicuous illustration. He em-

ployed all the resources of his critical acumen to prove
that the date of the fourth Gospel could be carried
back through Justin Martyr and the earliest Gnostics
to A. D. 125. But what avails all this, if John had been
dead fifty years! The vital weakness of Dr. Abbot's
essay is that it *assumes the historical credibility of a
mass of legends*. He accepts "the uniform tradition
supported by great weight of testimony, that the evangelist John lived to a very advanced age, spending the
latter portion of his life in Asia Minor, and dying there
in the reign of Trajan not far from A. D. 110." But
what is "this great weight of testimony" which Dr.
Abbot quietly assumes to be veracious? Simply the
"uniform tradition" of legends that had grown up
in the course of centuries, and, as has been shown, have
no historical foundation and are utterly discredited by
critical scholarship. Looked at from one side, Dr.
Abbot's historical arch seems firm. I myself regarded
it as such twenty years ago. He starts from historical
ground, namely, the historical existence of the fourth
Gospel in the latter part of the second century. On
this pillar he attempts to carry his arch across half a
century through Justin and Basilides to some historical
support on the further side. But in fact his arch stops
in the air. It cannot reach firm historical ground.
There remains, after all his efforts, a gap which cannot
be crossed. It is no wonder that he laid hold of legendary materials which fifty years ago were supposed to
be trustworthy, and tried to build on them. But the
"uniform tradition" of the third and fourth centuries
on which such men as Alford and Abbot relied has crum-
bled to dust, and the arch so carefully constructed between Irenæus and the Johannine legend of a long old
age at Ephesus lies to-day in ruins. Dr. Ezra Abbot was
one of the most learned and skillful exegetes of the last

generation, but the historical and critical spirit had not fully mastered him, and it is plain that he accepted the legends connected with John and the other disciples without due examination. For myself, were the external argument stronger than it is, and if all and more than all of Dr. Abbot's claims were allowed, it would not change the conviction to which I am brought on internal grounds. For it is my belief that the study of the Gospel itself and of its place in the historical evolution of christological thought is decisive in regard to the question of Johannine authorship. But I cannot leave the claims of Dr. Abbot and others concerning the evidence of the acquaintance of Justin Martyr and Basilides and Valentinus with the fourth Gospel without entering a strong demurrer. The effort to convince myself that Justin Martyr used the fourth Gospel has utterly failed, and the longer I have studied the question, the clearer becomes my conviction that he never saw it. Great reliance has been placed on the passage concerning the new birth. But if this was a quotation from the fourth Gospel, why did Justin not declare it such, as he did in the case of quotations from other gospels used by him? Justin clearly had in his hands certain gospels. His quotations from them are numerous, and he always refers to "the Memoirs of the Apostles" as the sources. from which he drew. These quotations are apparently from Matthew and Luke and besides some unknown gospel, perhaps the Gospel of the Hebrews, fragments of which have been preserved. But no extract from the fourth Gospel appears among them. When he recited the passage concerning the new birth, why did he not also refer it to "The Memoirs of the Apostles," if the fourth Gospel was one of those in his hands? Why should he have referred it directly to Christ? "For Christ also said." When we bear in

mind that many oral traditions of Christ's sayings were
floating in the air in Justin's day, as is shown by sayings drawn from such sources by Justin himself, and
still later by Irenæus and others, and that oral tradition
was still regarded by Papias, a contemporary of Justin,
as more trustworthy than written gospels, and when we
further note how inaccurate, as a quotation from the
fourth Gospel, is the passage put by Justin into Christ's
own lips, it is much more easy to believe that Justin
drew it from oral sources than from a written gospel
to which he never once alludes and of which he shows
no knowledge. But there are much stronger positive
grounds against Justin's acquaintance with this Gospel.
Surely if he had possessed it he would have made ample
use of it in setting forth and justifying his Logos doctrine which forms so original and marked a feature of
his writings. On the contrary, he shows no knowledge
of the remarkable proem of the Gospel, and never alludes
to its existence, or in any way connects his own Logos
doctrine with it. Nay, further, he makes it plain that
his Logos ideas are drawn directly from the Platonic
and Stoic philosophies. In fact, the Stoic spermatic
Logos doctrine is the very foundation of Justin's peculiar view, that all the ancient sages, such as Heraclitus
and Socrates and others, had a part of the Logos which
was in the world before Christ, and of which Christ
alone had complete possession. It was on this ground
that Justin declared such ancient sages to be Christians
before Christ's coming. Besides, the differences between
the Logos doctrine of the fourth Gospel and that of
Justin, instead of being merely superficial, as has been
urged, are profoundly radical, and in view of them it
is difficult, if not impossible, to believe that Justin could
have had the proem of the fourth Gospel before him
when he elaborated his own Logos christology. Still

more difficult is it to believe that, if he had it in his hands and supposed it to be Johannine, he could have failed to quote it frequently, so highly must he have regarded its apostolic authority. The result of historical investigation then must be, it seems to me, that Justin did not borrow his Logos doctrine from the fourth Gospel, and that the doctrine of that Gospel had its source in common with that of Justin in Greek philosophy.

So, in regard to the claim made that the earliest Gnostics, Basilides and Valentinus, quoted from the fourth Gospel, the failure to sustain it is in my view still more complete. To realize this one only needs to read carefully, and without any dogmatic prepossessions, the accounts given by Irenæus and Hippolytus of the different Gnostic doctrines. In doing this it must be borne in mind that Irenæus wrote half a century after Basilides and Valentinus, and that Hippolytus was nearly half a century later still. The first thing that strikes one is the fact that the two writers are dealing, not so much with individuals as with schools of thinkers, and that the names of the chief leaders are often used as synonyms for the schools of Gnostic speculation that took their origin from them. So far is this confusion of individual names and of the schools that afterwards assumed them carried, that singulars and plurals, " he " and " they," are made to follow each other not only in contiguous sentences, but even *in the same sentence*, showing that there was no idea or purpose of distinguishing the original Gnostics from their later followers, and that the sole intent all along was to state the general doctrines of the various Gnostic sects as a whole. Such being the patent fact, which one that runs may read, it is simply preposterous to fix on a quotation from the fourth Gospel which had been put into the

mouth of Basilides by Hippolytus, who wrote nearly a
century after him, and to infer from it that Basilides
himself had the Gospel in his hands, when it is plain
that Hippolytus is never distinguishing Basilides himself from the school that assumed his name, and when
it is allowed on all sides that the fourth Gospel had
been *in the hands of that school* for a generation or
more. It is difficult to characterize such a method of
argument, and I can only explain it as illustrating the
power of a fixed theological presupposition over even
scholarly minds. Perhaps a worse case still is that of
Resch in his attempt by a minute analysis of the earliest
Christian writings to glean out phrases and words which
seem to indicate a knowledge and use of the fourth Gospel. Such a method, when carried far enough, might
prove not only that Bacon wrote Shakespeare's plays,
but that Shakespeare wrote Bacon's " Advancement of
Learning."

The conclusion, then, to which one seems forced to
come is that the date of the fourth Gospel cannot be
proved to be earlier than the middle of the second century, and it still remains doubtful whether one is justified in assigning a date even as early as that. It is
quite likely that the fourth Gospel may have been
written several years before its appearance in what is
now known as history; but if evidence of it is lacking,
such a likelihood cannot be made the basis of an assumption that it was actually so written, and of the conclusion that John was the author, and then of the still
further conclusion that its christology is apostolic and
an authentic part of Christ's teaching. It was one of
the most vicious elements of the old method of reasoning
on this question, to take the ground that the traditional
view of the Johannine authorship of the fourth Gospel
should be accepted until its spuriousness was proved.

This assumption underlies the fixed presupposition that runs all through the efforts to prove that Justin Martyr and the earliest Gnostics were acquainted with the fourth Gospel, namely, that John *really was the author of it*, and that it must have been in their hands. Thus the method of the defenders of tradition has been largely to confine themselves to "refuting the arguments which were brought forward by the skeptical critics." But the burden of proof is always on the side of the affirmative in historical as truly as in all other matters. To insist that all the traditional claims concerning the fourth Gospel should be religiously accepted till they have been clearly proved false is against the fundamental laws of scientific and historical methods of investigation. It is a part of the old *a priori* deductive method which has suffered collapse. But it may be said that such a scientific method rigidly carried out would involve the rejection of almost all the so-called history that has come down to us from the ancient times. Certainly it has led to the rejection of a mass of legendary traditions which an uncritical age had allowed to be mingled with historical facts. But such a sifting of legend from history does not destroy history itself; rather it plants all real historical events on clearer and firmer ground. It is true that the scientific method when applied to history cannot give us absolute certainty in regard to any supposed historical events. All historical evidence is only probable; it can never reach demonstrative or necessary truth, like a geometrical or algebraic formula. But it cannot be inferred from this that therefore a mere historical likelihood can be accepted as a historical certainty. The true meaning of "probable" as applied to historical evidence is "having more evidence for than against." Everything depends upon the degree or weight of probability. There are high degrees of probability that are practically conclusive, and low degrees that have no weight at all. A person accused of crime is not convicted except on evidence that is, in legal phrase, beyond all reasonable doubt. Yet even such evidence has led to the conviction of innocent persons, because it is only probable, and thus may fail of arriving at truth, — the more reason, therefore, for the most rigid scientific method of investigation, that the highest possible degree of probability may be reached. It is not enough, then, that there is some degree of probability in favor of any supposed historical event. The science of history demands that the probabilities in favor of such an event should overbalance, even beyond all reasonable doubt, the probabilities against such an event. This is the prime difficulty with the evidence for the early date assigned by some to the fourth Gospel. There may be a low degree of the likelihood of such a date, but the probabilities against such a date are enormously greater, so that the historical critic is forced to decide for the later date rather than the earlier.

It was another vice of the old method of defending tradition that it insisted on the acceptance of all tradition as true until some other historical explanation could be found that would supplant it. So ripe and liberal a scholar as Dr. C. R. Gregory, of the University of Leipzig, in a recent review of Harnach's "History of Early Christian Literature"[1] surprises me by declaring that "It is unscientific to give up a tradition that is not positive nonsense, before we have a theory that has at least as good a support in history and that offers fewer difficulties." The reviewer applies this dictum to Harnach's criticism on the genuineness of the first Epistle of Peter. It would be equally applicable to the Johannine question. According to Dr. Gregory, the tradition

[1] *American Journal of Theology*, July, 1898.

that the Apostle John wrote the fourth Gospel should
be accepted until some other theory or explanation of
the authorship of that Gospel can be offered that is more
acceptable and presents fewer difficulties. But such a
principle, when applied to historical investigation, would
utterly overthrow the whole scientific method. It makes
it the duty of the historical critic to provide a good historical substitute for every myth and legend and unhistorical tradition that he finds. A heavy task surely!
It seems, then, that the historical student should accept
the historicity of Constantine's vision of the cross in the
sky at midday, with the Latin words, *hoc vince*, blazing
beside it, until he can satisfactorily explain the origin
of the legend, and decide whether it was a legendary
growth, having its source in some natural phenomenon,
or a pure legend from the beginning, and not only decide between the two explanations, but also give satisfactory reasons therefor. How much room would there
be for the exercise of historical criticism under such
conditions? If a rational historical explanation of all
the mythological and legendary growths that have fast-
ened themselves on historical events must be given before such growths can be cut away by the critic's knife,
then his work is at an end. The growth of legend is as
spontaneous and as lawless as the growth of weeds in
spring. The only fact that is historically clear concerning the story of Constantine's vision of a supernatural
cross, with its attendant *hoc vince*, is that it is a legend
lacking any historical foundation. Beyond this historical critics are utterly at sea. Neander, for example,
suggests four different explanations or theories of the
story, but does not decide between them any further
than to throw out the view that accepts its historicity.
This is as far as the critic need go. He cannot be
expected to explain how a legend began to grow. So

in the case of the question concerning the Johannine authorship of the fourth Gospel, the problem is whether the Apostle John wrote it. Who actually wrote it, supposing John did not, is an entirely different question, and does not directly concern the historical critic. Dr. Gregory requires him to accept the tradition of Johannine authorship until he can show who did write it, if John did not, or at least satisfactorily explain how it came into being. But this is an eversion of the scientific inductive process. The only vital question inductively is whether there is convincing evidence that the Gospel was written by John. When the inductive method has found an answer affirmatively or negatively, the critical work is done. Dr. Gregory, here following the old method of dealing with the problem, has confounded two distinct questions together, as if the historical settlement of the one involved also the settlement of the other.

Before we pass to our final division of the subject, it may be well to compare more directly the two divisions already considered, and note their relations to each other. Such a comparison may leave the result to which we have arrived more clear in the mind. The historical facts concerning the Apostle John left him still in Palestine, a rather inconspicuous member of the twelve Apostles, with a purely Galilean background and environment, and without any evidence of rabbinic or Greek culture; and all the historical light accessible makes it highly probable that his death occurred soon after A. D. 70, if not some years before. Turning to the fourth Gospel, we find a writing that is dominated by a distinct dogmatic motive, plainly the work of a Greek scholar versed in the deepest speculations of Greek philosophy, and representing an evolution of christological thought that marks it as a product of about the middle of the second century. This result of internal evidence corresponds to the date of its first appearance in history; for even the conservative critics do not carry it back of A. D. 125, and the whole tendency of criticism is to place it considerably later.

Let us now bring these two classes of facts together and see how they fit each other. An illustration will help us. Several years ago a young man was tried in New Haven for murder, and was convicted on this single bit of evidence. A knife with the blade broken was found in his pocket. The broken end was found in the body of the victim. The two pieces of the blade were produced in court, and under a microscope there was shown an exact fitting of them together. Suppose it had been revealed by the microscope that though there was a considerable closeness of correspondence, it was not complete, the prisoner would have been acquitted at once. It was the *exactness* of correspondence that fixed his guilt. Any want of exactness would have so far testified to his innocence. Now how is it with the relation of the character and history of the Apostle John, and the character and history of the fourth Gospel? What does our historical microscope say? Does it not emphatically declare that the two supposed parts of a single blade cannot be fitted together? There can be but one answer. How can the Aramaic "unlearned" character of John be made to fit into the highly learned Greek philosophical character of the fourth Gospel? How can the historical limit of John's life be made to cover a period of fifty or seventy-five years and fit into the date of the Gospel? It may be comparatively easy, by means of reliance on tradition to establish a loose connection between them, but the microscope reveals historical gaps that no sophistry can hide. Our illustration also helps us to see the sophistical character of Dr. Gregory's dictum. Suppose, in the case referred to, the broken piece had failed to fit that found in the prisoner's pocket, and that the attorney for the state had urged that before the accused could be cleared the defense should show to what knife the broken piece belonged. What would have been the quick judgment of the court? A man tried for murder is not compelled to show who committed the murder in order to prove that he did not commit it himself. No more is the historical critic compelled to show who wrote the fourth Gospel in order to decide on the evidence that John did not write it.

III. The *third* division of our subject, namely: when and how the tradition of the Johannine authorship of the fourth Gospel arose, may be dispatched with comparative brevity. Theophilus, who was the first to quote from the fourth Gospel as such, was also the first to name John as its author. Irenæus, perhaps a little later, was the first to describe our four gospels as written by Matthew, Mark, Luke, and John. This was in the last part of the second century. It would seem that the name of John was attached to the Gospel not long after its appearance, if not at once. Assuming, as we now do, that sufficient historical evidence is wanting for the Johannine tradition, the question arises, how it came to be attributed to the Apostle. Of course no conclusive answer can be given. But there are two views that may be taken of it. Either the writer, whoever he was, assumed the name of John the Apostle in order to gain for his work the authority of an apostolic name, or the Gospel may have been written by another John, namely, John the Elder, to whom Papias refers as one of his contemporaries, who became confounded with the Apostle. This last view has in its favor the fact that these two Johns whom Papias so clearly distinguished were actually confounded by Irenæus, and it is quite supposable that the confusion started by him may have been extended to others. It is on this ground that Harnack rules out Irenæus as a credible witness on the Johannine question, and concludes that the fourth Gospel was written by "John the Elder." But when it is considered how common was the custom in that period, especially among the Alexandrian Jews, to write anonymously and to seek the authority of some illustrious name, it is quite as easy to look in this direction for the true explanation. Let it be remembered that the Synoptic gospels are anonymous, though ascribed by tradition to Matthew, Mark, and Luke. The same is true of the Epistle to the Hebrews, attributed to Paul, and of the Apocalypse directly ascribed to John in the introductory verses, though what John is not clear. It should not, then, cause surprise that a gospel should appear anonymously and yet under the assumed name of the Apostle John. Authorship, editorship, authenticity, genuineness, anonymity, and pseudonymity were much more elastic words in those days than now, and the law of ethics in relation to them was much less strict. The great object of the Alexandrian Jewish writers, and equally so of the Christian writers, was to secure as high authority as possible for their works. This was especially true among the Christians in the second century and after. The question that decided whether a gospel or epistle or other writing should go into the growing canon of sacred scripture was whether or not it was written by one of the Apostolic circle. If the new gospel was to win such a place it must have some apostolic sponsor. The traditions that had been growing around the Apostle John might have recommended him as a suitable person to represent the peculiar mysticism of this Gospel. Legend had distinguished him as the Apostle of Love. This view explains, perhaps better than any other, the curious absence of John's name from the Gospel. The other apostles are mentioned by name again and again, but John is conspicuous by his absence until the very end. Then he mysteriously appears, not by name, but as "the disciple whom Jesus loved," or "another disciple," or "that other disciple," or "the other disciple." Why, we cannot help asking, all this unwillingness to call this disciple by his name? Was it modesty on the part of John himself, supposing he was the author? A strange modesty, indeed, that which could not allow him to appear under his name, and yet could allow him to describe himself as "the disciple whom Jesus loved," and introduce scenes in which he was highly distinguished above all the other disciples. The delicacy which some have discovered here I cannot see. But if some unknown writer wished to assume John's name, by way of indirect suggestion, the singular method adopted is at least not wholly unnatural, and at present I lean to this view. Still, when one realizes how easily in these times legends grew, of authorship as of other events, one is ready to conclude that after all the probabilities are not so slight that the connection of John's name with the fourth Gospel was the mere result of chance legendary tradition, which, once started, no matter how, speedily grew widespread and unanimous. Such a legend is no more surprising than the other legends that finally gathered around his name.

B. A CRITICISM OF PROFESSOR A. V. G. ALLEN'S "CONTINUITY OF CHRISTIAN THOUGHT."

In my account of Augustine's theological position, on page 69, I say: "Thus the Stoic, New Platonic immanence, with Augustine, supplants the Platonico-Aristotelian and Athanasian transcendence." Professor Allen, in his "Continuity of Christian Thought," assumes the very opposite of this statement as the keynote of his whole book. In his Introduction he says: " The Augustinian theology rests upon the transcendence of Deity as its controlling principle, and at every point appears as an inferior rendering of the earlier interpretation of the Christian faith." What this earlier interpretation is, he sets forth in the chapter on the Greek theology. Athanasius, he declares, "labors to retain the Stoic principle of immanent Deity without confounding God with the world. Like his predecessors, Clement and Origen, he builds his thought on the divine immanence, not on the transcendence of God." Elsewhere he speaks of Athanasius as "reproducing the teaching of Greek philosophy, and more especially that of the Stoic school." The only evidence that Professor Allen gives for this assumption is Eusebius's statement that Pantænus, whose pupil Clement was, "had been first disciplined in the philosophical principles of those called Stoics." Pantænus himself is scarcely more than a tradition, and nothing further is known of Clement's relation to him. There is not a single explicit allusion to Pantænus in Clement's voluminous writings. The whole theory that Clement, Origen, and Athanasius drew their philosophical ideas especially from the Stoics, and thus developed a doctrine of divine immanence in the world in place of the Platonic doctrine of the divine transcendence, is utterly without historical or philosophical foundation. How Professor Allen could have been brought to it is to me a puzzle. He seems to have been carried away with the idea that modern thought is returning along the lines of the new science to the ancient conception of God. This is the note that he continually strikes. Modern theology, he thinks, is reacting from the transcendental dualism of Augustine to the immanence of the Greek Fathers, Origen and Athanasius. It is a pleasant dream, but has no counterpart in fact. Origen is indeed once more in the ascendant; this is not, however, on account of his trinitarian doctrine, but because of the nobleness of his character, his grand spirit of tolerance, and his scholarly and spiritualizing method of dealing with truth.

As to Professor Allen's assumption that Augustine held to a dualistic doctrine of transcendence, it is as fallacious as the counter assumption concerning Origen and Athanasius. Origen was a philosophical Platonist, and so was Clement before him and Athanasius after him. Their whole Logos doctrine, which Professor Allen seems to misunderstand entirely, was based, as we have seen, on the Platonic dualism. Augustine, on the other hand, drew his ideas from New Platonic or Stoic sources. A double confusion runs through Professor Allen's book. First, he confounds two kinds of divine immanence, a theistic, and a pantheistic. Plato and the Greek Fathers held to a theistic immanence of God in the world, that is, a doctrine of divine providence and agency. But their dualism and doctrine of God's transcendence kept them from pantheistic tendencies. The doctrine of Augustine also fell short of strict pantheistic immanence. He did not wholly confound God with nature. But his view of God's efficient operation in nature was thoroughly Stoic in its tendency, as we have seen, leading to an elimination of strict second causes and of miracles as supernatural infringements of natural law. Nothing could be further from the truth than Professor Allen's statement that Augustine's theology is "built upon the ruling principle that God is outside the world and not within," and that "His being would be complete without the creation or humanity or the eternal Son." Neander in his "History of Christian Dogmas" puts it rightly. "Augustine's conceptions of the relation between the creative and upholding agency of God were determined by his idea of creation. Creation was not to be thought of as a temporal act, beginning and ending, but as ever continuous; hence God's upholding agency came to be regarded as a continued creation. His religious consciousness led him to the same view, by giving him the idea of the perpetual, absolute dependence of the creature on God in opposition to the deistical notion of the relation of God to the world." This view of the creation as without a temporal beginning is distinctly New Platonic and monistic, and is closely related to the Stoic pantheistic doctrine of the divine immanence. The only thing that saves Augustine from complete pantheism is his view, drawn from the Scriptures, that the world is a free creation of God, though not in time, while the New Platonic and Stoic pantheism makes the world a necessary evolution from deity. That Augustine's theology was "built upon the ruling principle that *God is outside the world, and not within*," as Professor Allen declares, is wholly foreign to Augustine's point of view, which started from his New Platonic Monism rather than from the Platonic Dualism. So far from holding such a deistic view, Augustine rather made the world and mankind to be the essential expression of God's eternal nature and the theatre of his unending working. Such was his interpretation of "My Father worketh hitherto." Augustine even found, as we shall see, in creation itself and in man, illustrations and reflections of the divine Trinity, showing his conception of the intimate connection of God and his universe. What Professor Allen attributes to Augustine quite accurately expresses the dualistic transcendence of Athanasius. How Professor Allen could find in Athanasius's treatises, "Contra Gentes" and "De Incarnatione Verbi," to which he refers, "the Stoic doctrine of the divine immanence," is to me simply inexplicable. How can the Stoic pantheistic immanence be drawn from such a passage as this ("De Incarnatione Verbi," 17): "He is at once distinct in being (ἐκτος κατ' οὐσίαν) from the universe, and present in all things by his own power, — giving order to all things, and over all and in all revealing his own providence, and giving life to each thing and all things, including the whole without being included, but being in his own Father alone wholly and in every respect," — where the difference between a theistic Platonic immanence, which is in complete harmony with the Platonic dualism, and the Stoic pantheistic immanence, is accurately drawn. Or take a passage in "Contra Gentes," 40, where there is a distinct allusion apparently to the Stoic view: "But by Word I mean, not that which is involved and inherent in all things created, which some are wont to call the seminal principle, — but I mean the living and powerful Word of the good God, the God of the Universe, the very Word which is God, who while different from things that are made, and from all Creation, is the one own word of the good Father who by his own providence ordered and illumines this universe." By the "seminal principle" Athanasius means the Stoic doctrine of the σπερματικὸς λόγος, which is eternally immanent as a vital force in the world, and in no possible sense separable from it. Athanasius in his writings twice refers to the Stoics and their immanent doctrine, in one case (Second Oration against the Arians, 11) charging his Arian opponents with a Stoic leaning, and in the other case (Fourth Oration against the Arians, 13) charging his Sabellian opponents with a similar leaning. The stout dualism of Athanasius led him to a strict acceptance of a creation *in time*, involving the view that " God's being would be complete without the creation," the very thing which Professor Allen applies to Augustine, misrepresenting him entirely, as Neander shows. Professor Allen does injustice to Arius as well as to Augustine, treating the dualistic view of God and creation, which he attributes to both, as " Jewish Deism." Arius and Augustine were as far apart as the two poles, as *I* have already shown. Arius was a philosophical dualist, agreeing with Athanasias perfectly in his Platonic transcendence. The real issue between Arius and Athanasias was not whether there are two worlds, separated by an essential chasm, but to which of the two worlds Christ belonged. I am not quite sure that I understand Professor Allen's view of New Platonism. He must be aware of the fact that Augustine's whole theology is steeped in New Platonic thought. But he seems to regard New Platonism as a refined form of transcendent dualism, instead of being what it actually is, a complete system of pantheistic thought combined with an evolutionary mediating principle which connects it with Platonism, while losing sight entirely of the dualism of Plato himself. Augustine, as I have said, is only saved from pantheism by his insistence on God's personality, and on the eternally active efficiency of God in the world. But his thought runs as far toward pantheism as it is possible for it to do without deserting his theistic starting-point.

This misunderstanding of Augustine's general position leads Professor Allen into further confusion as to Augustine's doctrine of sin and moral evil. Augustine was no Manichean, as Professor Allen charges. His conversion from the Manichean dualism to the monistic New Platonism was complete. His "Confessions" gives the whole story. To be sure, Augustine draws the line sharply between actual sin and holiness, and carries the division into the eternal state. But he did not treat evil as a positive principle. On this point he was thoroughly New Platonic and Stoic. "Sin," he declares, "is not a substance, but only a *defect* of substance." It has only a negative existence. So afraid was he of a Manichean dualistic conception of sin that he would not allow that the hereditary sinfulness and corruption of nature which passed from parent to child was itself a substantial element of nature, but he declared that it was merely a *quality* or *accident* of nature, as if such a quality or property of nature were not necessarily a substantial and inherent part of it. When all the qualities or attributes of a nature or substance are taken away, what is left? New Platonism and Stoicism also holds that there is but one eternal substance in the universe. Matter, sin, and all evil are but modifications of this one substance, having no positive, independent existence. Augustine held the same philosophical view. So for him sin could have no substantive existence. Good only was substantial. Sin was only a falling away from good. This, however, is on the straight road to a monistic pantheism, and utterly away from dualism, which allows a positive material world and an equally positive moral evil.

Professor Allen also gives a wrong view of Augustine's doctrine of grace. He treats it as dualistic, involving the necessity of external means, such as sacraments, as if God could not act directly on the soul.

He also declares that the Greek theology rested more in its doctrine of grace on the divine immanence, making the mediatorial mission of Christ the great source of gracious influence. I must dissent entirely from this view. The Greek church held to sacramental means of grace quite as strongly as the Latin. In fact, the whole later Latin system of sacraments was borrowed from the Greeks. It is true that Augustine accepted this traditional system; but his doctrine of grace was wholly monistic. He viewed grace as a direct exercise of God's efficiency upon the individual soul. The *means* of grace were secondary and might be dispensed with. Augustine's doctrine of grace was in close relation with his doctrine of nature and miracle. God is the direct efficient cause of all things in the realm of spirit as well as in that of nature. Regeneration is as much the result of such divine efficiency as creation or miracle. In a remarkable passage ("De Gen. ad Lit." ix. 18) he states this directly. Unfolding at length his theory of miracle as simply a special operation of divine causation "by which He manages as He wills the natures that He constituted as He chose," he adds, "and *there* is the grace by which sinners are saved." The whole passage shows that Augustine regarded the action of grace on the soul as the miraculous result of direct divine agency. This is very far from sacramental dualism. Some color of truth is given to Professor Allen's theory in the development of the external church system of the Middle Ages. But this was the effect of the universal ignorance and superstition that reigned; and, moreover, it had its birth, not in the West, but in the East, the original home of Christianity.

I should not feel called to make these strictures on a book that has many excellent qualities, were it not that its fundamental assumptions, which I regard as wholly false and misleading, are being accepted in certain quarters as true, apparently on Professor Allen's authority. The influence of this book has been singularly pervasive, and its theory of Greek Athanasian immanence and of Latin Augustinian dualistic transcendence is still employed by writers, as if it were historically true. Dr. John Fiske in his book on "The Idea of God" made it the historical key of his whole line of thought, and plainly drew it from Professor Allen, quoting from him *in extenso*. It seems strange, to one acquainted with the writings of Athanasius and Augustine, to have Athanasius described as holding that God was "immanent in the universe and eternally appearing through natural laws," when the truth is that Athanasius held that the universe and its laws were created in time, whereas God himself existed from eternity in the transcendent ideal world; and, if possible, still more strange to have Augustine described as so completely in the power of "Gnostic thought" as to "depict God as a crudely anthropomorphic being far removed from the universe and accessible only through the mediating offices of an organized church." Even Dr. Fiske's new book, "Through Nature to God," contains the same false reading of history; nor is he without good company. Professor Allen evidently has a large English following. Rev. J. B. Heard, in the preface to his Hulsean Lectures for 1892 on "Alexandrian and Carthaginian Theology Contrasted," relates the "joyful discovery" he made, by reading Professor Allen's book, "that the so-called new theology of modern thinkers was nothing more than a fresh draught of the oldest of all theologies." The lectures are amazing reading. Augustine is described as "steeped in dualism long after he had shaken off his early Manicheanism." "God was external to his works, the transcendent Lord of the universe, who could only

act-on the finite through some medium or channel which
He chose to personify as 'grace.'" It would be difficult
to misstate Augustine's real doctrine more completely.
"Grace" with Augustine was no instrumental, sacramental "medium or channel" of God's efficiency, but
that efficiency itself, acting directly and immanently on
the soul. Nor has the leaven of Professor Allen's book
yet ceased to work. The Hulsean Lectures for 1899, by
Rev. J. M. Wilson, on "The Gospel of the Atonement,"
just issued from the press, adopts the same theory.
"Two types of theology" are described, "that of the
Greek and that of the Latin Fathers." "The fundamental and dominant note of the one is the divine indwelling, that of the other is the divine transcendence."
It is pleasant to hear one true note struck from Oxford
itself. Rev. Aubrey Moore, in "Lux Mundi," page 83,
called attention to the mistake made by Dr. Fiske,
tracing it to Dr. Allen's book. He truly says: "It is
almost incredible to any one who has read any of
Augustine's writings, that, according to this view, he
has to play the rôle of the unintelligent and unphilo-
sophical deist who thinks of God as 'a crudely anthropomorphic being far removed from the universe and
accessible only through the mediating office of an organized church,'" quoting Dr. Fiske's language already
given.

I will only add that I am compelled to believe that
the πρῶτον ψεῦδος of Professor Allen and his associates is
a failure to apprehend the real character of the Greek
Logos doctrine, which is based on the Platonic dualism and transcendence. The Logos or Son of God was
regarded by Athanasius as a transcendent Being who
entered this lower world through the medium of a
human nature in order to bridge the chasm between the
transcendent world from which he came and the created

world of time. The incarnation, however, did not change the Logos from a transcendent being to an immanent being. His immanence was only in his human life, not in any change of his divine nature. If I understand Professor Allen, he supposes the Logos must be an immanent being by virtue of his incarnation; which is not the doctrine of the Greek theology at all. See Erdmann's "History of Philosophy," vol. i. pp. 274–276, for an account of Augustine's immanent pantheistic tendency, and of his theory of direct efficient grace. Also, see Schwegler's "Handbook of the History of Philosophy," p. 143, for an explanation of the monistic character of Christian Scholasticism, with the result "that Monism has remained the character and the fundamental tendency of the whole of modern philosophy."

C. PROFESSOR PFLEIDERER'S ARTICLE IN THE "NEW WORLD."

I have assumed the genuineness of the words here attributed to Christ (see p. 290); but I am in sympathy with the view taken of the passage by Professor Pfleiderer in an article on "Jesus' foreknowledge of his sufferings and death," in the "New World," September, 1899. Professor Pfleiderer gives quite convincing reasons for doubting whether Christ actually said the words "give his life a ransom for many," as well as the words in the Synoptic account of the last supper in which Christ connects the supper with his death. He holds that these passages are essentially Pauline, and are the result of "later dogmatic reflection on the death of Jesus as a means of redemption," and he shows that the Pauline doctrine of a "substitutional atoning sacrifice" is "quite remote from the circle of thought of Jesus himself."

"Jesus everywhere made the forgiveness of sins dependent on the penitent and humble disposition of men, together with their own willingness to forgive, without anywhere intimating that it presupposed, as a condition, a preceding propitiation of God by a substitutional atonement. The parable of the prodigal son is, in this respect, very instructive." The reader will perceive how closely in accord Pfleiderer is with my own views. His article appeared after the twelfth chapter of this book was written.

In general I would further say that when we consider how many plain interpolations, not only of single words or clauses, but of whole passages, have been brought to light and properly excluded from the New Testament in consequence of recent critical investigations, it ought not to be regarded as anything strange, should further interpolations be found even of a radical character. Suppose a fresh Greek manuscript of the gospels were to be discovered, dating a century or two earlier than the Sinaitic or Vatican manuscripts, is it not more than probable that not a few important corrections would be made in our present revised text? When we bear in mind the many remarkable changes that have been made in the *Textus receptus*, on which the King James's English version was based, necessitating the recent revised version, we need not be surprised at the results of any new archæological find. It is also to be noted that the further back we go in our textual investigations, the more numerous the interpolations and changes may be expected to be, — an expectation amply sustained by the history of textual criticism. So that it may be readily seen that the genuineness of no portion of New Testament literature can be absolutely relied on. It has been assumed by certain theologians that the most accurate text now attainable should be piously guarded as containing the real words of Christ. But it is impossible to sustain such an assumption. Even if we were absolutely certain that our present gospels have come down to us in their exact original form, which of course is far from true, we should not then be sure that we had Christ's words as they were uttered. Our gospels were not reduced to writing until more than a generation after Christ's death, even according to the most conservative estimate, and historical evidence wholly fails to justify this conclusion, and postpones the date at least a generation later. The first generation of Christ's disciples were dependent on oral tradition for their knowledge of his teachings. Paul, whose death occurred more than thirty years after that of Christ, gives no hint that any gospel had been written in his day, which probably explains the fact that he makes so little allusion to the life and teachings of Christ. Further, the Synoptic gospels themselves give clear internal evidence of being gradually developed compendiums and recensions of different oral traditions and written gospels, and of being in this way so intimately related to each other as to indicate some common origin. The later tradition that they were written by apostles or their attendants lacks historical proof. The tradition itself does not appear until near the middle of the second century, and not in its fully developed form till near the end of that century. Irenæus, who wrote about 180, that is 150 years after the death of Christ, is the first Christian Father to name Matthew, Mark, Luke, and John as the authors of our four gospels. How such a tradition arose is an obscure question. But it evidently grew out of the tendency to seek apostolic authority for certain written gospels, and it is not unlikely that there was some foundation of fact behind it, though the present form of the tradition is without his-

torical proof. When we leave tradition and seek for
historical light from the post-apostolic writings themselves concerning the date of our four gospels, no clear
trace can be found earlier than the middle of the second
century, though detached passages are given which bear
a likeness to corresponding passages in our gospels;
but such passages are not quoted from any of our gospels, and it is probable that they represent oral tradition
rather than any written gospel. A remarkable proof of
this is found in a statement of Papias, who wrote about
A. D. 140–150, his death occurring about A. D. 155 or
later. In the fragments of a work on the "Sayings of
Christ," Papias tells us how he attained his knowledge
of the gospel, declaring that he was careful to question
every one who had learned anything from those who
had been themselves hearers of Christ's own disciples,
that he might thus learn from their very lips "what
Andrew or Peter said, or what was said by Philip, or
by Thomas, or by James, or by John, or by Matthew,
or by any other of the Lord's disciples." " For I im-
agined that *what was to be got from books was not so
profitable to me as what came from the living and
abiding voice.*" How clearly this fragment shows that
more than a hundred years after Christ's death, *oral
tradition* was still holding its ground against certain
written gospels that were beginning to be circulated,
such as are referred to in the proem of Luke's Gospel.
There is no evidence that Papias had any of our present
gospels in his hands. Much has been made of a fragment from him in which an account is given of Matthew's writing the sayings of Christ in the Hebrew language, but this cannot be our Greek Gospel of Matthew,
as all admit, and Papias does not quote from it. Then
his account of a gospel written by Mark cannot be
made to square with the character of our present Mark.

These allusions to gospels by Matthew and Mark are the first references to any names of gospel writers that appear in the post-apostolic Fathers. The gospels thus referred to by Papias probably belong to the list of earlier gospels which were being written and used in his day, and later gave way to our present gospels. Clear evidence of such lost gospels appears in the early Christian literature. But Papias does not seem to have used them, being prejudiced against them in favor of oral tradition. With these facts in mind, how can it be claimed that the teachings of Christ, that have come down through such a long period of oral tradition and slowly developed reduction to writing, are the exact words that fell from his lips? It is also to be remembered that Christ spoke Aramaic and not Greek, so that our earliest and most authentic Greek manuscripts are only a translation, and cannot therefore always precisely represent the original, — the Semitic Hebrew and the Aryan Greek differing so radically in roots, structure, and idiom. Surely, under such circumstances, critical scholars, like Pfleiderer, may be permitted to doubt whether Christ actually uttered certain words or phrases, where internal exegetical evidence is against it, and where such statements are out of harmony with his general teachings.

INDEX

ABBOT, EZRA, essay on "Authorship of Fourth Gospel," 354; seeks to carry back the date to 125 A. D., 355; argument rests on "uniform tradition," 355; examination of claims as to acquaintance of Justin Martyr, Basilides, and Valentinus with fourth Gospel, 356–359; not fully mastered by the critical and historical spirit, 356.

Abbott, Lyman, 125, 126, 144, 150, 168, 206, 284, 286.

Acton, Lord, 195.

Acts, the Book of, 7.

Alford, Dean, 331.

Allen, A. V. G., 1; theory of Athanasian immanence and Augustinian transcendence, 368; criticism of, 369–377; view of New Platonism, 372; charges Augustine with Manicheanism, 373; view of Augustine's doctrine of grace, 373.

Allen, J. H., 2.

"American Journal of Theology," 9, 361.

Anselm's "Cur Deus Homo," 84, 94, 95; foundation of mediæval doctrine of atonement, 297.

"Apocalypse, The," 330.

Apollonius, 324.

Apostle's creed, 24, 32.

Aramaic, original language of Gospel, 19.

Arius, 36, 372.

Athanasius, 24, 36; trinitarianism of, 38–45; not a tritheist, 47; not Stoic but Platonist, 371; quotation against the Stoics, 371, 372.

Athenagoras, 23.

Atonement, three stages of doctrine in New Testament, 288; as a substitutional sacrifice, of Ethnic and Jewish origin, 292; doctrine of Epistle to Hebrews, 296, 297; doctrine of Irenæus, Anselm, Thomas Aquinas, Calvin, 297; governmental and moral theories, 298; debasing effect of material sacrifices, 302; Christian, is spiritual at-one-ment, 307.

Augustine, 3, 58; culture of, 64; philosophical views, 67–70; trinitarianism, 65, 70, 77; contrasted with Athanasius, 71, 77, 79, 81; results of Sabellianizing tendency, 83–93; credulity of, 324, 325, 330; what saved him from pantheism, 372; not a Manichean dualist, 373; monistic definition of sin, 373.

BARTOL, C. A., 1, 2.

Basil, 55.

Beard, Charles, 203.

Beecher, H. W., 144.

Berry, G. A., 145.

Bethlehem, 8.

Bible, as a medium of divine revelation, 269.

Bradford, A. H., 126, 127.

Brooks, Phillips, 127, 130, 131, 283.

Bunyan's "Pilgrim's Progress," 234.

Burnet, Bishop, 99.

Bushnell, Horace, 111, 112.

CALVIN, JOHN, 80, 95; want of appreciation of nature, 264.

Carlyle, Thomas, 56.

Channing, W. E., 107.

Choate, J. H., 219.

Christology, 19; Chalcedon definition of, 279; contradiction involved, 280; why it has been a doctrine of theology rather than of anthropology, 280; effect of inductive method, 281.

Christopher, St., legend of, 326.

Church, the, in what sense a medium of revelation, 270.

Cicero, 89, 178.

Clarke, Samuel, 99.

Clementine Homilies, a legendary romance, 327.

"Congregationalist," the, 181.

Cook, Joseph, 1, 118-125.

Creeds, historical, 311.

Critical spirit, distinctive mission of, 224, 225.

Criticism, historical, 186, 187; of the Bible, 187-189; final aim of, 174; providential work of, 207.

DANTE, 253.

Deductive method compared with inductive, 237.

Diderot, 195.

Dionysius of Rome, 23.

Dogma, not of the essence of religious faith, 204, 205; its function in religious experience, 205.

Dorner, I. A., 114, 116.

EDWARDS, JONATHAN, 103, 235.

Emerson, R. W., 130, 153, 157.

Emmons, Nathaniel, 104, 148; trinitarianism of, 105-106.

Erasmus, 179.

Erdmann, "History of Philosophy," 377.

Eusebius, correction of Irenæus, 338.

Evolution, historical laws of, 175.

FAIRBAIRN, A. M., 136; address in Boston, 302; defence of sacrificial view of atonement, 303, 305.

Faith, a free movement of moral consciousness, 201; independent of dogma, 201; evil effects of confounding it with dogma, 201, 203; word used in two different senses, 207, 311; confining it to its evangelical meaning a boon to theology, 217, 218; sign, of speedy revival of, 248.

Fichte, 136.

Filioque, 57, 97.

Firmin's Tracts, 98.

Fisher, G. P., 109, note; argument for Johannine authorship of fourth Gospel, 331.

Fiske, John, 375.

Fourth Gospel, 6, 25, 26, 32, 33; latest battle-ground of the critics, 191; contrast with Synoptics, 342; substitutes Logos for Messiah, 342; comparison of its Logos doctrine with that of Justin Martyr, 343; doctrine of the essence of the Christian life compared with that of Synoptics, 343; evidence of Philonic and Gnostic influence, 346; mysticism of, 346; historical difficulties, 348; question of historicity, 350; writer's object, 350, 352; religious idealism of, 352, 353; first historical appearance in latter part of second century, 353; date not proved to be earlier than middle of second century, 359; Theophilus the first to name John as author, 365 (see Johannine problem); how Gospel came to be attributed to John, 365; Harnack's view, 366.

GIBBON, EDWARD, 187.

Gloag, "Introduction to Johannine Writings," 26, note.

Gnosticism, 33, 346.

God, old definitions of, 271; inductive view of, 272.

Gordon, G. A., 131-134.

Gore, C., 90.

Gospels, the four, first alluded to by name by Irenæus, 365; question of authorship, 379; not in the language of Christ's original teachings, 381.

Gregory, Nazianzen, 78.

Gregory of Nyssa, 54.

HAECKEL, ERNST, 154, 155.

Harnack, Adolf, 56, 89, 366.

Harris, George, 236.

Harris, Samuel, 236-246; definition of God, 238; doctrine of Christ, 245; of Trinity, 245, 246.

Hartranft, C. D., indictment of science, 258-260.

Heard, J. B., "Hulsean Lectures" (1892), 375.

Hebrews, epistle to, 18; view of atonement, 296.

Hedge, F. H., 2, 130.

Hegelianism, 136.

Hell, the old dogma of, 253, 255;

in pictures of mediæval churches, 303.

Hilary, 61, 62.

History, peculiar position of, as a science, 218; a medium of revelation, 265, 314; theistic, 309; essential optimism and idealism of, 315, 316.

IGNATIAN Epistles, 12, note.

Induction, the law of, 228.

Interpolation, in New Testament, 378.

Irenæus, view of atonement, 297; imperfect character of text of work "Against Heresies," 332; lack of critical spirit illustrated, 234; reminiscences of Polycarp, 337; confounded two generations of disciples, 339; conclusion concerning historical credibility of, 341; first to describe the four Gospels as written by Matthew, Mark, Luke, and John, 365.

JEROME, 120; credulity of, 329.

Jesus Christ, birthplace, 8; tradition of miraculous birth, 11, 12; historical foundation of the new Christianity, 198, 201; not a dogmatist, 202; characteristics of moral consciousness, 265-269; protest against Jewish sacrificial atonement, 289; his own teaching of moral at-onement, 291; spoke Aramaic, not Greek, 381.

Johannine problem, 6, 25, 319.

John, the apostle, 19; historically accredited facts concerning, 319-322; plays a small part in New Testament narratives, 320; defects of disposition and character, 321; disappears early in the Acts, 321; not mentioned by Paul in later epistles, 321; testimony of Papias concerning manner of death, 322; in Post-Apostolic age becomes centre of legendary growth, 322; no historical basis for tradition of great age, 330; not identified with seer of Patmos, 330; not author of fourth Gospel, 356, 365.

John of Damascus, 78, 80.

John the Elder, 338, 365, 366.

John, Gospel of, see "fourth Gospel."

Justin Martyr, 10; argument for Christ's miraculous birth, 13; logos doctrine derived from Greek philosophy, 29; character of doctrine, 29-32; account of Simon Magus, 327, 328; no clear historical proof of acquaintance with fourth Gospel, 354-358.

Καταλλαγή (reconciliation), use in New Testament, 288.

Kenosis, 281.

Kepler, 232.

LEGENDS concerning the Apostles, 322; causes of growth, 322, 323; unhistorical character, 324, 325.

Lessing, 140.

Logos, 18; doctrine of, 25; origin of doctrine, 27; character of, 29.

Lucretius, "De Natura Deorum," 233.

Luke, Gospel of, 8, 10.

Luther, ix.

MAN, consubstantiality with God, as a scientific doctrine, 286.

Marcellus, 44.

Mark, Gospel of, 11, 380.

Mary, mother of Jesus, 10, 13; immaculate conception of, 13.

Materialism, one phase of monistic pantheism, 309; protest of moral consciousness against, 309.

Matthew, Gospel of, 8; genealogy of first chapter, 8, 10; testimony of Papias concerning a Hebrew gospel of, 380.

Media, the, of divine revelation, 264-270.

Μεσίτης, 18.

Messiah, 5, 8; in Old Testament, 7, 15.

Methodology, 250.

Milton, John, 254.

Monism, 129; philosophical, distinguished from scientific, 154; idealistic, distinguished from materialistic, 155-159; versus dualism, 159; essentially unitarian, 166.

Moore, Aubrey, 370.

Mysticism, 274.

NATURE, a medium of revelation, 264.

Neander, A., ix. 12, note, 249, 370.

Newman, J. H., 149.

New Platonism, 65.

"New World," v.

Nicene creed, 23, 58, 167.

Niebuhr, 187.

Ὅμοιος (like), 38, 63.

Ὁμοιούσιος (like in essence), 37, 63.

Ὁμοούσιος (completely like in essence), 37, 63 ; meaning theologically, 45-51.

Origen, 24, 34 ; doctrine of eternal generation of the Son, 34, 35.

Orthodoxy, presuppositions of, 249, 250.

Οὐσία (essence), 52-54.

Pantænus, 368.

Pantheism, 87 ; result of philosophical monism, 308.

Papias, distinguishes two Johns, and three generations of early disciples, 337 ; preference of oral tradition to written gospels, 380 : no evidence of use of present gospels, 381.

Patmos, 330.

Paul, 5, 17 ; doctrine of God and of Christ, 21 ; new element introduced into doctrine of atonement, 293 ; mixture of Jewish and Greek ideas, 295.

Peter, 19 ; historical knowledge of, ends with New Testament, 326 ; the legend of, 326-329 ; no historical proof that he ever visited Rome, 328 ; story of visit rests on fiction of Simon Magus, 328 ; supposed tomb under St. Peter's church, 328 ; tradition of martyrdom a pure legend, 329.

Pfleiderer, Otto, article in "New World," 377-381 ; view of Christ's doctrine of atonement, 378.

Plato, quotation from "Republic," 301.

Platonism, contrasted with Stoicism and New Platonism, 66.

Plotinus, 87 ; "Enneads" of, 88 ; pantheism of, 90, 91 ; present influence on New England thought, 138.

Plumptre, J. H., article on John in Smith's "Bible Dictionary," 324.

Polycarp, 20, 336 ; no allusion in "epistle" to John or fourth Gospel, 338 ; no allusion to Holy Spirit or Comforter, or Logos, 339 ; "Martyrdom of," filled with miraculous and legendary elements, 339.

Protestant Reformation, 177-179.

"Quicunque Vult" (Pseudo-Athanasian creed), 98.

Raphael, 227.

Reason, the, double meaning of the term, and consequent confusion in theology, 221-223.

Sabatier, Auguste, 210 ; view of difference between faith and dogma, 210 ; view of dogma as essential to religious life, 211 ; criticism of view, 212-216.

Sabellianism, 75.

Salmasius, 246.

Schaff, Philip, 89 note, 329 note.

Schleiermacher, 110.

Schwegler, Albert, "Handbook of History of Philosophy," 136, 377.

Science, not in conflict with religion, 230.

Semo Sancus, a Sabine divinity, 327 ; confounded by Justin with Simon Magus, 328 ; discovery of pedestal with inscription to Semo Sancus, 229.

Septuagint version, 12.

Shedd, W. G. T., 114 ; description of hell, 255.

Sherlock, 99.

Simon Magus, 328.

Sinaitic Syriac manuscript, 9, note.

Smith, H. B., 114, 115, 117.

Stephen, Leslie, testimony to fallacious character of memory, 339.

Strong, A. H., 136, note.

Stuart, Moses, 107-113.

Tatian's "Diatessaron," 9.

Tertullian, 10, note, 61, 62 ; account of John's miraculous escape from death, 324.

Theism, an intuition of moral consciousness, 308.

Theology, a science, 217, 257 ; should be allowed full scientific freedom, 218 ; the old, materialistic, 310 ; the new, theistic, 308 ; the new, spiritualistic, 309 ; the new, distinguishes faith as a religious act from belief as an intellectual act, 311; the noblest department of philosophy, 312; its golden age in the future, 313.

Tradition, unanimity of, not a sufficient ground of historicity, 322; oral, held ground for a hundred years after Christ's death, 380.

Trinitarian, versus Unitarian, no longer a live issue, 277, 278.

Trinitarianism, the Nicene, four stages of evolution, 24; three divisions of history of, 97; the "new," 165, 169; versus the new Unitarianism, 169–171; two opposite forms of, 276; traditional dogmatic, how viewed by the new inductive theology, 277.

Trinity, the, in the Ethnic religions, 275; the Christian, historical, and philosophical origin, 275.

'Υπόστασις (concrete being), distinguished from οὐσία, 54.

VICTORINUS, M., 89.

WATERLAND, 100–102.
Watts, Isaac, 102.
Whiton, J. M., 134, 135.
Whittier, hymn quoted, 283.
Wilson, "Hulsean Lectures" (1899), 376.
Wordsworth, quoted, 264.

ZELLER, E., 87.

The Riverside Press
PRINTED BY H. O. HOUGHTON & CO.
CAMBRIDGE, MASS.
U. S. A.

CPSIA information can be obtained at www.ICGtesting.com
Printed in the USA
BVOW060439050712

294371BV00003B/328/P